MARX
An Introduction

MARX
An Introduction

W. A. Suchting

Senior Lecturer in Philosophy, University of Sydney

New York University Press · New York *and* London
1983

Copyright © W. A. Suchting, 1983

Published in the U.S.A. by New York University Press,
Washington Square, New York, NY 10003

Library of Congress Cataloging in Publication Data
Suchting, W. (Wallis)
  Marx, an introduction.

  Bibliography: p.
  Includes index.
  1. Marx, Karl, 1818-1883. I. Title.
HX39.5.S92 1983   335.4′092′4   83-8034
ISBN 0-8147-7831-3
ISBN 0-8147-7832-1 (pbk.)

Manufactured in Great Britain

An die ferne Geliebte

The biographers like best to give Marx a miniature barricade as a writing-desk in his study, or at least as a knick-knack on his writing-desk. When we could much more easily rather build a barricade from this writing-desk!

Brecht

Contents

Preface

1

It is not difficult to understand why people should want to learn about Karl Marx. After all, his work is one of the basic sources for the ideas which have helped shape the contemporary world. In one place people are gaoled, tortured and killed for being 'Marxists', and in another they suffer similarly for not being such. Any contemporary social thinking that has not seriously encountered Marx can safely be dismissed as irrelevant on that ground alone. No wonder then that of the making of many books on this subject there is no end.

But why add to the heap with this one? A sufficient answer must be that I do not know of any quite like the one I have tried to write, and that such a book I think may be useful and — hopefully — interesting to a number of readers. I have, in fact, tried to produce a book on Marx which has a number of characteristics possessed in differing measure by various available works but not combined in any I am acquainted with: specifically, a book which is genuinely introductory and, in being so, both comprehensive and reasonably brief. In aiming at being introductory it aims to be elementary, not in the sense of being oversimplified, but in trying to treat the main elements of the subject rather than the details. Of course, this is an impossible combination of aims, so compromises have been everywhere necessary. But if it serves some readers as a stepping stone to more extensive treatments or to more detailed aspects of the subject then it will have done its job.

2

As regards mode of presentation, I believe that the ideal one (certainly that in accord with Marx's own programme) would show how Marx's work, both theoretical and practical, arose from a pre-existing situation and in turn changed that situation. As regards the theoretical aspect anyway, it would work on the assumption that a certain stage of theoretical development has thoroughly concrete historical presuppositions but that the body of thought which arose in that context has also to be understood and assessed in its own terms and not merely as an 'expression' of the historical tendencies of the time. This is, I think, the only way of avoiding the twin pitfalls of separating thinking from its historical roots ('theoreticism') or of simply reducing it to them ('historicism'). The book can make no pretension to seriously attempting to follow this counsel of perfection: at best it merely gestures towards such a presentation and the emphasis is on Marx's ideas.

3

Debts are owed in the first place to many of the sturdy labourers in the field of Marx-studies — writers like Auguste Cornu and Maximilien Rubel — whose often not very spectacular toil is quite simply indispensable to anyone seriously engaged with Marx's work.

Of the more 'interpretive' literature, I have learned most from the writings of Louis Althusser and then from a number of writers who have been influenced by him.

More personally, my main obligation is to my colleague and friend John Burnheim, with whom I have discussed many issues — in the first place ones concerning Marx and Marxism — over several years, and from whom I have had constant instruction, in particular about the primacy of the idea of practice and about the centrality of the notion of problem-solving in understanding social and historical affairs. I am also indebted to him for comments on an earlier draft of this book, as I am to the following for similar help: Randall Albury, Michael Matthews and Ross Poole. These people are responsible for some of whatever merit there may be in the book but for none of its deficiencies. Des Burke's acute eye and fine feeling for the English language greatly eased the burden of proof-reading and eliminated many a solecism and infelicity.

A fragment by Brecht on Marx yielded the epigraph,[1] and

Preface

that acerbic master of line and word Patrick Cook allowed me
to use one of his cartoons.[2] Last but by no means least my
thanks are due to Patricia Bower for her always intelligent
and skilful typing.

For the rest, I have been occupied with Marx and Marxism
for some time now and must have accumulated many debts
which have slipped my mind. To any such neglected creditors I
can only extend my gratitude and express my apologies. In the
words of some of Coleridge's doggeral:

> 'Tis mine and it is likewise yours;
> But an if this will not do,
> Let it be mine, good friend! for I
> Am the poorer of the two.[3]

Sydney
September 1982

Notes

1 See Brecht, B. *Gesammelte Werke in 20 Bänden* (Frankfurt a. M.,
  Suhrkamp Verlag, 1967), Vol. 20, pp. 74f.
2 Taken from the reprint in his collection *Coming Soon* (Sydney,
  Currency Press, 1977), p.53.
3 From the preface to 'Christabel'.

To the reader about using this book

This book is a whole in the sense that it is tied together by an underlying method and by developing themes. But parts of it can be read independently of the others even if a certain amount of their significance will be lost by doing so. In particular someone more interested in the later (roughly: post-1850) Marx could begin with Part II or even Part III. Certainly Part I is — unfortunately for these as initial chapters — the most difficult, at least for readers without some background in the history of philosophy. Someone who begins with Part II or Part III and then, having finished, returns to the first part, should have less trouble with it.

A note on references
to Marx's writings

Please note the following points:

1 Where a passage from Marx or one of his works referred to in this book has appeared in a volume of the Marx-Engels *Collected Works* now being published from Moscow, the reference is to this. If it has not yet appeared there, but is in the Pelican Marx Library, then this is cited. Otherwise references are to the *Selected Works in Three Volumes* by Marx and Engels (Moscow) or to other editions as specified at the place.

2 The principal abbreviations used are as follows: full bibliographical details will be found in the list of literature at the end of the book.

C, 1, 2, 3	:	*Capital*, Volumes, 1, 2, 3
CW	:	(Marx-Engels) *Collected Works*
EW	:	*Early Writings* (Pelican Marx Library)
G	:	*Grundrisse*
PW, 1, 2, 3	:	*Political Writings*, Volumes 1, 2, 3 (Pelican Marx Library)
SW	:	(Marx-Engels) *Selected Works in Three Volumes*

When the edition in question is in more than one volume the reference is to the volume number followed by a colon and page number (unless otherwise specified). For example, 'CW 2:36' refers to Marx-Engels, *Collected Works*, volume 2, page 36.

3 English translations of Marx's writings are very frequently patchy in quality, and sometimes simply unreliable. I have therefore had to revise a very considerable number of the passages cited. This has been done without notice, as re-

marking upon each change would have fairly littered the text with such notes.

Changes of this sort have been made by reference to the standard Marx-Engels *Werke* (Berlin, Dietz, 1956ff) except in the case of the *Grundrisse* where the text used has been the standard Dietz edition, Berlin, 1953.

Introduction

This book is about Marx, not about 'Marxism'.

Why make such a distinction?

One answer would be that Marx himself made it: Engels reports that 'Marx said of the "Marxism" that was all the rage among certain Frenchmen towards the end of the 70's:... "all I know is that I am no 'Marxist'"'.[1] In fact what is generally referred to by the term 'Marxism' is demonstrably not even an approximately unitary body of theory or practice. This is obvious enough just from a consideration of the very concrete contemporary conflicts between various nations all of whose governments claim to be adhering to the principles of Marxism, and between various Communist parties in different capitalist countries. The point is only reinforced by going backwards in stages and considering the struggles within the Soviet Union, especially between the death of Lenin and the expulsion of Trotsky; the conflicts between the Bolsheviks and the survivors of the Second International; and then the clashes between the factions within the latter up to the beginning of World War I. Or, looking at the more theoretical scene, there is simply no single body of doctrine in the works that have historically been called 'Marxist' — ones which you might expect to figure in a book called, say, *A History of Marxist Theory*.

The fact is that 'Marxism' cannot properly be thought of as a simple (or even complex) theoretical datum which can be more or less straightforwardly presented and then interrogated for truth or falsity, adequacy or inadequacy in terms of this or that theoretical or practical task. It has always been a *construction*, and in the first place an *historical* construction. The various doctrines — the major ones at least — calling themselves such

xvii

have always been theoretical responses to various historical circumstances, with definite practical consequences. Of course each of them has called upon various texts from Marx for canonical legitimation; and it is largely this common claim that gives them the 'family resemblances' necessary for them all to be said to be part of the history of a common doctrine. Nor does what has been said mean that these various theories are not subject to assessment regarding their adequacy to their theoretical subject-matter and practical tasks; it just means that this is a matter of considering different (even if related) views.

2

But could 'Marxism' not be characterized exclusively by reference to Marx's own writings? The diversity and indeed inconsistency in great part, one with another, of many of the historical forms of 'Marxism', or particular doctrines therein, might then be explained as a result of misrepresentation, distortion — in general 'revision' — of Marx's own thought. The authority of references to his texts does not count against this, for it is well known that the Devil can cite scripture for his (or her) purpose.

But if anything is clear from the discussions of the past couple of decades about Marx it is surely that there is no single, homogeneous body of doctrine in his writings taken as a whole. These works contain different and indeed conflicting positions not only when the works in question are considered chronologically but frequently even when each is looked at individually. (I shall say something further about these different positions presently.)

Of course it is still possible to claim that even Marx himself was not always faithful to the 'essential' core of his thought, which has to be disengaged from its natal detritus or from the various matters that came to adhere to it in the course of its growth. But then the questions arise: Who is to say what is 'essential' in Marx? How would a claim of such a sort be defended in any but a thoroughly dogmatic way? There is certainly a unity in Marx's life and work but it is the unity not of a particular set of doctrines but of a political commitment:

the destruction of capitalism and its replacement by a communist society of 'freely associated producers'.

3

However, the sole alternative to a rigid essentialist presentation of Marx's thought is not a limply descriptive relativism that confines itself to cataloguing the various strands. What can be done further is to evaluate the positions referred to earlier with regard to their aptness for certain ends, and one or other of these may as a result be emphasized in a presentation of Marx.

This is in fact one of the methodological points of departure of the present book, and it is necessary to say something more about it here.

In brief, I see three principal strands in Marx's writings taken as a whole. The first is what may be called the 'essentialist-teleological' thread. By this I mean a procedure of explanation and criticism which starts from certain alleged intrinsic natures or 'essences' of things. These are conceived of as tending towards certain goals, as realizing themselves in appropriate ends, or, in short, as having inherent teleologies. The second is what may be called (though perhaps with some danger of misunderstanding) the 'structuralist' strand, according to which primacy is accorded not to individual essences but to (social) relations defining structures which confer on individuals what characteristics they have and which have tendencies to develop in certain ways. The third strand takes the crucial concept for the understanding of the social world to be neither individuals nor relations but the material transformative activities, the *practices* in which human beings engage.

These three strands are not neatly exemplified in the works of just one particular chronological period or in specific works, though certain writings are to some degree exemplars. Thus the *Economic and Philosophical Manuscripts of 1844*, in which a theory of the essential nature of human beings (their 'species-essence') functions as a criterion for evaluating existing institutions, is an excellent illustration of the first approach; large parts of the *Manifesto of the Communist Party* and some parts of *Capital* are exemplifications of the second; the 'Theses on Feuerbach' are strongly in the direction of the third. But most of Marx's main works contain at least traces of more than one.

Though each of these approaches is noted in the course of this book, it is written from the viewpoint that the third is the one of most contemporary relevance, both theoretical and practical, and it is this which occupies the foreground. Any concern that this might make the work, considered as a presentation of Marx, to some extent one-sided, may be mitigated by the consideration that this aspect of Marx's thought has not yet been represented in the literature nearly as much as the other two.

4

It has been well said that Marx's work is systematic without forming a system.[2] I understand by this that on the one hand he did not leave a fully articulated and in principle complete set of substantive views about all aspects of the relevant subject-matter (somewhat in the way in which the great systems of classical philosophy were intended). But on the other hand he did proceed in accordance with certain leading ideas which could, in principle at least, be applied to other aspects of the relevant subject matter.

This idea might indeed be expressed somewhat in terms of Lakatos's notion of a 'research programme'.[3] This is, roughly, a set of principles, of different degrees of generality, set up for application to problems arising from different aspects of its subject-matter, together with various pieces of information as to how those principles might be applied. Such a programme is not to be evaluated by this or that particular success or failure but in terms of its longer-term fertility, especially in the light of competing programmes.

Such a conception, applied to Marx's work (more precisely to one or more of the main strands of Marx's work) avoids two major pitfalls. On the one hand, it rejects the canonizing of everything Marx ever wrote (even within the limits of the aspect concentrated upon). On the other, it makes it inadmissible to see the essence of the doctrine simply as a method which can survive any number of inadequacies in the result of its use.

Marx's own application of the programme I have in mind was fragmentary and attended by different degrees of success as regards various subject-matters. At one end of the spectrum the political economy is the best worked out part of the project; at the other the theory of ideology (say) scarcely exists (the theory that is, as distinct from concrete analyses and hints at a theory); the treatment of the domain of politics stands somewhere between. I have sought to keep within the limits of what is in Marx's own texts and to resist the temptation to fill out some of the lacunae there from the works of later writers, even where this entailed incompleteness in the presentation, though I have not eschewed amplification here and there in what has seemed to me to be both the letter and spirit of the text.

5

Karl Marx drew his first breath in 1818, his last in 1883; his life was thus almost bisected by the period of revolution marked by the date 1848. He was born into a world which was already decisively marked, socially and intellectually, by the two upheavals whose results introduced 'modern times': the Industrial and the French Revolutions. Hobsbawm has called the first 'probably the most important event in world history, at any rate since the invention of agriculture and cities', and the second 'ended the European Middle Ages'.[4] The development of the Industrial Revolution during the period ending in 1848 created the economic conditions for the great take-off by capitalism after the middle of the century; and the social changes consummated in that year, by completing the social transformations begun in 1789, created the political conditions. The period from 1848 to the end of the main working period in Marx's life (about 1873) saw the triumph of capital, the regrouping of the working-class after the defeats of 1848, and also the first long-lasting economic crisis in the last half of the 1870s. In brief, Marx's life spanned the period in which the roots of the contemporary age were formed and he reflected upon it all unrelentingly. It is no wonder that Marx's thought is still the unavoidable entrance to the understanding of the present — and, many would hold, to leading ideas about how to transform it.

Notes

1 W 22:69. For a very detailed discussion of the background of this remark see Draper, H. *Karl Marx's Theory of Revolution*, Vol. II (New York and London, Monthly Review Press, 1978), pp. 5ff. (From Marx's own pen see the second draft of his letter to Vera Zasulich of 8 March 1881, in which he speaks similarly of 'Russian "Marxists"' — W 19:397.)

2 Balibar, E. *Cinq Etudes du matérialisme historique* (Paris, Maspero, 1974), pp. 45f.

3 See Lakatos, I. *Philosophical Papers*, Vol. I (eds. J. Worrall and G. Currie) (Cambridge University Press, 1978), esp. Chapter 1.

4 Hobsbawm, E. J. *The Age of Revolution 1789-1848* (New York, Mentor, 1962), pp. 46, 113.

PART I: 1818-1845

Chapter 1
Student and radical democrat

1

Karl Marx was born on 5 May 1818 in Trier, Germany's oldest city, situated in the southern Rhineland. France had occupied and annexed the Rhineland during the Napoleonic wars, sweeping away the feudal regime and generally winning the support of the populace by its style of government. It was unwillingly rejoined with Prussia in 1814. This resulted in Marx's father, a barrister in the public service, converting to Christianity, as the family was a thoroughly Jewish one (indeed with rabbinical ancestry) and Prussia had re-introduced anti-Semitic laws, in particular relating to employment, done away with during the period of French rule. The elder Marx was strongly imbued with the literature of the French Enlightenment and had some connections with liberal trends in the Rhineland.

Karl entered the Trier secondary school in 1830, where he had the 'humanities' style of education standard for the time. Five years later he passed the school leaving examinations, for which he wrote various compositions, seven of which have survived. That of main biographical interest is the German essay on a subject of the writer's choice, in this case 'Reflections of a young man on the choice of a profession', a piece filled with edifying sentiments the character of which is sufficiently illustrated by the concluding words:

If we have chosen the position in life in which we can most of all work for mankind, no burdens can bow us down, because they are sacrifices for the benefit of all; then we shall experience no petty, limited, selfish joy, but our happiness will belong to millions, our deeds will live on quietly but perpetually at work, and over our ashes will be shed the hot tears of noble people. (CW 1:8f)

In the autumn of 1835 Marx matriculated as a student of law

at the University of Bonn, the intellectual centre of the Rhineland. Besides courses in law he attended others including ones on classical mythology, history and history of art. He also wrote poetry. In August of the following year he obtained his 'Certificate of Release' from Bonn. October saw him enrolled in law at Berlin, then the leading German university, though, as he wrote later, he pursued this as a subject 'subordinate to philosophy and history' (EW 424). He continued to write poetry; but its quality does not make quotation of samples exigent.

One of the main sources for knowledge of Marx's activities during this time in Berlin is a long letter to his father (with whom he had a very close relationship) written in November 1837. He tells here how he tried to unite his studies of law and philosophy in a work on the philosophy of law, in connection with which he went over from a study of Kant and Fichte to that of Hegel. He writes further that 'the grotesque craggy melody' of Hegel's writings did not appeal to him at first, though he eventually got to know them 'from beginning to end, together with most of his disciples' (CW 1:19). He refers in particular to the members of a group calling itself the Graduate Club (*Doktorklub*), intellectuals with strong Hegelian leanings, including in particular the brothers Bauer— Edgar and Bruno.

We must pause then to look briefly at the intellectual background of Marx's time in Berlin. But this in turn demands some appreciation of the social background, going back at least towards the end of the eighteenth century, on the eve of the French Revolution.[1]

2

What was called 'Germany' at that time was basically a congeries of essentially independent principalities and powers whose unity was mainly that of geographical position and historical origin, an aspect of which was a fundamentally common language. It was subject to an Emperor and Diet, but the power of both was only formal. Internally the states and towns were tyrannized by nobility or petty bourgeois elements.

Germany was invaded and partly occupied by the French

during the Revolutionary wars that began in 1792. One of the main effects of this was to accelerate the decomposition of the social structure of feudal-absolutist Germany and as a consequence contribute to the development of capitalism and a national bourgeoisie.

The immediately subsequent history of Germany was structured and determined by the consequences of these events. The basis was the conflict between the feudal-manorial system of old Germany on the one hand, and, on the other, the new capitalist organization of production. This was reflected in a conflict between feudal-conservative ideas, and ones looking towards the future, in the first place liberal thought.

The 'Wars of Liberation' against the French called up a spirit and a movement that pressed towards two main goals: national unity and liberal-democratic social structure. This reached its high point at the Wartburg Festival in October 1817, attended by many thousands of people. Some members of the student associations (the *Burschenschaften*) took to individual terrorism. The murder in March 1819 of the poet Kotzebue, widely thought to be an agent of Tsarist absolutism, gave the government the opportunity to begin a thorough-going repression of national and democratic movements, a political state of affairs which nevertheless went along with steady, economic development, especially in the west, and particularly in the Rhineland.

3

Hegel was the indisputably dominant force in German philosophy from his call to the University of Berlin in 1825 to his death in 1831. He was nineteen in 1789; his first great published work, the *Phenomenology of Spirit*, was completed on the eve of the Battle of Jena in 1806; the first volume of his *Science of Logic* was published in the year of Napoleon's Russian campaign of 1812. But a good deal more important than these chronological coincidences were the objective tendencies of his work, which may best be understood in terms of the tension within it between two strands.

According to his system the fundamental character of the world is of a nature that Hegel calls Mind or Spirit. In order to

5

manifest itself as what it really is in itself it has to go through a process of development which might be compared in some respects to the growth of a full-grown tree from its seed. This development involves the self-division of Spirit into finite spirits, human beings, on the one hand, and, on the other, a world which is apparently quite independent of and indeed alien to them, and which because of this limits their freedom. Through their actions human beings strive to overcome what seems to them the sheer otherness of the objective world. They eventually break through to the insight that the natural and social world is, in fact, identical in nature with Spirit, so that humanity is not limited by anything foreign to it and is therefore absolutely free. The realization of this final state of things, of 'reconciliation' between finite and infinite Spirit, Hegel sees as, if not completed, at least made possible and foreseeable, by a form of constitutional monarchy similar in many important respects with the Prussian state.

The whole contradictory scene in Germany is reflected here: on the one hand, Hegel's system represents the most comprehensive philosophy of *change* and *freedom* ever excogitated up to that time, and one which, moreover, worked over philosophically the entire experience of the two social revolutions (the French and the Industrial) that created the bases of modernity; on the other hand, a highly conservative philosophy functioning as such not only in Hegel's own hands but objectively also.

4

As already mentioned, Hegel died in November 1831. He was working at the time on an article about the draft English Reform Bill which was passed in 1832. This in a sense corresponded to the most significant set of events of that time, namely, the revolution in France in July 1830 (the year Marx entered high school in Trier). This toppled Charles X, the Bourbon king restored after 1815 and installed Louis Phillipe, thus assuring the supremacy of capitalist interests in France.

The July revolution in France had a powerful effect on Germany, helping to revive active movements for national unity and liberal-democratic reforms, a movement that reached a first peak at the Hambacher Festival in May 1832 attended by about 25,000 people. Reactionary forces in Germany moved to block this movement as it had the earlier. But it was not so easy this time, mainly because of the solid base the movement had in the economic development that had occurred in the meantime.

This development had at least two consequences: a growth of the bourgeoisie on the one hand, and, on the other, an impoverishment of middle strata and the formation of a more extensive proletariat. These two segments, united by their hostility to feudal absolutism, generated two different types of opposition. What there was of a working class here and there provided a basis for communist ideas. But this was by no means as significant at the time as the liberal-democratic movement rooted in the bourgeoisie. This expressed itself in a number of ways. One was a literary movement with direct political significance which called itself 'Young Germany', the chief figures in which were Ludwig Börne and Heinrich Heine. Another, of more importance for our purposes, was the 'Young Hegelian' movement.

5

The persistence of the precarious unity in Hegel's system between the two trends I have distinguished depended upon a favourable social milieu. After 1830 the movement destroyed this and the changes right after his death brought out the inner tensions. The Hegelian heritage became divided between the Right Hegelians, seeking to hold to the letter of the Master's teachings, and the Left or 'Young' Hegelians holding to what they considered the spirit of his work whilst trying to appropriate it from the point of view of liberal-democratic trends.

The issue in terms of which the battles were fought was, in the first place, the interpretation of religion in the Hegelian system. Religion was the focus because in a Germany suffering from political repression issues of political significance were frequently refracted through the somewhat less sensitive prism of controversies over religion.

In the Hegelian system what religion and philosophy referred to were held to be the same, namely, Absolute Spirit;

it was just that religion referred inadequately through images whilst philosophy (the Hegelian philosophy anyway) did so adequately by means of pure concepts. Shortly after Hegel's death David Strauss published his *Life of Jesus* (1835-36) in which he argued that the gospel narratives should not be looked to for a coherent doctrinal or historical picture. Instead they should be interpreted as myths expressing the messianic aspirations of the early Christian communities. Whilst the Right stood by the original Hegelian view of the truth-claims of religion, the Left or Young Hegelians followed a line inspired by Strauss and held that religion was simply an historically ephemeral form of consciousness, the real meaning of the Hegelian philosophy being said to consist in the affirmation of the endless progression of Spirit. According to this view the self-consciousness of humanity constantly expresses itself in forms which it does not see as its own creations and which, like religion, thus stand as apparently external constraints on the further free development of self-consciousness. The task of 'critique' is to expose these pseudo-objective formations for what they really are and thus free the human spirit for further progress.

Amongst other important contemporary influences now forgotten except by historians of ideas (e.g., August von Cieszkowski) must be mentioned one who certainly is not. This is Ludwig Feuerbach, a former student of Hegel who had brought his first (though by no means last) objections to his teacher together in a piece called 'Towards a critique of Hegel's philosophy' which was published in 1839 (the year in which Marx began research for his doctoral thesis). What Feuerbach opposed to Hegel was not, as the young Hegelians did, a revised philosophy of self-consciousness, another brand of idealism, but a resolute (if traditional) materialism.

Feuerbach's works (amongst others) were highly influential with the Young Hegelians whose literary focus was the *Halle Annals (Hallische Jahrbücher)* edited by one Arnold Ruge. On the death of the Prussian king Friedrich Wilhelm III and of his relatively liberal minister Altenstein in the spring of 1840 the *Halle Annals* became, in early 1841, the *German Annals (Deutsche Jahrbücher)*. Meanwhile the Graduate Club had been transformed into The Libertarians (*Die Freien*), a Young Hegelian circle.

6

In April of the following year, 1841, Marx submitted his doctoral thesis and the degree was granted in the same month.

The subject of the thesis was the *Difference Between the Democritean and Epicurean Philosophy of Nature*. Together with this there has survived the fragment of an appendix and a large number of notebooks filled with preparatory materials. Some of these are simply extracts and summaries of relevant authors, but others contain passages of no little significance for Marx's intellectual biography.

The very choice of subject matter for the thesis was significant in a number of ways. To start with, the mere fact of taking aspects of the history of *materialism* as the theme is notable: materialism has had a 'bad press' in the history of philosophy. For Hegel in particular Democritus and Epicurus were minor figures in the evolution of Spirit, and Epicurus had been put down as just one aspect of the decadence of Greek philosophy. But Marx strongly affirmed the 'humanism' of Epicurus — in particular his defence of freedom against the necessitarianism of Democritus and his 'this-sided' ethics against the moralism of Plutarch.

Furthermore, for Marx the Epicurean period presented important analogies with his own time. (He actually intended the study of Epicurus to be only one part of a much more extended study of Hellenistic philosophy, including Stoicism and Scepticism.) This parallel is the subject of some rather obscure passages in the notes to the dissertation and also in the preliminary notebooks. Thus Marx writes that:

the theoretical mind, once liberated in itself, turns into practical energy, and, ... as *will*, turns itself against the reality of the world existing independently of it .... But the *practice* of philosophy is itself *theoretical*. It is the *critique* that measures the individual existence by the essence, the particular reality by the Idea. (CW 1:85)

This is very Hegelian: the practice of philosophy falls within the domain of theory and consists in assessing a given reality (e.g., a form of state) against the standard given by its essence, which is determined by its place in the ideal system which

9

realizes rational freedom. A little further on Marx writes:

When philosophy turns itself as will against the world of appearance, then the system is lowered to an abstract totality, that is, it has become one aspect of the world which opposes another one.... Inspired by the urge to realise itself, it enters into tension against the other.... The result is that as the world becomes philosophical, philosophy also becomes worldly.... (CW 1:85)

In other words, when philosophy reveals the gap between the essence and the inadequate realization of the essence, it becomes an 'abstract totality': a 'totality' insofar as it limns the essential structure of the world, but 'abstract' insofar as it coexists with an inadequate embodiment. To the extent that the world becomes, as a result of action, a more adequate embodiment of the essential structure, the latter itself takes on the character of empirical reality. In the notebooks there is a passage which is very similar in many respects, making particularly explicit the underlying comparison between the post-Aristotelian and post-Hegelian periods: Aristotle's philosophy comprehended the world in a total system and was followed by the practically oriented philosophies of the Hellenistic period. 'The same now with the philosophy of Hegel' (CW 1:491). Thus, Marx seems to be saying, the appropriate behaviour for a philosopher of the post-Hegel period is to turn to the practice of philosophy, to 'critique', to help bring the actually existing world into harmony with the exigencies of the complete system.

At least one further point deserves remark as being relevant to what has just been said and also to what is to come. Marx has defined the task of post-Hegelian philosophy to be the critique of what exists from the point of view of the demands of philosophy. Hegel was of course politically conservative. This was an aspect of his life and work that the Left Hegelians had rejected, considering it something that could be dropped whilst maintaining, in all essentials, the rest of his doctrine. Marx disagrees, considering that the conditions for the possibility of a conservative 'accommodation' between the system and the world as it is must be sought for in the very principles of construction of the system itself:

It is quite thinkable for a philosopher to fall into one or another apparent inconsistency through some sort of accommodation: he himself may be conscious of it. But what he is not conscious of is the possibility that this apparent accommodation has its deepest roots in an inadequacy or in an inadequate formulation of his principle itself. Suppose therefore that a philosopher has really accommodated himself, then his pupils must explain *from his inner essential consciousness* that which *for him himself* has the form of *an exoteric consciousness*. (CW 1:84)

Marx was to return to this problem in the very near future.

7

After the award of the doctorate Marx returned to Trier until the beginning of July of the same year, when he moved to Bonn. Here he planned, with Bruno Bauer and Ludwig Feuerbach (whose work *The Essence of Christianity*, which had just appeared, he was studying) to bring out a periodical called *Atheist Archives* (*Archiv des Atheismus*) of a radically left-wing cast. He was also hoping to win a university teaching post as Bauer had. But these plans became increasingly unrealistic.

In December 1841 the new king, Friedrich Wilhelm IV, had issued revised censorship instructions which further curbed the freedom of the press; moreover, Altenstein was replaced by the hard-line Eichhorn, and the liberal Hegelian Professor of Law at Berlin, Gans, by the right-wing Stahl. The general offensive against Hegelianism had been announced in Schelling's inaugural lecture in November 1841 and continued in his Berlin lectures during the early months of 1842. (The audience here included Kierkegaard, Bakunin and Engels.)

Bauer had published his *Critique of the Evangelical Gospels* in three volumes over 1841-1842. As a consequence of this, and of his general left-wing politics, he was suspended from his post for the winter semester 1841-1842 and in May 1842 he was dismissed. All in all the writing was very clearly on the wall for Marx as regards his hopes for an academic career.

Meanwhile in January 1842 he had written, for the *German Annals*, his first article, 'Remarks on the latest Prussian censorship instruction'. This was a swingeing attack on the new regulations of late December 1841; it fell victim to the censorship it attacked. In April he began writing (from Bonn) articles for the *Rhenish Gazette* (*Rheinische Zeitung*). This was

11

a new paper which had been founded in Cologne in January. Its backers were mainly elements of the oppositional Rhineland bourgeoisie, and its main object — indicated by its subtitle: 'For politics, commerce and industry' — was to push for changes that would assist the development of industry and trade. In October he moved to Cologne and became editor of the paper, which thereby gained an increasingly pronounced radical-democratic policy (it had tended to be an organ of the Young Hegelians) and a greatly enlarged circulation.

8

In the articles which he wrote for the paper before he assumed the editorship, Marx put into effect the 'practice of philosophy' which he had sketched in the passages from his dissertation already cited. He is engaged in 'critique' as there defined and as repeated in only slightly different words now. 'We must', he writes, 'take the essence of the inner idea as the measure to evaluate the existence of things' (CW 1:154). The 'essence of the inner idea' of humanity is, following Hegel, rational freedom, which is 'the natural gift of the universal sunlight of reason' (CW 1:151). A free press is the expression and instrument of this freedom. 'The essence of the free press is the characterful, rational, moral essence of freedom' (CW 1:158). The state and its laws are, when they correspond to their essences, vehicles of rational freedom and hence cannot but permit and encourage freedom of the press:

Laws are...the positive, clear, universal norms in which freedom has acquired an impersonal, theoretical existence independent of the arbitrariness of the individual.... the state [is]...the great organism, in which legal, moral and political freedom must be realised, and in which the individual citizen in obeying the laws of the state only obeys the natural laws of his own reason, of human reason. (CW 1:162,202)

In a later autobiographical sketch Marx recalls how as editor of the *Rheinische Zeitung* he found himself 'in the embarrassing position of having to discuss what is known as material interests' (EW 424), and how the work on articles on such questions first turned his attention to economic matters.

By far the most important of the pieces to which he alludes are 'Debates on the law on thefts of wood', and 'Vindication of the correspondent from the Moselle'. In these for the first time Marx tackles socio-economic as distinct from the more or less purely political questions of his earlier pieces. What results is an increasing tension between a continuing Hegelian-idealist conception of state institutions on the one hand, and, on the other, the beginnings of an insight into the way in which 'material interests' systematically underlie their operations, an insight thus generated not by abstract theoretical analysis but by his treatment of concrete issues.

The earlier view of law and the state is still present from first to last during this period[3], but co-existing with it is a very different view of what they are really like, the contradiction being blunted by the idea that the existing forms are merely inadequate embodiments of their essential character. Thus Marx writes that the customary right of the poor to collect fallen wood:

has been turned into a *monopoly* of the rich... . Since private property does not have means to raise itself to the standpoint of the state, the latter is obliged to lower itself to the irrational and illegal means of private property.... The state ... stoops so low as to act in the manner of private property instead of in its own way. (CW 1:235, 241)

What is the solution to this problem of a conflict of interests? It is ... a free press:

In the realm of the press, rulers and ruled alike have an opportunity of criticising their principles and demands ... on terms of equality ... no longer as individuals, but as intellectual forces, as exponents of reason. (CW 1:349)

9

In view of all this it is not surprising that there is no breath of socialist — far less of communist — ideas in Marx's articles of this period, even though there was a small but not insignificant native German communist literature (e.g., the works of Moses Hess and Wilhelm Weitling) and reports of movements of similar tendencies in France (e.g., a then well-known book by

Lorenz von Stein). His position can perhaps best — and with appropriate vagueness — be summed up as one of 'radical democracy': democracy because of his view that 'the law is the conscious expression of the popular will, and therefore originates with it and is created by it' (CW 1:309), and radical because he allows no limitation on this from considerations of, say, the alleged incapacity of some to exercise freedom because of 'immaturity' (CW 1:153).

As regards socialism and communism, Marx says in the same autobiographical sketch already referred to that about this time

an echo of French socialism and communism, slightly tinged by philosophy, was noticeable in the *Rheinische Zeitung*. I objected to this dilettantism, but at the same time frankly admitted in a controversy with the *Allegemeine Augsburger Zeitung* that my previous studies did not allow me to express any opinion on the content of the French theories. (*loc. cit*)

The article to which Marx refers is 'Communism and the Augsberg *Allegemeine Zeitung*', his first article as editor of the *Rheinische Zeitung*. In it he replies to a charge by that paper that his own is a mouthpiece of communism. The article concludes:

... the real *danger* lies not in *practical initiatives*, but in the *theoretical elaboration* of communist ideas, for practical initiatives, even *mass initiatives*, can be answered by *cannon* as soon as they become dangerous, whereas *ideas*, which have conquered our intellect and taken possession of our minds, ideas to which reason has fettered our conscience, are chains from which one cannot free oneself without a broken heart; they are demons which human beings can vanquish only by submitting to them. (CW 1:220f)

Marx, in fact, began studying the writings of French socialists like Fourier, Cabet, Dézamy, Leroux, Considérant, as well as Proudhon, between his taking on the editorship and the beginning of 1843.

10

The *Rheinische Zeitung* had suffered from censorship during the whole of its existence, several of Marx's articles having been sacrificed. Then on 19 January 1843 a decree was issued banning the paper as of 1 April, and imposing rigorous censorship for the period till that date. A number of factors led to this step, not least a complaint from the Tsar regarding an article published on 4 January about Russian absolutism; but the immediate pretext was the appearance of the first of Marx's projected series on the peasantry of the Moselle Valley whose vineyards were the core of the South Rhineland economy.

Marx protested against the shareholders' decision to try to ward off the hand of the Prussian government by moderating the policy and tone of the paper, but to no avail. He resigned in March just before the axe actually fell. Indeed, as he wrote later, 'I eagerly grasped the opportunity to withdraw from the public stage to my study' (EW 424).

His first move after his resignation was to arrange to co-edit with his friend Arnold Ruge a radical periodical (Ruge's *German Annals* had been banned in January) involving that co-operation between German and French writers which had been envisioned on the German left for some time. It would be called accordingly the *German-French Annals* (*Deutsch-Französische Jahrbücher*). The business connected with it was concluded in May 1843.

A correpondence related to it, including three letters from Marx to Ruge, was later included in the *Annals*. The letters are filled with denunciations of conditions in Germany, but the tone is optimistic: 'Let the dead bury their dead and mourn them. On the other hand, it is enviable to be the first to enter the new life alive; that is to be our lot' (CW 3:134).

Marx married in June 1843 and spent the summer and autumn of that year in the small provincial town of Kreuznach.

Notes

1   An excellent sketch of German history as relevant to German philosophy in the nineteenth century will be found in the first chapter of Lukács, G. *The Destruction of Reason* (London, Merlin Press, 1980).
2   See, for example, CW 1:230, 231, 306, 345.

Chapter 2
Philosophical communist

1

The period which immediately preceded Marx's move to Kreuznach had ended by posing him three tasks. First, he had to acquire a deeper knowledge of the political and social matters which had been forced on his attention by his experiences both of the theory and practice of state censorship and of 'material interests'. Second, the same experiences made urgent the critique of the Hegelian conception of the state and politics which had influenced him so deeply and a reckoning with which he had mooted shortly after his first newspaper article on the Prussian censorship instructions. Third, if his notion of political action as 'critique' was rooted in his social and political ideas, then an alteration of the latter would naturally require a rethinking of the question of the correct programme of political action. Marx addressed himself to all these during his summer in Kreuznach.

With regard to the first he plunged into a study of the relevant literature, working through the history of the French Revolution, through books on the contemporary social scene, especially that in capitalist societies far more developed than the German (for example, Thomas Hamilton's *Men and Manners in America*), and also through the classical writings in the history of political economy and philosophy (including Rousseau, Montesquieu, Machiavelli and de Tocqueville). From the tackling of the second task came the most important single work of this period, a long manuscript (not published till this century) consisting of a paragraph by paragraph critique of central parts of the sections on the state in Hegel's *Philosophy of Right*. (Heine once wrote that 'a great genius forms itself through another great genius less by assimilation than by friction'[1]. If this is so then Marx's *Critique of Hegel's*

'*Philosophy of Right*' is a striking illustration.) These two projects were the main business of the period up to August. In the direction of the third question was the last (written in September) of three letters to his friend Ruge which concerns the programme of political intervention. The final work of the period, written towards the end of his stay in Kreuznach, was a pair of articles 'On the Jewish Question' in which all of the above paths of work came together.

2

I have already commented on the meaning of the idea of 'critique' in Marx's writings of the preceding period. Briefly, it is an examination of some aspect of reality in terms of the concept appropriate to it, that which expresses the relevant essential nature; for example, a law is subject to 'critique' insofar as it is interrogated for its consistency with the ideal function of law as means to rational freedom.

At the present stage of Marx's writings it means something different. Fortunately at one point in the work on Hegel Marx gives an unusually explicit indication of what he means by it. He contrasts what he calls 'vulgar' or 'dogmatic' critique with 'true' or 'truly philosophical' critique:

Vulgar critique falls into... *dogmatic* error... . It finds contradictions everywhere...*fights* with its subject-matter in the same way in which formerly the dogma of the Holy Trinity, say, was demolished by the contradiction of one and three. True critique, by contrast, shows the inner genesis of the Holy Trinity in the human brain. It describes the act of its birth. So...truly philosophical critique...not only shows up contradictions as existing; it *explains* them, it comprehends their genesis, their necessity. (CW 3:91)

This gives the decisive clue to the structure of the method of Marx's 1843 critique of Hegel. He not only subjects Hegel's text to a devastating internal criticism but also works to show how the contradictions and non-sequiturs are actually generated, thus demonstrating both that they are not merely accidental blemishes that might be eliminated, and how they arise necessarily from the theoretical framework itself. Thus Marx, in effect, aims to fulfil the project sketched in his work

17

on the doctorate regarding the explanation of Hegel's
'exoteric' political accommodation on the basis of his 'esoteric'
consciousness.

3

Hegel's doctrine of the state is situated in his central pre-
occupation with the separation between personal, individual
life on the one hand, and political life on the other. This he
thought to have been absent from the ancient, or at least the
classical Greek world but to have been definitively instituted by
the revolutions which had brought about the modern state.
Hegel saw the central task of political theory as the working
out of a model in which the two aspects of life could once more
be brought back into unity without sacrificing the developments of each which had occurred since antiquity.

In Hegel the distinction is marked by that between the
sphere of 'civil society', the domain of purely private endeavours, on the one hand, and the sphere of political life, the
state, the sphere of common, universal life on the other. (It is
essentially Rousseau's distinction between the sphere of
l'homme or *l'homme privé*, and that of *le citoyen*.) In the
Philosophy of Right he seeks to show how the two spheres may
be reconciled by a form of political organization which
includes a monarch, 'estates', and an 'assembly of estates'.

The monarch comes to the throne by birth, and thus
independently of political considerations. An 'estate' is a
group of people having a similar occupation or enjoying the
same legal, economic or social status. Two of the civil estates
are called 'unofficial' because their political significance
accrues to them not directly by virtue of the very conditions by
which they are constituted but indirectly by virtue of their
being represented in the relevant chamber of the legislature.
The first is the 'substantial' estate, which embraces the rural
class and whose principal membership is the landed gentry and
aristocracy. The other is the 'acquisitive' estate, which is the
industrial and commercial class. The grounds of unity, both
within the two estates, and between them and the state, are,
respectively, the principle of primogeniture in entailed
property, and the 'corporations'. The latter are a variety of

trade, professional and municipal organizations, both economic and political in nature. They organize the workings of civil society and represent the latter against the state. The former provides the members of the relevant estate with the stable basis of economic independence which allows for a disinterested political spirit. Finally, in the Assembly of Estates all the elements of society are represented and deliberate about the common weal of society. These universal aims of the state are the business of the estate which consists of the bureaucracy of salaried civil servants, which is thus an estate with both civil and immediately political significance.

4

Marx's criticism consists in the first place in pointing out contradictions within Hegel's doctrines. For example, as regards his identification of landed private property governed by primogeniture as a principle of socio-political unity, he argues that the economic independence of the landed gentry is based on a form of private property which is independent of the state, of civil society and even of the family, and thus independent of all social bonds. In general private property is the force that makes not for cohesion but for lack of it, and thus does not help to unify but precisely to sunder. As for the Assembly of Estates Marx argues that it is a contradictory notion. On the one hand, the relationship of the Estates to civil society makes the state itself a *dependent* extension of civil society (because in them the legislature's essence is guaranteed by independent private property and its existence guaranteed by the privileges of the corporation). On the other hand, that relationship is intended to guarantee the *independence* of the state relative to private interests, for the members of the Estates are supposed to abjure the interests of their civil situation in favour of the universal interests of the body politic.

5

In opposition to all this Marx takes the *people* to be the real subject of political consciousness, and thus sets up the demand for a constitution which is adequate to the will of everyone to be actual members of the state, to affirm in practice the political nature of the species. This is essentially the demand for democracy, which presupposes universal suffrage. But this elevates civil society directly to political significance and thus in effect dissolves it as a separate sphere — which means, correlatively, the disappearance of its complement, the political sphere of the state, which no longer has any rationale. Now the principle of civil society is private property, so the abolition of civil society presupposes its abolition also. Thus the split between civil society and the state which is the problem that Hegel's *Philosophy of Right* set out to solve can be adequately approached only by abolishing the real terms of the problem itself, that is, in the final analysis, by the abolition of private property. But this is just communism.

It is sufficiently clear just from this how far Marx has come in his thinking in only a few months, for his political position now points towards a relation between politics and *economics*: the demand for a certain change in the economic structure has an immediate political consequence and the demand for a certain change in the political structure has an immediate economic precondition. As he said in a later autobiographical sketch, his examination of Hegel's *Philosophy of Right* led him to the conclusion that legal relations and political forms 'originate in the material conditions of life, the totality of which Hegel...embraces within the term "civil society"'. And, he goes on, 'the anatomy of civil society is to be sought in political economy' (EW, 425). Thus the path to a study of political economy is opened up.

Nevertheless Marx is still working at this point with conceptions which he will soon drop. What is fundamental to his thinking is the idea of human beings as sharing an essence:

If...in the exposition of the family, civil society, the state, etc., these social modes of man's existence are regarded as the actualisation, the objectification, of his essence, then the family, etc., appear as qualities inherent in a subject. The human being remains always the essence of all these entities, but these entities also appear as people's *actual* generality, and therefore also as *something people have in common*. (CW 3:39f)

6

So much for the first manoeuvre in Marx's critique, the exhibition of contradictions. What now of the second, the attempt to see the 'conditions of the possibility' of these internal contradictions, and other theoretical difficulties?

Marx locates the theoretical key to Hegel's errors in his *idealism*, that is, as he was to characterize it over twenty years later, in Hegel's view that 'the process of thinking...is the creator of the real world, and the real world...only the external appearance' of thinking (C 1:102).

For the clue to the specific means of production of that idealism Marx turned to Feuerbach. Already in his 'Towards a critique of Hegel's philosophy' (1839) Feuerbach had diagnosed the fundamental move of Hegel's idealism as an *inversion of subject and predicate:* whilst in fact the real world is the subject of predication by universals Hegel turns the universal predicates into subjects (or at least aspects of an all-embracing subject, the 'Idea') and regards the real as accidents of that subject[2]. In *The Essence of Christianity* (1841) Feuerbach had applied this 'transformative method' of criticism to religion, which, he argues, transforms certain predicates of the human species (collective omniscience, omnipotence and so on) into ones pertaining to an imaginary subject, God. And in his 'Preliminary theses for the reform of philosophy', published in February 1843 (in time for Marx to read before he began his Hegel critique) Feuerbach had repeated his point.[3]

Marx takes over this method of criticism. Hegel starts, he writes, not with what is real, the particular subject of an affirmation, but with a thought-entity, a universal, the predicate. Thus Hegel says not 'The monarch is sovereign' but 'The sovereignty of the state is the monarch' (CW 3:25). Thus being is identified as the universal, of the nature of thought, and the real as an accident of the universal. Then, in a subsequent move, the real having been first transmogrified into thought, it is then recovered by presenting it as a product of thought, so that the real becomes an appearance of the ideal world (e.g., CW 3:23f).

The provenance of the contradictions, non-sequiturs and other inadequacies in Hegel's argument then becomes clearer.

For since the basic content of the 'ideal' domain with which Hegel is operating is derived from the real, to the extent that Hegel strives to produce conclusions which are in fact excluded by the structure of the real he must fudge his arguments. In other words, Hegel's arguments have certain constraints which are pre-given from outside the domain of these arguments, namely, by the character of the real subject-matter which his idealist approach distills into concepts alleged to be prior to and productive of that reality. So the argument is condemned either to reproduce in thought the problems of the real or, insofar as it attempts to go outside the framework set by the real, to do so at the expense of consistency and coherence.

This then is Marx's answer to the question posed in his work on his doctoral dissertation regarding Hegel's political accommodation: its source was to be located not in merely accidental personal features of that particular thinker but in the very principle of production of his philosophy. It also explains the force of the conservative element in Hegel: to the extent that the real appears to be given birth to by the ideal, the real in all its actual susceptibility to change is given the appearance of the universality and necessity proper to the domain of pure concepts (CW 3:39, 83).

7

During the period of Marx's work on the critique of Hegel he was also corresponding with his friend Arnold Ruge. In the third, the most important letter, written in September, shortly before his departure from Kreuznach, Marx begins by saying that there is no disagreement among 'truly thinking and independent minds' about what is to be done away with (in the first place the current state of things in Germany). But about the shape of the future there is not only no agreement but not even much individual clarity.

In particular the current idea of communism, considered as equivalent to the abolition of private property is too narrow. For, he says in effect, people are oppressed, dehumanized in ways other than ones which could be removed simply by altering the distribution of property. Contemporary communist doctrines are 'dogmatic' insofar as they simply confront the world with a set of ready-made ends for the realization of which people must cast around for the means. To this Marx opposes what he calls the 'critical' approach, which simply seeks to reveal, through an analysis of the given situation, what its inner tendencies are:

It is precisely the advantage of the new trend that we do not dogmatically anticipate the world, but only want to find the new world through critique of the old one. Hitherto philosophers have had the solution of all riddles lying in their writing-desks, and the stupid, exoteric world had only to open its gob for the roast pigeons of absoute knowledge to fly into it .... But ... constructing the future and settling everything for all times are not our affair.... (CW 3:142)

If this general statement of method is accepted then the further, more concrete question arises: 'We want to influence our contemporaries, particularly our German contemporaries .... How are we to set about it?' (CW 3:143). Marx begins his answer by saying that it is undeniable that the subjects which form the main interest among contemporary Germans are religion followed by politics. Thus, in accordance with the prescriptions of the 'critical' method, the right move is to take these just as they stand and, without confronting them with some ready-made system, to analyze them in such a way as to show the potentialities for human emancipation that they contain.

This is the message of a couple of difficult but crucial sentences heavy with their Hegelian heritage:

Reason has always existed, but not always in a rational form. The critic can therefore start out from any form of theoretical and practical consciousness and from existing reality's *own* forms develop the true reality as what existing reality ought to be and what its final goal is. (CW 3:143)

The continuity between this and Marx's writing during his very recent period of journalism is very sharply expressed in the fact that the sense of the first sentence is already there in a passage in that earlier work (CW 1:155). The meaning is that the essence of human being is freedom, which is equivalent to conformity to the principles of Reason. Thus human beings cannot exist without Reason's existing. So 'Reason has always existed'. But it has not always existed 'in a rational form'

23

because, for example, some people may have used their freedom to try to suppress the freedom of others. So what the social critic has to do is to start from some actually existing form of consciousness and, by analysis, to show the way in which Reason, existing as always, even if not in a rational form, can be emancipated, so that the form is adequate to the principle of Reason. This process of making the form adequate to the principle then becomes an internally defined and not merely externally imported definition of the goals of the present.

Marx goes on to specify this general point more closely with an eye to the contemporary situation which is to be the field of their coming activity:

As far as real life is concerned, it is precisely the *political state* — in all its *modern* forms — which, even where it is not yet consciously imbued with socialist demands, contains the demands of reason. And the political state ... everywhere ... assumes that reason has been realised. But precisely because of that it everywhere becomes involved in the contradiction between its ideal function and its real prerequisites. From this conflict of the political state with itself, therefore, it is possible everywhere to develop the social truth .... the *political state* is a register of the practical struggles of mankind .... Therefore the critic not only can but must deal with ... political questions (which according to the extreme Socialists are altogether unworthy of attention). (CW 3: 143, 144)

We can see from this just how close Marx still is at this point to the positions he held during his period as newspaper editor, but also how far he has distanced himself from them. The state is still conceived of as having a certain ideal function, an essence, namely that of expressing the interests of the human community. That it should truly perform this function is a demand of Reason. But there is an existing contradiction between this essence of the state and the presuppositions for its realization (e.g., the lack of a free press). So the truth is to be revealed by uncovering the lack of correspondence between the essence and the reality. For example, the essential point underlying the difference between the social estate system and the representative system is that between rule by private property and rule by human beings. So the criticism of the former involves a programme of struggle against private property insofar as this stands in the way of realization of the human essence. Extreme socialists despise politics as a means for the realization of fundamental social aims (and — Marx might have added — others pursue politics in abstraction from such aims). His programme is to bring the two together: to struggle for fundamental social reorganization through politics.

Thus, in sum:

We develop new principles for the world out of the world's own principles.... We merely show the world what it is really fighting for.... The reform of consciousness consists *only* in making the world aware of its own consciousness, in awakening it out of its dream about itself, in *explaining* to it the meaning of its own actions..... Hence, our motto, must be: reform of consciousness ... by analysing the mystical consciousness that is unintelligible to itself, whether it manifests itself in a religious or a political form. It will then become evident that the world has long dreamed of possessing something of which it has only to be conscious in order to possess it in reality.... It is a matter of a *confession*, and nothing more. In order to secure remission of its sins, humanity has only to declare them for what they actually are. (CW 3:144f)

Thus the 'reform of consciousness', the new aim, is conceived as something going on basically within consciousness, being simply a way of making people aware of the true origins and nature of what they think, believe and do. A dream vanishes when it is recognized as a dream, and religious and political mystification vanishes once it is recognized *as* mystification. Just as a sin is erased with the confession of it, so remission for humanity's 'sins' — failure to realize the coincidence of reality and the demands of Reason, inadequate consciousness of itself and its actions — is gained just by the act of declaring what it has done and failed to do. It is this process of helping to make humanity conscious of its real situation that the new journal is intended to forward.

8

Work in accordance with this programme is ideally exemplified in the last major writing of the Kreuznach period, a pair of articles 'On the Jewish question', which unites the topics of religion and politics and brings together all the main themes in the work with which Marx had been most recently preoccupied.

The immediate context of the articles was this. Whilst the French Revolution had brought complete social and political emancipation for Jewry, for the first time in Europe, the regimes of the Restoration after 1815 had striven to reverse this. (I have mentioned earlier how Marx's father had felt the effects of this.) In 1843 the Rhenish parliament had voted for Jewish emancipation once more, but this had been quashed by the king. Bruno Bauer had just published two pieces, allegedly from the standpoint of the Left. In the first he argued that Jews cannot seriously expect civil-political emancipation within a state to whose fundamental religion they are hostile; furthermore that, insofar as all they are asking for is the rights of Christian subjects, they thereby accept, in effect, the oppressive character of the state as such and do not deserve to be supported. In the second he argued that in fact Judaism is a religion that renders those adhering to it less capable of becoming free than Christianity does.

Marx's argument in his first article is essentially this. Jews' being politically emancipated, that is, its being the case that their religious beliefs are no barrier to enjoying political rights, just means that people's religious beliefs in general do not constitute any part of their qualifications for political rights. But this, far from being inconsistent with the nature of the modern political state, is totally in accord with it. For this form of state rests on a sharp separation between, on the one hand, the sphere of the private individual — into which falls the question of religious belief — and, on the other, the sphere of what is common to individuals as members of humanity (its 'species-life'). The former is the domain of civil society, the latter of the state. People's real, everyday lives are led in civil society and they live an ideal life in an imaginary sphere of universality, the state. In this respect civil society has a relation to the state similar to that which secular life has to heaven. Political emancipation is to be supported unconditionally because it does away with all privileges based on the special characteristics of individuals considered just as individuals, and to that extent in fact affirms their species-character. But this sort of emancipation must not be confused with 'human' emancipation which consists precisely in the freeing of human beings from the situation in which their lives suffer a diremption into two quite separate domains, in one of which they live in a merely imaginary fashion. Referring to Rousseau (whom of course he had been recently studying) Marx concludes:

Only when the real individual person re-absorbs in himself the abstract citizen, and as an individual human being has become a species-being in his everyday life, in his particular work, and in his particular situation, only when humanity has recognised and organised his 'forces propres' as *social* forces, and consequently no longer separates social power from himself in the shape of *political* power, only then will human emancipation have been accomplished. (CW 3:168)

9

In the second part of his article Marx argues that it is just the separation between the sphere of the pursuit of purely individual interest on the one hand the the sphere of communal interest on the other which is at the basis of religion itself. Furthermore, the root of the distinction between the two spheres is the existence of civil society, which is the real factor and whose nature is such as to require an ideal counterpart in the state. But the principle of civil society is buying and selling, which finds its concentrated expression in *money*, the reified embodiment of people's essential powers. As such it is the common root of the alienated 'ideal' forms of which the principal types are the political and the religious domains:

Money is the estranged essence of people's work and people's existence and this alien essence dominates them, and they worship it. . . . Just as people, as long as they are in the grip of religion, are able to objectify their essential nature only by turning it into something *alien*, something fantastic, so under the domination of egoistic need they can be active practically, and produce objects in practice, only by putting their products and their activity, under the domination of an alien being, and bestowing the significance of an alien entity — money — on them. (CW 3:172, 174)

So the two parts come together. The first defined the conditions for the political emancipation of Jewry, that is, for

Jews to be able to enjoy full civil rights. These were the conditions which obtain in the modern state, involving a complete separation between the sphere of civil society and that of politics, between the world of purely individual interest and that of putative common interest. Now Marx identifies the world of civil society as precisely that which generates Judaism as a typical religion. So just as the condition for the political emancipation of Jewry is a separation of the sphere of civil society from that of the state, the condition for the abolition of Jewry as a religion, and hence the 'human' or 'social' emancipation of the Jew, is the subsequent doing away with that separation.

The article concludes:

Once society has succeeded in abolishing the *empirical* essence of Judaism — huckstering and its preconditions — the Jew will have become *impossible*, because his consciousness no longer has an object, because the subjective basis of Judaism, practical need, has been humanised, and because the conflict between people's individual-sensuous existence and their species-existence has been abolished. The *social* emancipation of the Jew is the *emancipation of society from Judaism*. (CW 3:174)[4]

10

'On the Jewish question' was significant in Marx's development on a number of counts. It strikingly exemplifies the programme, set out in the letter to Ruge presented above, of linking particular political goals with wider ranging ones concerning social reorganization (political emancipation of Jewry with abolition of private property). Again, it shows Marx's newly found materialistic method at work. Bauer's discussion of the question of the political emancipation of Jewry and of the emancipation of society from religion was in religious terms; it is replaced here by an inquiry into the social bases of each. In the second article especially, the idea of the products of human activity gaining a power over their producers brings forward the idea of 'estrangement', which will be developed in the next period of Marx's work. Finally, an economic concept — money — enters here for the first time, even if in philosophical garb, once more pointing the way to the importance of political economy.

11

Marx's last letter to Ruge, commented upon in some detail earlier, announces his imminent departure from Germany and fairly breathes relief and anticipation. 'Whether the enterprise' — the idea of a jointly edited Franco-German periodical — 'comes into being or not, in any case I shall be in Paris by the end of this month, since the atmosphere here makes one a serf' (CW 3:142).

Notes

1   Heine, *Sämtliche Schriften*, ed. H. Briegleb (Munich/Vienna, Hanser Verlag, 1976), vol. 5, p. 561.
2   *The Fiery Brook. Selected Writings of Ludwig Feuerbach* (trans. Z. Hanfi) (Garden City, New York, Anchor Books, 1972), pp. 81f. At least one remark in the preliminary notes to Marx's dissertation (CW 1:458) makes it very likely that he had already read passages like this.
3   Feuerbach, *op. cit.,* p. 168.
4   It is important to remember in reading these two articles that Marx uses 'Jew', 'Judaism', etc. in a somewhat ambiguous way. He uses them sometimes in a quite literal manner, but sometimes (in particular in the passage to which this is an explanatory note) in a way perfectly common at the time (as it is to a lesser extent today) to signify a type of orientation to the world, roughly, one dominated by trading (especially petty trading) and desire to make money. Listen for example to what Heine (himself a Jew of course) wrote round about this time:

> 'Jews' and 'Christians' are for me words thoroughly related in meaning in contrast with 'Hellenes', by which name I similarly designate not a definite people but a mental tendency and way of looking at things which is both inborn and a result of upbringing. ... Thus there were Hellenes in the families of German parsons and Jews born in Athens and perhaps tracing their descent from Theseus. The beard does not make the Jew or the tail of a wig the Christian. (Heine, *op. cit.*, vol. 7, p. 18)

There is a detailed treatment of the whole matter in Draper, H. *Karl Marx's Theory of Revolution*, vol. I (New York and London, Monthly Review Press, 1977), pp. 591ff.

Chapter 3
Revolutionary communist

1

'Freedom is a new religion, the religion of our age', wrote Heine about this time:

The French are the chosen people of the new religion, the first gospels and dogmas were penned in their language. Paris is the new Jerusalem, and the Rhine is the Jordan which separates the land of Freedom from the land of the Philistines.[1]

Paris was indeed the ideal place for Marx to acquire that knowledge, both theoretical and practical, of contemporary socialist-communist movements, the lack of which he had admitted during his period of journalism and which was made more pressing by the programme of political intervention laid out in the September letter to Ruge.

France (and indeed Western Europe) was still living in the shadow of 1789. The 'Restoration' of 1815 was very largely one in name only. The victors over Napoleon tried to impose from above a political order which would take Europe back to the relative equilibrium of pre-Revolutionary Europe. But the economic and general social tendencies which had given rise to the French Revolution were still working in the ground. If 1848 was to be the volcanic explosion that released the forces which had been building up since the artificial equipoise established in 1815, 1830 stands in the middle of the period not only chronologically but in real terms too. Especially in France with the fall of the Restoration king Charles X as a result of a workers' insurrection it meant the definitive defeat by the bourgeoisie of its former aristocratic opponents. (In Britain the process was characteristically more peaceful with the Reform Bill of 1832.) But precisely because this victory had been won by the workers it meant the emergence of the working class as an independent and self-conscious force. From then on, with the feudal-absolutist enemy effectively off the battlefield it was a question of the confrontation of two classes which, since they had been united in opposition to the common enemy before, had not clearly constituted themselves *as* classes. The period from 1830 to 1848 was thus one of contestation.

The period obviously provided an ideal culture for socialist and communist currents. This is not the place to try to sketch their earlier sources. One was the Industrial Revolution. The social problems and potentialities of this were the main springs of the 'Utopian' socialism represented in England by Robert Owen (1771-1858) and in France by St Simon (1706-1825) and Fourier (1772-1837). This combined with the other, which was the French Revolution and in particular the Left revolutionary Jacobin secret societies and Parisian workers' clubs stemming from the tradition of Babeuf, especially as transmitted in the writings of his comrade-in-arms Buonarotti, which had sought to carry through consistently the egalitarian tendencies of the Revolution. This stream of French communism had a continuous history from the later period of the French revolution. Secret societies of a socialist-communist nature were a continuing feature of French political life in the face of the repression which political opposition faced under the 'July monarchy' of Louis Phillipe, successor to Charles X, and they were associated with a series of workers' uprisings from 1831 onwards.

Such societies also existed in the large German colony in Paris consisting mainly of migrant workers and refugees. The latter had formed the 'League of Outlaws', the left wing of which had broken away in 1836 to form the 'League of the Just'. Marx and his family actually lived with one of the leaders of the latter (Germain Mäurer), and he immediately established contacts with various tendencies in the French communist and socialist movements. From the end of 1843 to March 1844 he also made an intensive study of the French Revolution (with a view in particular to writing a history of the Convention).

31

2

The impact of his new experience is evident in Marx's first major writing after his arrival in Paris, the 'Contribution to the critique of Hegel's philosophy of right. Introduction', which came out in February 1844 in the first issue (a double number) of the *German-French Annals.*

The title of the article very naturally suggests that it is a preliminary to the long commentary on Hegel's theory of the state, some major aspects of which were surveyed in the preceding chapter; and indeed this is how Marx represented it later (EW 425). In fact it is a quite independent piece, politically well in advance of what he had written hitherto, and in particular of the critique of Hegel written at Kreuznach. It is a highly transitional work. On the one hand, it presents a revolutionary rather than philosophical communist position, identifying the working class as an actual agent for the communist reorganisation of society. On the other, the conception of social change in it is still very idealist in character, despite his decisive embracing of a general materialistic position in the earlier Hegel-critique. These two elements exist in a symbiosis the essential lines of which I shall now briefly trace.

The article begins with a famous passage on religion which is one of the high-points of rhetorical prose in world literature. Religion having been revealed to be generated by and a response to secular conditions, the next task is the critique of these and the formulation of a programme for changing them. And since the political arena for Marx is primarily Germany, Marx plunges at once into an analysis of the state of affairs in Germany.

Germany's political backwardness, Marx writes, is explained by the fact that it never experienced, as England and France did in the seventeenth and eighteenth centuries respectively, a revolution which brought the bourgeoisie to power in a way corresponding to its economic development. What is has is essentially a capitalist economy with a feudal state. But, he goes on, if Germany is behind the advanced nations in its actual political situation, it is contemporary with them as regards the state of its philosophy, in the sense that what England and France attained to in social reality Germany achieved in thought, in philosophy, with its central concepts of Reason and Freedom.

How does this advanced philosophy relate to the state of politics in Germany? He distinguishes two directions here. The 'practical' one (Marx doubtless has in mind German communist writers like Weitling) 'demands the *negation of philosophy*'; but they forget that '*you cannot supersede philosophy without making it a reality*'. However the 'theoretical' group (most probably the Young Hegelians) '*thought it could make philosophy a reality without superseding it*'. Marx does not spell out what he means here, but it can be put as follows. Philosophy (like religion) is a product of a certain sort of world, namely one which, not allowing the practical realization of certain human goals like free self-activity, diverts preoccupation with them into their purely theoretical elaboration and contemplation. The 'practical' party does not realize this and thinks that philosophical speculation can be done away with just by a gesture of rejection. But the only way to get rid of philosophy (as of religion) is to abolish the situation which gives rise to it, that is, to bring about a state of affairs in the world which realizes in practical terms what philosophy realizes only in the mind, and hence to make unnecessary the purely speculative completion of the real. But, conversely, the 'theoretical' party does not see that once speculative philosophy's ideal demands are realized in practice philosophy's whole rationale is at an end, for its very existence depends upon the gap between reality and humanity's deepest aspirations. Thus the basic political task is the realization, the making real, of the demands of philosophy. Germany's revolutionary past consists in the Reformation. 'As the revolution then began in the brain of the *monk*, so now it begins in the brain of the *philosopher*.... *Our status quo* will be shattered against philosophy' (CW 3: 182, 183).

Of course 'the weapon of criticism cannot... replace criticism by weapons, material force must be overthrown by material force; but theory also becomes a material force once it has gripped the masses' (CW 3: 182). So the question is: What, if any, is the element in Germany that can be gripped by theory, that can actually use the weapons that critical philosophy has to hand? Now 'theory can be realized in a people only insofar as it is the realization of the needs of that people' (CW 3:183). Thus the question becomes: Is there a group in Germany whose practical needs are such that only a total social revolution such as is envisaged by philosophy can satisfy them? Such a group must be one which not only has no stake in existing society but whose 'universal suffering' stems wholly from existing society, so can be removed only by the total destruction of the latter and thus entail the emancipation of other groups too. The only class that fills this bill is the proletariat. So philosophy and the proletariat complement one another: 'As philosophy finds its *material* weapons in the proletariat, the proletariat finds its *mental* weapons in philosophy... . The *head* of... emancipation is *philosophy*, its *heart* is the *proletariat*' (CW 3:187). And all this fits together neatly with Marx's criticisms of the 'practical' and the 'theoretical' parties. For the proletariat is the agent of realization of philosophy, and the realization of philosophy (i.e., the realization of the ideals it proclaims), entails the total overthrow of the prevailing order, and thus the disappearance of the proletariat. Therefore philosophy's being made a reality on the one hand, and the abolition of the proletariat on the other are coincident.

As I indicated at the beginning the article is a highly transitional one. On the one hand, Marx passes beyond the mere philosophical deduction of communism from the demand for the realization of the species-being of humanity and looks to the working class as the agent that will, material weapons in hand, bring about communism. On the other hand, ideal factors — in particular philosophy — are still seen as the inner force of that revolution, articulating the needs of the suffering mass that is the proletariat; indeed the identification of the working class as the agent of change proceeds by a purely speculative deduction.

3

We have seen that one of the consequences both of Marx's work as a journalist and also of his critique of Hegel's doctrine of the state was to impel him in the direction of acquiring a knowledge of 'political economy'. This was, in Marx's time, a heterogeneous body of writing which had originated in the seventeenth century, on the one hand in England (Mercantilist theories) and on the other in France (the Physiocrats). The substantial tie was the common project of comprehending the capitalist society of their different times and forming the basis for practical interventions on the part of various interest-groups. France was also a very favourable place for Marx to study this political economy, both because of the native French contribution to it and also because much of the English literature on the subject (in particular the work of the two giants Adam Smith and David Ricardo) was available in French, Marx's English still being shaky. Accordingly, between the time when he arrived in France at the end of 1843 and March 1844 he began a systematic study of the subject, filling many notebooks with extracts and commentaries (notably a dissertation on a French translation of James Mill's *Elements of Political Economy*). His work was decisively stimulated by one of the essays recently published in the *German-French Annals*, namely, 'Outlines of a critique of political economy' by one Friedrich Engels.

Marx continued these studies from April 1844 onwards through the spring and autumn, writing a work which he laid down unfinished in August of that year. It did not, in fact, see print for nearly a century and then under the editor's title, *Economic and Philosophical Manuscripts of 1844* (also sometimes referred to simply as *The 1844 Manuscripts* or *The Paris Manuscripts*).

As we have seen, there had been three main streams of theoretical endeavour in Marx's intellectual history so far: philosophy (mainly German, and particularly Hegel and Feuerbach), socialism and communism (mainly French), and political economy (mainly English). All ran together at this point into a synthesis which was no less significant for being a merely very temporary station on Marx's theoretical journey. It goes without saying that it is the major work of his Paris period.

Not all of what Marx did write of this work has come down to us. What we have are three manuscripts (or four, depending on how they are divided up). Broadly speaking they have three themes — the ones mentioned above — which occur in the inverse order to that which they have in Marx's intellectual biography. The strictly economic theme, that of the political economy of capitalism and its critique, takes up the first two manuscripts and the middle part of the third; the political theme, discussion of the communist alternative to capitalism, occupies the first part of the third manuscript; and philosophical themes, mainly relating to Hegel, conclude it. I shall now indicate something of the main content of the work. (All page references till further notice will be to CW 3.)

4

The first manuscript consists of four major subsections, of which the last, that on 'estranged labour', is the one most read and anthologized, the first three indeed being seldom considered with any real care. But just a little attention to them reveals that, if they do not have major systematic significance in the light of Marx's later work, they are of the first importance from the point of view of his theoretical development.

What is new here is very largely encapsulated in the very first words of the first manuscript: 'Wages are determined through the antagonistic struggle between capitalist and worker' (235). These are simple words, but fateful in marking important breakthroughs for Marx. First, he is here concerned with *wage* labour and not just labour in general performed to earn a living, which is what he has been preoccupied with so far. He is here talking about developed capitalism, about industrial, factory labour (293). Second, and of course intimately connected with this, he is definitively within the context of *class* analysis: the wage is a matter of a relation between two basic classes, workers and capitalists (266, 270). Third, the relationship between the classes is one of *struggle*: the idea of class struggle has already been there in Marx's writings, but now it has been given a name (260). Moreover the wage-labour / capital antithesis is conceived as an *active* principle, representing a *contradiction* in modern society; it is an internal, constitutive relation between the classes, not a merely accidental one (293f, 312, 237). Thus the working class is depicted here quite differently from the way it was in the article surveyed earlier in this chapter, where it was presented just as 'a class with *radical chains*', a class marked out by 'its universal suffering' (186). Further, the resolution of the contradiction consists in a *revolution* which is thus conceived as a working out of inner tendencies of capitalist society and in particular by way of basically inner tendencies in the *economy* (270, 297).

But for all this Marx's use and presentation of the received political economy is still very undeveloped in comparison with what he will do with it later. He has no independent theory of the economic domain (this will not be achieved for another dozen years) and hence no *theory* of its developmental tendencies which are registered just as the obvious fact of the progressive polarization of wealth and poverty. Thus the economic analysis is still at a primitive level and the vacuum which thus exists is filled by moral critique. In fact Marx basically accepts the received economics: he just thinks that it does not really understand what it is doing deeply enough, what the significance of its results is, and therefore does not draw appropriate political conclusions. As he writes at the beginning of the last subsection:

We have proceeded from the premises of political economy. We have accepted its language and its laws . . . . Political economy starts with the fact of private property; it does not explain it to us. It expresses in general, abstract formulas the *material* process through which private property actually passes, and these formulas it then takes for *laws*. It does not *comprehend* these laws, i.e., it does not demonstrate how they arise from the very nature of private property. (270f)

It is as an attempt to 'explain', to 'comprehend' the results of political economy that Marx presents the section on 'estranged labour'.

5

Marx says here that he proceeds from 'an *actual* economic fact', namely, that:

The worker becomes all the poorer the more wealth he produces, the more his production increases in power and size. The worker becomes an ever cheaper commodity the more commodities he

37

creates. The *devaluation* of the world of human beings is in direct proportion to the *increasing value* of the world of things. (271f)

Marx proceeds to list four ways in which this 'economic fact' depends on what he calls 'estranged labour' (272ff):

1   Workers are deprived of the *product* of their labour and, in the hands of capital, it confronts them as a hostile power. Indeed workers are separated from their very means of life and labour, which, again in the hands of capital, become a power over and against them.

2   This 'estrangement' from the material preconditions of their producing and from their product depends in turn upon an estrangement involved in the *act of production*: what Marx calls 'self-estrangement'. This is a matter of the productive activity's being alien to workers in the sense that it is not, in general, a way of expressing and developing themselves. Thus labour is 'forced labour': what should be an end in itself, as the constitutive property of the species (self-objectification) becomes a mere means to an end, namely, avoiding labour. The labour is not what it should be, namely, what is most intimately the workers' own, but the property of someone else, becomes a possession of others (capital).

3   In turn, 1 and 2 above imply a third mode of estrangement, that of the worker from the *species*. The life of the species is essentially constituted by the universal appropriation of nature by means of free productive activity. Insofar as workers cannot freely appropriate their product and do not engage in free productive activity they are estranged from the species; the nature of the species becomes alien to them. What constitutes the intrinsic end of the species becomes merely a means to other ends.

4   Finally, by virtue of 1, 2 and 3 above, and most proximately the last, workers are estranged from *one another*: people do not relate to one another as members of the species (since they do not relate to the species in terms of its essential character) but only as potential *means* for the private ends of each.

Now, Marx goes on (278ff), the task is to see 'how the concept of estranged, alienated labour must express and present itself in real life' (278). His argument is essentially this. If the product of workers' labour is alien to the worker, then it must belong elsewhere. But, for reasons which Marx sorts out to his own satisfaction, this must be other people. So the objects the worker produces are the private property of others. Thus the whole result of the argument, Marx says, is that:

> *private property* is ... the product, the result, the necessary consequence, of *alienated labour* .... Private property thus results by analysis from the concept of *alienated labour*. (279)

The discussion ends, after a few more pages, with the posing of two questions, the second of which is this:

> We have accepted the *estrangement of labour*, its *alienation*, as a fact, and we have analysed this fact. How, we now ask, do *human beings* come to *alienate*, to estrange, their *labour*? How is this estrangement rooted in the nature of human development? (281)

The manuscript breaks off unfinished before any attempt to answer this question. (I shall return to this theme in the next chapter in a discussion of the theme of communism in *The German Ideology*.)

6

The concept of private property is the point of transition from the political economic strand to the political, to the treatment of communism, for this is just the abolition of private property. But private property can be abolished (or 'negated') in one of two ways. It is abolished negatively by 'a *generalisation* and *consummation* of it'. That is, private property is brought to its *highest form* by being made *common* property — *common* property is still *property*:

> This type of communism — since it negates the *personality* of human beings in every sphere — is but the logical expression of private property, which is this negation. General *envy* constituting itself as a power is the disguise in which *greed* re-establishes itself and satisfies itself, only in *another* way. ... Crude communism is only the culmination of this envy and of this levelling-down proceeding from the *preconceived* minimum. It has a *definite limited* standard. How little this annulment of private property is really an appropriation is in fact proved by the abstract negation of the entire world of culture and civilisation, the regression to the *unnatural* simplicity of the *poor* and crude person who has few needs and who has not only failed to

39

go beyond private property, but has not yet even reached it. (295)

Private property can only be abolished positively, and true communism established, when the very root of private property is destroyed. According to the analysis of the preceding part this is estranged labour. Therefore the positive negation of private property is a matter of the abolition of estranged labour. In turn, estranged labour is essentially productive labour which is separated from its object (the means of labour and the product of the labour) and from the subject (the activity of labour does not realize and develop the producers). So the negation of estranged labour is labour which does not suffer from either of these features. It is a form of productive activity in which the freely produced and appropriated object is a realization of the self, the mirroring of the self in objective situations (humanization of the natural). And it is a productive activity in which the self reflects the object insofar as it is a question of developing human powers adequate to the appropriation of objects according to their own characteristics (naturalization of the human). With this the individual is once more united with the species and with other individuals. Private property identifies appropriation in all its forms with *possessing*: all modes of interaction with the world are reduced to this single, primitive relation.

7

These twin themes of estranged labour and its overcoming through the instituting of free productive activity leads to the third main theme of the *Manuscripts*, namely, the critique of philosophy, but, more especially, the critique of Hegelian philosophy. Marx here brings together the relevant themes in his writing up till now and develops others. It is his last real reckoning with Hegel.

Marx has essentially two things to say about Hegel, one positive and the other negative and critical. The positive thing (a new element in Marx's Hegel critique up till now) is that Hegel made an immense contribution to conceiving history in terms of the way in which humanity becomes what it is at a time through a process of labour: at every point in its development humanity realizes and develops its collective powers by an activity of objectifying itself in the natural and social world.

The negative, critical point is, to begin with, that Hegel, using *mental* labour as his paradigm, sees this whole developmental process as occurring entirely within the realm of thought (even if transindividual thought) so that the whole conception is irremediably idealist in character. According to Hegel the odyssey of humanity consists in Absolute Mind's self-recognition. In the course of history Absolute Mind objectifies itself, by means of productive activity, in a series of forms. The agents of this objectification, human beings, do not recognize these as forms of Mind, but take them to be irreducibly objective, alien to Mind. But in the final event the opacity of the apparently wholly objective is broken and subject and object are recognized as being one.

Marx's objection is that Hegel here confuses *estrangement* with *objectification*. Certainly humanity has, under the regime of private property, been estranged from the results of its own activity, from its self-objectifications, its own creations having escaped from its control and taken on a life of their own. But the recovery of the world of *estranged* objects is still the recovery of a world of *objects*, whereas for Hegel the overcoming of the appearance of the alienness of objects in history is identical with an overcoming of the idea of their essential otherness with respect to humanity.

Marx then recurs to the point that he had made already in the 1843 critique of Hegel, namely, that insofar as Hegel rejects the shapes of humanity's objectifications only to the extent that their presumed objective character is denied, the shapes themselves are allowed to persist, and religion, the state, and so on are left essentially as they were. 'Here *is* the root of Hegel's *false* positivism, or of his merely *apparent* criticism' (339). That is, just as positivism straightforwardly and as a matter of programmatic principle confines itself to an account of things as they are, Hegel really does the same, only covertly. So once more the point is that Hegel's conservatism was not some in principle accidental feature of his position which might be dispensed with in order to preserve the rest, but

41

an essential consequence of the very principle of his method.

8

The first number of the *German-French Annals*, which appeared in February 1844, also proved to be the last. It folded for various reasons: the hoped-for co-operation between French and German writers did not eventuate; there was a heavy loss due to a seizure of a large number of copies at the German frontier; and there was a gradual falling-out on both personal and political grounds between Marx and Ruge, principally connected with Marx's going over to revolutionary communism.

This schism was consummated by an article which Marx published in early August 1844 just as he was finishing work on the *Manuscripts*. The article was entitled 'Critical marginal notes on the article "The King of Prussia and social reform. By a Prussian"', the 'Prussian' being Ruge. The background was this. In June 1844 there had been a rising of a large number of Silesian weavers, a wretchedly exploited group of domestic handicraftspeople. They had destroyed the homes of some of their masters, and, using only weapons like sticks and stones, won a battle against troops sent to quell them, before being crushed by vastly superior forces, and subjected to savage repression. In his article Ruge had downplayed the significance of the events and presented a generally very pessimistic view of the perspectives for social change in Germany.

There is no question of even summarizing Marx's complex and sulphurous reply. Just two points may be made about this article which represents a significant advance in Marx's thinking in several respects. First, whilst it has clearly discernible overtones of the article surveyed at the beginning of this chapter there is a crucial change in regard to it: now it is not German philosophers or philosophy that are the bearers of revolutionary theory but the people themselves:

The German proletariat is the *theoretician* of the European proletariat.... A philosophical people can find its corresponding practice only in socialism.... Confronted with the first outbreak of the Silesian workers' uprising, the sole task of one who thinks and loves the truth consisted not in playing the role of *school-master* in relation to this event, but instead in studying its *specific* character. (CW 3:202)

Second, the article shows a notable change in what Marx had had to say thus far on the nature of the state, namely, that it represents in an imaginary way the species-being of humanity the members of which are in fact separated by the regime of private property and money. In this article the state is still based upon the contradiction between public and private life, between general and individual interests. But now the sphere of the latter is identified with that of 'trade...industry... mutual plundering'. He concludes that the '*slavery of civil society* is the natural foundation on which the *modern* state rests...the existence of the state and the existence of slavery are inseparable' (CW 3:198).

9

The main event in August was to prove one of the most important in Marx's life. At the end of the month one Friedrich Engels passed through Paris on a trip home to Germany, and the two met. They had already made each other's acquaintance in 1842 whilst Marx was editor of the *Rheinische Zeitung*. But the meeting was not cordial on Marx's side as he associated Engels with The Libertarians in Berlin (where Engels had been both following up his literary and philosophical interests and doing his military service), a set from whom Marx had dissociated himself. Meanwhile Engels has been working in the family business in Manchester and, amongst other things, had contributed two pieces to the *Annals*, one of which especially (that on political economy), Marx thought very highly of, both at the time and later. When they met for this second time they found that they agreed on all essential points concerning their views on society and history. Thus commenced one of the great friendships and collaborations.

In September they began their first work together. Marx in fact wrote most of it, Engels having begun at the same time an already projected work. (This was published the following year — *The Condition of the Working Class in England*.) The joint work was finished by November 1844 and published in

February 1845: *The Holy Family or Critique of Critical Critique. Against Bruno Bauer and Company.*

The title of the book gives more than a hint both of its subject matter and literary character. It is in fact basically a dissection of work by some of the post-Hegelian epigones, particularly the Bauer brothers, detailed often past the point of any interest to a present-day reader who does not have specialist interests in such matters, and written in a tone of mockery which is often very funny and effective but also often heavy-handed and tedious. The reader who is familiar with Marx's writings up to this point will not find a great deal that is new in the book though there are some notable excurses on particular themes.[2] Feuerbach is still a dominant influence.

10

Marx had published his article against Ruge in *Vorwärts*, a German newspaper in Brussels on the editorial board of which he served. In January 1845 he and a number of other German migrants in Paris who were collaborators on the paper received an expulsion order from the French government. This was a result of pressure from the Prussian government, which had already accused Marx of 'high treason and *lèse majesté*' on account of his articles in the *Annals* and had issued a warrant for his arrest should he enter Prussian territory. After some toing and froing it was agreed that the paper should cease publication in return for a recision of the expulsion order. But Marx chose to leave. February 1845 saw him and his family resettled in Brussels.

Notes

1 *The Prose Works of Heinrich Heine* ed. H. Ellis (London, Walter Scott, n.d.), pp. 64f. (The passage is from Heine's *Travel Pictures*, Part IV, section entitled 'The Liberation'.)

2 These include an attack on the idealist view of history at the beginning of Chapter VI, the brief history of modern materialism in Section 3 of the same chapter, and the long analysis of Eugene Sue's *The Mysteries of Paris*, which forms Chapter VIII (Marx's most extended discussion of morality).

PART II: 1845-1850

Chapter 4
Historical materialism and communism

1

Just before leaving Paris Marx had signed a contract with a German publisher for a book to be called *A Critique of Economics and Politics*, the deadline being the summer of 1845. Only what is probably a set of headings for the political part of this work survives (CW 4:666). Engels proposed the idea of a critique of the economist Friedrich List as a representative of the aspirations of the German bourgeoisie, and also a series of translations of the Utopian socialists. A long draft of an article on List from Marx's pen has been found (CW 4:265), as has a plan for a 'Library of the best foreign socialist writers' (CW 4:667); but that is all. For the rest Marx worked hard at his reading on economic and social matters. The most famous of the few writings of this period is a set of brief remarks published posthumously by Engels as 'Theses on Feuerbach', a concise sketch of themes to be developed in *The German Ideology* (about which more presently).[1]

Engels arrived in Brussels in April. The two worked together on their new conception of history. In July they took a six week trip to England, the 'classic' capitalist economy of the time. They stayed there till September, studying English political economy, meeting the English Chartist leader George Harney and leaders of German workers' organizations in London, and on one occasion attending a meeting of the Chartists and representatives of various revolutionary groups called to consider the idea of founding an international organization, the 'Fraternal Democrats'.

47

2

Back from England Marx decided to interrupt his work on the *Critique* in order to write — as he told his publisher — 'a polemical piece against German philosophy and current *German socialism*' which would precede the presentation of his (and Engels') own positive views and thus prepare the public for the *Critique* with its radically different standpoint (W 27:448f). As we have already seen, they had criticized the Young Hegelians and others in *The Holy Family*. But this had been before they had arrived at their conception of history in the form in which they now had it, and also whilst they were still strongly under the influence of Feuerbach. So it was necessary, they thought, to have a final show-down with the Young Hegelians from their present standpoint, which would also have to be presented. It was furthermore necessary to take a clear critical distance from Feuerbach in the light of a recent reply by Bruno Bauer to *The Holy Family* in which he had referred to Marx and Engels as Feuerbachians. Finally, a Young Hegelian anarchist Max Stirner had published in November 1844 what soon became an influential book, *The Ego and Its Own*, and this contained amongst other things a criticism of Marx and Engels.

The two worked on the project from the winter of 1845 to late summer 1846. Unforeseen difficulties arose with regard to publishing the manuscript which was finally 'abandoned . . . to the mordant criticism of the mice' (EW 427). (The manuscript was not published as a whole, or substantially so, till 1932.)

The work was called *The German Ideology* and subtitled *Critique of Modern German Philosophy According to Its Representatives Feuerbach, B. Bauer and Stirner, and of German Socialism According to Its Various Prophets*. This, in fact, gives an accurate indication of its contents which is divided into three main parts, the first and most important a critique of Feuerbach in the framework of a presentation of the new materialist conception of history, the second an attack on Bruno Bauer and (especially) Max Stirner, and the third a criticism of German socialist literature.

3

It is worth emphasizing that the materialist conception of history is essentially a product of this period no matter how much preliminary work had already been carried out. This emerges from an examination of the key ideas of the new theory. It is also what Marx himself says in the brief auto-biographical sketch contained in the Preface to the later *Contribution to a Critique of Political Economy*. He writes here (EW 425) that his examination of Hegel's *Philosophy of Right* led him to the conclusion that legal relations and political forms originate in material conditions the 'anatomy' of which is to be sought in political economy. He goes on to say that 'the study of this, which I began in Paris, I continued in Brussels'. He then summarizes, in an oft-cited passage, 'the general result' at which he arrived as a consequence of these studies and which became 'the guide' of his further studies.

Presentation and discussion of the main ideas of the new analysis of society and history contained in the 'Theses on Feuerbach' and *The German Ideology* will be one of the main themes of the next part of this book. It must suffice here to sketch in just a few words the essential idea.

This was, most centrally, that the way in which a society produces and reproduces its material means of life is the most primary determinant of the other characteristics of that society. This replaces the point of view of the *1844 Manuscripts* according to which humanity is ascribed certain essential characteristics which are, amongst other things, used as a criterion with which to judge social arrangements:

The premises from which we begin are not... dogmas, but real premises.... Human beings... begin to distinguish themselves from animals as soon as they begin to *produce* their means of subsistence. (CW 5:31)

Talk of 'alienation' and 'estrangement' as the Young Hegelians and Feuerbachians understood it (and as Marx had done not long before) is pitilessly mocked; though the terminology is used at various places it is ascribed a quite new content. Only a year or so later Marx writes about how the Germans, interpreting French Communist literature in terms of German philosophy 'wrote their philosophical nonsense beneath the French original. For instance, beneath the French criticism of the economic functions of money, they wrote "Estrangement of Humanity"'; and in the same place he writes how the same Germans thought of themselves not as representing the interest of definite groups but of 'Human Nature, of Man in General, who belongs to no class, has no reality, who exists only in the misty realms of philosophical fantasy' (CW 6:511). At a still later time he would recall this period and its '*humanism*, the catch-phrase with which all the muddle-heads in Germany...have covered up their embarrassment' (CW 11:270).

More specifically, what, according to this conception, has been crucial about the modes of production and reproduction of material life over the most significant part of human history has been the fact that the means by which production has been carried on have been controlled by one group of people but worked by others, with the result that the former could live off the labour of the latter. This has meant that there has existed a set of practices and associated organizations and institutions a central function of which is the maintenance of this state of affairs. It also determines the character of the ways in which the members of a society represent that society and themselves. But the time is ripe for the abolition of this situation of oppression, for the reorganization of society along communist lines.

4

Marx's thinking about communism at this stage in fact requires a somewhat fuller treatment.

The basic contrast in the work is that between what Marx calls 'natural' (*naturwüchsige*) society and communist society. The first signifies a state of society the cause of which is not 'subordinated to a general plan of freely combined individuals' (CW 5:83) and hence where 'people's own deeds become an alien power opposed to them, which enslaves them instead of being controlled by them' (CW 5:47). The second, communism for the first time consciously treats all naturally evolved [*natur-wüchsige*] presuppositions as the creations of hitherto existing human beings...and subjugates them to the power of united individuals. (CW 5:81)

What, more particularly, is the character of communist society? This is, negatively speaking at least, specified by the absence of what Marx locates as the fount and origin of all aspects of natural society: the *division of labour*. The beginnings of this he finds in the sexual act and then in the division which develops spontaneously by virtue of natural predispositions like physical strength. The head of the family has the power of disposing of the labour-power of wife and children and of the product of the use of that labour-power. But this is just to say that he possesses private property. So Marx grounds private property precisely in the division of labour.

This may be seen as an answer to a problem posed in the *1844 Manuscripts*, to which I have already drawn attention. We have seen that Marx there regards private property not as the cause but as the effect of estrangement, though he gives no explanation for the existence of this estrangement. *The German Ideology* can be viewed as taking up this question again in quite different terms and, though not using the theoretical apparatus of the *1844 Manuscripts*, again seeing private property as an effect, but this time of the division of labour which, as we shall see, Marx presents as having consequences which add up to what was previously identified as the state of estrangement.

This connection between division of labour and private property having been made a number of further considerations follow. Division of labour ramifies both into broad areas like that of the division between town and country and then within individual branches. The process of exchange of products from the various sectors means that the result of the individual acts of exchange is a power which works independently of the will of anyone: the movement of the market. A related effect is generated by the great division between mental and manual labour: ideas free themselves (or appear to) from their moorings in material practices, and may even appear to determine the character of the very soil from which they sprang. In other words we have ideology (especially in the sense given it by Marx in *The German Ideology*). Further there comes about a distinction between, on the one hand, the interests of separate individuals and families, considered in their separateness, and, on the other, their common interests. Both are real, but the first asserts itself the more powerfully in quotidian life, whilst the second is represented as a 'general' interest which inhabits a special sphere and is the pre-occupation of the members of a special slot in the division of labour, namely, the State. Indeed, whilst the State claims to represent the common or general interest it really represents the special interest of dominant groups or classes. (The continuity and also the difference between this account and that in 'On the Jewish question' will be evident: the latter presented the state as the representative of the general interest which had no embodiment in everyday life, but left very vague the origin of this state of affairs, a question which *The German Ideology* tackles.)

So in Marx's presentation the division of labour is at the bottom of humanity's being dominated by forces which it itself generates — though without being aware of it and is thus dominated by them — in particular those of the economy (the movements of the market) and of the political (the State). But the individual *qua* individual is also thus dominated. For an individual belongs to a class by virtue of certain relations defining membership of that class. But in general the specific conditions of class membership will coincide only in part with the specific qualities that go to constitute that particular individual. So once more individuals are dominated by structures over which they have no control. Not only that but — in a related point — people are thus subject insofar as they find themselves expending their labour-power within slots in the division of labour which are pre-given and do not necessarily correspond to those abilities and interests.

What are the conditions for the overcoming of natural society and the coming of communism? Marx's answer is along two broad lines. In the first place, such a change presupposes a high level of development of the productive forces, and this for a variety of reasons: so that a revolutionary situation will obtain by virtue of the glaring opposition of progress and poverty; so that the revolution can distribute plenty rather than generalize want (which would generate tendencies to counter-revolution as various groups sought to gain control over scarce goods); so that the revolution will be general rather than local (in which case there would be merely revolutions of limited scope able to be crushed by nations not undergoing a revolution); so that people will have available to them the unlimited resources for development vouchsafed by the world-wide integration of the productive forces; so that the advanced character of the productive forces will call forth the sorts of developed capacities (to use them) suitable for many-sided human beings. In the second place a communist revolution must be made by the working class and not by some other group acting on its behalf, because not only must the old order be overthrown, but people adequate for the new must be created, and this can only be done in the practice of revolution which simultaneously transforms material circumstances and people.

5

Meanwhile both Marx and Engels had been involving them-selves in the everyday political life of the Belgian capital, which, like Paris, was a city with its own radical democratic movement. There was a German workers' colony there and it was also a gathering place for Polish and Italian revolutionary émigrés. Marx and Engels sought to gain influence for the views which they had just been working out, especially in *The German Ideology*. In pursuit of this aim and in an attempt to raise the level of communist political activity they established, at the beginning of 1846, a 'Communist Corresponding Committee' which would, Marx wrote, provide

both a discussion of scientific questions and a critical appraisal of popular writings and socialist propaganda that can be conducted in Germany by these means. But the main aim . . . will be to put German socialists in touch with English and French socialists, to keep foreigners informed of the socialist movements that will develop in Germany and to inform the Germans in Germany of the progress of socialism in France and England. In this way differences of opinion will be brought to light and we shall obtain an exchange of ideas and impartial criticism. (W 27:442)

The founding of this Committee led to attacks by Marx and Engels on various figures in the other socialist-communist currents in Brussels. Marx also tried to gain the co-operation of people in Paris, particularly the influential Proudhon. But this did not have much success.

The plan was not helped by Marx's bringing out a swingeing attack on Proudhon. The latter had published in 1846 a book called *System of Economic Contradictions. The Philosophy of Poverty*, a work which had no little success in both France and Germany. In December of that year Marx wrote a long discussion of it, including many valuable statements concerning the new theory of history, to a Russian living at the time in Western Europe, one P. V. Annenkov. He followed it up with the publication in July of the following year of a full scale attack on Proudhon (in French) entitled *The Poverty of Philosophy*, in which, as he wrote later, 'the salient points of our conception were first outlined in a rigorous though polemical form' (EW 427). Marx's book made little impact however.

Connections of a much closer sort were established with communists in London, particularly German ones. The main organization here was the 'League of the Just'. This was a secret society composed of former members of a similarly named society in France who had been expelled for taking part in an ill-fated uprising in 1839. The front organization of the League was the 'German Workers' Educational Union'. In May 1846 Marx made overtures to the London communists suggesting that they form a Corresponding Committee working together with that in Brussels. This suggestion was initially received with some reserve but in January 1847 Marx was invited to join the League; this he did. In June of that year a congress consisting mainly of the London section of the League and the Brussels Corresponding Committee was held in London. It was decided to found a new organization to be called the 'Communist League'. In August the Brussels Corresponding Committee reorganized itself as a branch of the Communist League, with Marx as president. Its front organization was the newly founded 'Brussels German Working Men's Union'. (In December Marx delivered a series of lectures on political economy to the Union. These were published in part the following year as *Wage-Labour and Capital.*) About the same time there was also founded in Brussels what was to become the 'International Democratic Association' modelled on the London 'Fraternal Democratics'; Marx was elected vice-president.

6

The second congress of the Communist League was held in London during November and December 1847. It directed Marx and Engels to prepare a statement of the League's aims; they immediately began work on it. Engels wrote a draft in catechism style called *Principles of Communism*. Material from this was used in the final work which turned out however to be quite different in form and style and came mainly from the pen of Marx. It was the *Manifesto of the Communist Party*. This actually appeared just after the Paris uprising in February 1848 which began an era of about two years of European revolution.

Without doubt the *Manifesto* is the best known and most influential single writing in the whole corpus of Marxism. The subsequent influence of the booklet makes it very easy to see its significance at the time of its first publication in a quite misleading way. Then it was just one more of the innumerable such manifestos and clarion calls to the world issued by various grouplets in different countries, and there was to some extent a simple, if historically dramatic, coincidence in the connection between its date of publication and the beginning of a period of revolution on the European continent. What distinguished it from most of the literature of the sort was not merely its distinctive literary élan, but the grounding of its political programme in the wide-ranging general account of society and history, as well as a distinctive view of capitalism, which had been the result of the theoretical work of Marx and Engels during the preceding period.

7

The *Manifesto* begins with a sketch of the history of modern, capitalist society. The bourgeoisie has developed the productive forces available to humanity to a degree undreamt of in previous times. But those very forces cannot develop further within the framework of capitalism, and indeed cannot be sustained at its present level, as shown by the facts of cyclical crises and of the constantly worsening condition of the working class. The working class has increased in numbers and has had its consciousness raised to a revolutionary level by the very progress of capitalist production and is now ready to overthrow the bourgeoisie and reorganize society along socialist-communist lines.

The Communists 'do not form a separate party opposed to other working-class parties'. The former are distinguished from the latter by just two facts:

1. In the national struggles of the proletarians of the different countries, they point out and bring to the front the common interests of the entire proletariat, independently of all nationality.
2. In the various stages of development which the struggle of the working class against the bourgeoisie has to pass through, they always and everywhere represent the interests of the movement as a whole.

Thus, in sum:

The Communists... are, on the one hand, practically, the most advanced and resolute section of the working-class parties of every country, that section which pushes forward all others; on the other hand, theoretically, they have over the great mass of the proletariat the advantage of clearly understanding the line of march, the conditions, and the ultimate general results of the proletarian movement. (CW 6:497)

By way of concrete programme what is envisaged is a conquest of the bourgeoisie in two broad stages. The first is a political victory. The problem here is 'to raise the proletariat to the position of ruling class, to win the battle of democracy'. (Note here the implication that the conquest of democratic rights for the working class will, given appropriate political activity, bring the working class political power.) The second step is to use that political supremacy firstly to take 'by degrees' all capital from the bourgeoisie and put it under the control of the workers' state and, secondly, to develop the productive forces as quickly as possible. The means towards the first end are presented as being what in later terminology would be called 'transitional demands'[2]: in the beginning capital cannot be wrested from the bourgeoisie

except by means of despotic inroads on the rights of property, and on the conditions of bourgeois production; by means of measures, therefore, which appear economically insufficient and untenable, but which, in the course of the movement, outstrip themselves, necessitate further inroads upon the old social order, and are unavoidable as a means of entirely revolutionising the mode of production. (CW 6:504)[3]

The measures will differ, it is said, from country to country (a point stressed by the authors in the Preface to the 1872 German edition), but ten are listed which, it is suggested, will be 'pretty generally applicable . . . in the most advanced countries'. These include abolition of property in land and application of all rents of land to public purposes, a heavy progressive income tax, abolition of the right of inheritance, centralization of credit, means of communication and transport in the hands of the State, gradual abolition of the distinction between town and country by the combination of agriculture and manufacturing industries and the more equable distribution of the population over the country and free education for all children in public schools.

Notes

1 There is a detailed exegesis of the 'Theses' in my contribution to *Issues in Marxist Philosophy*, Volume II (eds J. Mepham & D.-H. Ruben) (Brighton, Harvester Press, 1979).
2 See for example, Gorz, A. *Strategy for Revolution* (Boston, Beacon Press, 1967).
3 The words from 'necessitate' to 'order' were added, presumably by Engels, to the English edition of 1888.

Chapter 5
Testing years

1

1848 was a year of revolution over most of Europe. The analysis of the causes of its outbreak and the determinants of its subsequent course is a matter of the utmost complexity. Here it is impossible to do more than give the most schematic indications, and the focus must be on Germany where Marx (and Engels) spent the greater part of 1848 and 1849 and which formed the centre of their main political activity.

Put in its most general terms 1848 meant the completion, for important parts of Europe, of the basic tendencies of 1789, namely, the realization of the conditions for the full development of the industrial bourgeoisie, a programme whose consummation had been obstructed by the outcome of the Congress of Vienna in 1815.

The most immediate general trigger of the events of 1848 was the outbreak of an economic crisis in England in 1847, a crisis which fairly rapidly spread to Europe. To start with, the effects of this combined with other factors already present to detonate national liberation movements in the European periphery (Italy, Switzerland, Austria-Hungary, Poland, among the Czechs, Ireland and elsewhere), the success of which was necessary for the installation of bourgeois power.

In France the effect of the English economic crisis combined with an internal agricultural crisis to produce both a sudden worsening of the conditions of the masses and an exacerbation of the contradictions within the bourgeoisie. The overall result was a coalition of classes against the financial aristocracy who held the main political power and underpinned the constitutional monarchy of Louis Phillipe. There was a victorious working-class insurrection in Paris during 22-24 February which installed a provisional government of liberal parliamentarians and immediately introduced reforms such as a proclamation of the right to work and the opening of 'national workshops'.

In Germany the effects of the English crisis took place in an already thoroughly unstable situation. The rebellion of the Silesian weavers in 1844 was still fresh in the memory. There had been disastrous harvests in 1844-1845 and a potato blight in 1845-1846. The overall result was poverty, famine, epidemics, the closing of enterprises, high and increasing unemployment, and mounting civil disorders. In general the declining petty-bourgeoisie as well as the nascent working class were in a bad way and demanded governmental amelioration of their lot; the rising industrial bourgeoisie also demanded government assistance but, more globally, suffered from the restraints imposed on their free development by a state basically not aligned with their interests. The main political objective of the liberal bourgeoisie was to instal a constitutional monarchy which would open the door to political power for them without leaving open the real possibility of successful popular revolution.

A dispute in early 1847 between the King of Prussia and his parliament (Diet) over the voting of moneys led to an insurrection in Berlin during 18-19 March. The King agreed to the idea of democratic national unification and permitted the convocation of a central representative assembly in Frankfurt to take place in the coming May. During the same period liberal governments were formed in several German states (except Prussia and Austria) and uprisings occurred in the south-west of Germany.

2

There were some reverberations of all this in Brussels, where Marx was living, but a flexible though firm government policy kept the situation well under control. Nevertheless on 3 March Marx was ordered to leave Belgium within twenty-four hours. Fortunately, at the same time he received from the new government in Paris a recision of the expulsion order of three years before and an invitation to return to Paris; this he did without delay.

It was decided to move the seat of the Central Committee of the Communist League to Paris and Marx was made effective head there (later president). During the last week of March, Marx (and Engels) drew up a leaflet entitled *The Demands of the Communist Party in Germany*, which was distributed on a wide scale in that country. These demands represented an adaptation to the concrete German conditions of the transitional programme of the *Manifesto*. The most important were: complete unification of Germany as a republic; universal adult suffrage; payment of representatives of the people; universal arming of the people; abolition without compensation of all feudal obligations; nationalization of feudal estates, of mortgages on peasant lands, of banking and means of transport (CW 7:3ff).

Marx and Engels returned to Germany in April. They decided to settle in Cologne on account of various political advantages this city offered. Sufficient funds were gathered to launch a daily newspaper and the *Neue Rheinische Zeitung. Organ der Demokratie (New Rhenish Gazette. Organ of Democracy)* appeared for the first time on 1 June with Marx as editor-in-chief, the name of the paper of course recalling the paper that Marx had edited five years before in the same city.

3

Marx and Engels were to contribute between them about 230 articles to the paper, some of major theoretical significance and all of importance for following the events of that time. There is obviously no question here of tracing the reports and analyses contained in these articles or of following the course of events even in outline. As for the general political programme of the paper, it remained, from first to last, two-fold: the setting up of a unified democratic republic and war with Russia. As we have seen, even the *Demands* were not communist: Marx's view was that a destruction of absolutism on the basis of an alliance between all groups opposed to it was an indispensable condition for any further political gains on the part of the workers and their allies. The war against Russia was urged because Russia was the main bulwark of absolutism in Europe so that the destruction of its power to intervene was considered crucial for the success of the democratic movement in the west.

As well as editing the paper Marx participated actively in Cologne politics. His locating of the gravamen of the situation in the aim of achieving a bourgeois state brought him into some conflict with others in the radical movement who wanted an openly communist programme. The Communist League faded out (whether Marx actually engineered its dissolution is a matter of dispute among historians) since its *raison d'être*, clandestine propaganda, was out of place in the new circumstances, and its received programme was inconsistent with the merely democratic line of the paper.

By mid-1848 the prospects of the revolution were at best mixed. The severest reverses had come from France. Here the April elections for a Constituent Assembly had resulted in a triumph for conservative royalists and moderate republicans. The radicals and socialists staged a coup, the failure of which encouraged the government to go further. In particular it decided to close the national workshops that had been opened by the Provisional Government. This provoked an uprising of the Parisian working class on 23 June which was bloodily suppressed over the next few days. (It called forth some of the finest of Marx's articles for his paper. See CW 7:130ff.) New censorship laws were passed and the right of assembly suspended. Napoleon's nephew Louis Napoleon was elected president. The first great combat between the bourgeoisie and working class for political power was over.

The paper was banned in September 1848 and did not reappear till October. This interruption severely exacerbated the already grave financial problems of the paper caused by the desertion of the greater part of its liberal bourgeois backers.

By December 1848 Marx was convinced that the liberal bourgeoisie would not go beyond peaceful protest against absolutism. In such circumstances there was no point in continuing to advocate the tactic of a united front with the bourgeoisie and the policy of the paper changed. It published a programme which included resistance to the collection of taxes, the funding by levy of a people's defence force and foreshadowed the formation of committees of public safety.

This led to Marx's appearance before the public prosecutor

in November. He was again in court in February 1849 on charges of libel against state officials and in September on charges of plotting to overthrow the government. He defended himself on both occasions and was acquitted each time.

The revolutionary struggles continued to go badly throughout Europe and in Germany in particular, despite temporary successes here and there. On 16 May 1849 Marx received an order expelling him from Prussian territory and on 19 May the last issue of the paper appeared (printed entirely in red). It was headed by a statement over the names of members of the editorial board addressed to the workers of Cologne calling upon them not to be provoked into an uprising which would inevitably be defeated by superior force (CW 9:467).

Both Marx and Engels went to Frankfurt in an unsuccessful bid to revive the struggle there. Marx left for Paris at the beginning of June (Engels joined the fighting still continuing in Baden), establishing connections with the leaders of political clubs and workers' organizations there. But later in the month he was informed by the French government that if he wished to remain in France he would have to live in the provinces. As a result he left for London in August, confidently expecting a new round of revolutionary ferment in England, connected with a resurrection of Chartist agitation, and with a promise of funds to begin a new periodical.

4

A prospectus for this, to be called *Neue Rheinische Zeitung. Politisch-Oekonomische Revue (New Rhenish Gazette. Politico-Economic Review)* was published in early January 1850. This said that the periodical was to be considered a continuation of the newspaper of the same name. The review would have the advantage over a newspaper

of comprehending events in a broader perspective and having to dwell only upon the more important matters. It permits a comprehensive and scientific investigation of the *economic* conditions which form the foundation of the whole political movement.

It goes on:

A time of apparent calm such as the present must be employed precisely for the purpose of elucidating the period of revolution just experienced, the character of the conflicting parties, and the social conditions which determine the existence and the struggle of these parties. (CW 10:5)

Without much doubt the most important articles published were precisely of this description, namely, a series of three by Marx in the first number (appearing in March 1850) later collected as *The Class Struggles in France, 1848 to 1850*, one of Marx's major historical works.

Marx and members of the earlier London branch of the League of Communists now began the job of reorganizing the Central Committee, and joined the German Workers' Society in London which was led by the League of Communists. Marx became president.[1] In an effort to reconstitute the League in Germany the Central Committee sent a member there with a document composed by Marx and Engels entitled 'Address of the Central Committe to the League'. This both analysed the events of the revolutionary years just elapsed and set out a programme for the further struggles which they saw as imminent.

5

Amongst the numerous tactical and strategic ideas set out in the analyses of this time — particularly the above-mentioned 'Address' and *Class Struggles in France* — the following are particularly important. A central idea is that of 'permanent revolution'. The March document affirms that the role that the German liberal bourgeoisie played in 1848 *vis-à-vis* the people would be taken over in the next round of struggle by the democratic petty bourgeois which had come to have the same position in the opposition as the liberal bourgeoisie had in 1848. After the analysis of the composition of the democratic party, the 'Address' goes on to define what the workers' basic attitudes to it should be:

The relation of the revolutionary workers' party to the petty bourgeois democrats is this: it marches together with them against the faction which it aims at overthrowing, it opposes them in everything by which they seek to consolidate their position in their own interests. Far from desiring to transform the whole of society for the revolutionary proletarians, the democratic petty bourgeois strive for a change in social conditions by means of which the existing society will be made as tolerable and comfortable as possible for them. (CW 10:280)

In other words, 'while the democratic petty bourgois wish to bring the revolution to a conclusion as quickly as possible . . . it is our interest and our task to make the revolution permanent' (CW 10:281). The document concludes that for the German workers 'their battle cry must be: The Revolution in Permanence'.

One of the ways of doing this is to use the tactic of what was later to be called 'transitional demands', which we have seen foreshadowed in the programmatic pages of the *Manifesto*.

Compel the democrats to interfere in as many spheres as possible of the hitherto existing social order, to disturb its regular course and to compromise themselves as well as to concentrate the utmost possible productive forces, means of transport, factories, railways, etc., in the hands of the state . . . . They must carry to the extreme the proposals of the democrats, who in any case will not act in a revolutionary but in a merely reformist manner, and transform them into direct attacks upon private property. (CW 10:286)

Connected with this is another germinal idea in the addresses, developed over half a century later by the Bolsheviks as the concept of 'dual power'.[2]

Alongside the new official governments [the workers] must immediately establish their own revolutionary workers' governments whether in the form of municipal committees and municipal councils or in the form of workers' clubs or workers' committees, so that the bourgeois-democratic governments not only immediately lose the support of the workers but from the outset see themselves supervised and threatened by authorities backed by the whole mass of the workers. (CW 10:283)

Finally there is the clear expression of the fundamental political form of the transitional period from capitalism to communism, namely, the 'dictatorship of the working class' (CW 10:69). I shall leave the discussion of this idea till later (Chapter 21) when Marx discusses the significance of an historical approximation to it.

6

In June 1850 Marx and Engels issued another document over the name of the Central Committee of the League. This was a report on the state of the League in various countries. Its final words were highly optimistic: '... at this moment ... the situation is so critical that the outbreak of a new revolution can no longer be very far away' (CW 10:377).

Their views on this changed very soon. In the last issue of the *Review* they published a long and detailed analysis of contemporary economic and social trends from May to October 1850. The conclusion was a sobering one politically: the revolutions of 1848-1849 had been triggered by a trade crisis and in the conditions of economic recovery then prevailing it was totally unrealistic to expect the outbreak of a new revolution:

With this general prosperity, in which the productive forces of bourgeois society develop as luxuriantly as they can within bourgeois relationships, there can be no talk of a real revolution. Such a revolution is only possible in the periods when *both these factors*, the *modern* productive *forces* and the bourgeois *forms of production*, come *into collision* with each other.... *A new revolution is possible only in consequence of a new crisis. It is, however, just as certain as this crisis.* (CW 10:510)

It had begun to dawn on Marx that what he had not long earlier taken to be the death-throes of capitalism were in fact just the disorder of its real birth. Marx immediately drew certain political-organizational conclusions from this which were quite unacceptable to the faction within the Central Committee of the League which still thought in terms of an immediate taking of power by the working class. In a session of the Central Committee in September 1850 Marx argued that the opposition was substituting an idealism of the will as the decisive factor for a materialist standpoint which looked to appropriate material conditions as presuppositions of successful action. He argues that the working class had to go through a long period of patient political organization and class-struggle to prepare itself for the taking of power (CW 10:626).

The result was an open split in the League. Marx's group severed connections with related organizations and the two opposing factions worked as independent groups within the League, the Central Committee being transferred to Cologne. Marx left the German Workers' Society in London, the front organization of the League. The political life of the League was effectively at an end.

November 1850 saw the sixth and last number of the *Review*.

Notes

1 At the end of 1849 Marx made the acquaintance of the revolutionary faction of the declining Chartist movement known as the Fraternal Democrats and a couple of exiled leaders of the Blanquist party. The result was a drawing up of the statutes of a *Société universelle des communistes révolutionnaires* ('World Society of Revolutionary Communists') (CW 10:614f). But the idea never came to anything.

2 See e.g. Lenin V.I. 'The dual power', *Collected Works*, Vol. 24 (Moscow, Progress Publishers, 1964), pp. 38ff; Trotsky, *The History of the Russian Revolution*, Vol. 1 (London, Sphere Books, 1967), Chapter XI.

PART III: 1850-1864

Chapter 6
New directions

1

1850 marks the end of a decisive period in Marx's life and indeed a watershed in his life as a whole: whilst in the immediately preceding years he was in the first place a political activist and only in the second a theoretician, for the next almost fifteen years active politics was no longer a central concern and theoretical research takes first place. This is a reflection of the trends of the time which were dominated by two major factors: the triumphant progress of capitalist development and the quiescence (in comparison at least with the years just past) of the working class. Marx's assessment of the economic situation in the survey article in the *Review* already referred to was accurate to the extent that it registered an upturn in the economy. But he very much underestimated its extent. In the context of the preceding economic development and the defeat of the working-class during 1848-1849 capital was now poised for a triumphant sweep that would experience no serious long-term economic obstacle till the onset of a long depression which began in the early 1870s and no serious political challenge till the brief if significant events of the Commune of Paris in 1871. Marx was realist enough to see that the earlier revolutionary years and the organizations that had been part of this were finished. Though he had periodical bouts of optimism and kept in touch with current radical politics for the next fifteen years or so, he did not engage in any political work that can be compared with that of the preceding few years; significant political engagement did not recommence till the revival of working-class political activity, a result of which was the founding of the International Working Men's Association in 1864. For the rest his political writings mainly concerned the immediate past and the present — in the first place the fate of the Communist League.

Beginning in May 1851 members of the League began to be arrested in Germany and Paris. Amongst documents found in connection with these arrests was the March 1850 address by Marx and Engels, already referred to. A political trial was set in train with great publicity. It began in October 1851 and in November of the following year seven of the eleven defendants were convicted and sentenced. The Communist League was now effectively defunct and the formal *coup de grace* was delivered the same November. Marx had already sent detailed materials for the defence; by the beginning of December 1852 he had finished a full-scale book published the following year as *Revelations About the Cologne Communist Trial* which tore apart the prosecution case.

In mid-1852 he had also written (with Engels) a series of vignettes of some of the political figures of the German emigration entitled *The Great Men of the Exile*, a work of acidity and savage lampoonery only equalled by a book entitled simply *Herr Vogt* published by Marx in 1860. This was a detailed defence of himself (and others) against slanderous attacks by an individual of that name, and a counter-offensive on the theme of Vogt's being a Bonapartist agent, a claim that was later independently substantiated. At its worst the book is a tedious journey down the Byzantine labyrinth of contemporary émigré politics; at its best it is a fireworks display of irony and invective.

Of an altogether different theoretical significance is *The Eighteenth Brumaire of Louis Bonaparte* (1852) perhaps Marx's greatest and certainly his most scintillating historical work. It analyses in historical materialist terms the background and character of Louis Napoleon Bonaparte's *coup d'état* of 1852 and carries forward the analysis of French society since 1830 begun with the already mentioned and recently published *Class Struggles in France, 1848 to 1850. The Eighteenth Brumaire* did not merely deploy tools that Marx had already forged but developed new ones for treating the particular subject matter and it is one of the main sources for the study of Marx's thinking on politics.

Among the other writings on contemporary affairs during this period the main group is Marx's journalism. This consists of about 500 articles (they are only now being collected and edited as a whole) written mostly for various newspapers (the bulk for the *New York Herald Tribune*) and mainly on current affairs in England, Europe, the United States and the Far East. Though they were in general produced for bread and butter they are a precious commentary on the events and trends of the day and were a laboratory of historical materialism as also of political economy, on which Marx was working throughout this period.

2

I have already traced Marx's first serious studies of political economy in 1844 (bearing first fruit in the famous manuscripts of that year), through the contract signed in 1845 for a *Critique of Politics and Political Economy* to his labours in Brussels marked by *The Poverty of Philosophy* and the lectures and notes partly published as *Wage-Labour and Capital*.

The years 1848-1849 did not allow much time for reflection on fundamental issues of political economy. But we have also seen that by the end of 1850 he had decided that a renewal of the revolutionary movement was conditional upon economic downturn, and he spent parts of 1850-1854 reading the literature of political economy with an eye to a work (in which friends had interested a German publisher) to be laid out in three volumes on *A Critique of Economics*, *Socialism* and *History of Economic Thought*.

However this too went the way of previous projects of a similar sort and work in this direction was dropped till the beginning of 1856. That year saw the beginning of a serious economic recession, starting in the United States and spreading to England and Europe. This led to a revival of politics if not of revolutionary politics. At any rate it sent Marx back to the subject of political economy, and between August 1857 and June 1858 he produced a huge manuscript on the subject. This was published only in 1939-1941 as *Grundrisse der Kritik der Politischen Oekonomie (Rohentwurf)* — that is, *Outlines of a Critique of Political Economy (Rough Draft)* — and it is now known even in the English-language discussions of it simply as 'the *Grundrisse*'. It is a work that is important in many respects. For one thing it contains a long preliminary discussion — often referred to as 'the 1857 Introduction' — in which Marx lays out for the first and only time (at some length anyway) his methodological conceptions. For another it includes a plan for a proposed multi-volume treatise on political economy in the broadest sense, about the essentials of which he did not change his mind, though he was to alter the arrangement of the material somewhat. Putting this together with what he wrote elsewhere during 1858 about his plans we can say that basically what Marx proposed was a work in six major parts: on capital, landed property, wage-labour, the State, international trade, and finally on the world-market and crises. Though he was only to complete a small part of this, clues to the content of a good deal of the rest of it are to be found in the *Grundrisse*.

Marx resolved to rewrite the material of the *Grundrisse* and to present it in the form of a series of shorter works. Only the first of these was actually written and published, the *Contribution to a Critique of Political Economy* in 1859. The best known part of this is the Preface — often called 'the 1859 Preface' (not to be confused with 'the 1857 Introduction' referred to above). It was in the course of this that Marx sketched a brief intellectual autobiography, containing in particular the often quoted summary of his conception of the principles of historical materialism. The material in the main body of the *Contribution* was later rewritten for the first two chapters of the first volume of *Capital* in which indeed it is often cited.

Other affairs took Marx away from his economic studies for most of the next two years. But between 1861 and 1863 he completed another immense manuscript (which has only recently begun to be published in full). This comprises a draft of what later emerged as the first volume of *Capital*; what amounts to a critical history of the foundations of political economy from its origins in the seventeenth century to Marx's own time (published at the beginning of the present century as *Theories of Surplus-Value*); and work which was to go into the third volume of *Capital*. The last section Marx continued to labour at during 1864-1865.

3

This, in fact, brings the story of the coming to be of *Capital* to the limits of the period being surveyed in this chapter. But since I shall be treating *Capital* as a whole in the immediately subsequent chapters and since the history of its composition has some significance for the interpretation of its parts I shall overstep the strict chronology here and briefly sketch the course of Marx's later work in this direction.

In 1865 he delivered an address criticising some views current in the contemporary workers' movement in Britain (according to which it is impossible to raise wages above a certain level) under the title *Wages, Price and Profit* (published posthumously as *Value, Price and Profit*). This was Marx's first public exposition of his mature economic theory, and it is an incomparable introduction to it.

During the next two years he worked at the first volume of *Capital*, which finally came out in 1867. It caused no great stir (except in Russia) despite Engels' publicizing work on its behalf (mainly in the form of numerous reviews). The work as it stands ends rather abruptly; in fact Marx omitted a planned final chapter, a very long draft of which was published only in 1933 and translated into English much later as 'Results of the immediate process of production'.

Between 1872 and 1875 Marx worked on a French version of the work with his translator (J. Roy), revising the original text quite extensively and indeed writing that he considered the translation to possess 'a scientific value independent of the original' which 'should be consulted even by readers familiar with German' (C 1:105). A second German edition of the first volume appeared in 1873; amongst other things the original appendix (on 'The value-form') was omitted, its substance being worked into the much rewritten first chapter. (Third and fourth editions were published after Marx's death by Engels in 1883 and 1890 on the basis of the French translation and Marx's marginalia.)

Marx worked on the manuscripts of what was to be the second volume of *Capital* during 1867, 1868, 1870 and then again during 1875-1878; he also laboured further during 1873 on those designed for the third volume. But he never completed them for publication, and it was left to Engels, after Marx's death, to turn the disorderly heaps of manuscript, written in a hand all but totally incomprehensible to anyone else but his closest friend, into the second and third volumes of *Capital* as we have them today. (They appeared in 1885 and 1894 respectively.) It was an editorial *tour de force* without parallel.

4

Capital was the central work of Marx's life, in both a purely biographical and a systematic theoretical sense. We have seen that he conceived it, or at least the general project, some two decades before the first volume finally reached the public; he worked at it off and on during all of that time and afterwards almost to the end of his life. Its doctrines both underpin his conceptions about the nature and developmental trends of capitalist society, hence his ideas about the future and political strategy and tactics; they also afford the best illustrations from Marx's pen of methods of historical materialism.

For these reasons I shall, in the following chapters, reverse both the temporal and systematic orders and outline some of the leading ideas of *Capital* in advance of the relevant general categories of historical materialism which, chronologically considered, were to a great extent worked out, in rough form at least, in advance of the writing of *Capital* (as early as 1845-1846) and which, systematically speaking, are in a definite sense presupposed by *Capital*.

Chapter 7
What is *Capital* about?

1

To start with, two very general questions arise about *Capital*. First: What is the work actually *about*? And second: What *method* does Marx use? I shall try to answer the first straightaway. The second I shall say something about also, but leave further remarks on that head to the end, which will thus return to some of the themes of the beginning, as any treatment of it that could be helpful must necessarily presuppose much of the knowledge about *Capital* that this and following chapters are meant to convey.

The first question may seem a rather odd one. But the answer to it is not obvious and failure to search it out properly can lead to considerable misunderstanding of the work.

To begin answering it let us look in the first place at the full title of the book: *Capital. Critique of Political Economy*. Thus Marx announces the work as being about 'capital', but, at the same time, as being a critique not only of particular doctrines but of an entire subject or discipline. In this and the following two chapters I shall concentrate on the first aspect; I shall return to the second in Chapter 11.

What then is the book about considered simply as a book on 'capital'? In the Preface to the first volume he writes that what he proposes to examine is 'the capitalist mode of production, and the relations of production and forms of intercourse that correspond to it' (C 1:90); in particular it is 'the ultimate aim' of the work 'to reveal the economic law of motion of modern society' (C 1:92). He says further that 'England is used as the main illustration of the theoretical developments ... because it is the classic representative of capitalist production' (C 1:90, 349n.). Thus Marx makes a distinction between, on the one hand, what the central subject-matter of the work is, and, on the other, the illustrations of the analysis.

What then is 'the capitalist mode of production and the relations of production and forms of intercourse that correspond to it', and what is an 'economic law of motion'?

2

In order to understand what Marx means by 'the capitalist mode of production (etc.)' it is first necessary to understand what he means by a 'mode of production' as such. Unfortunately he uses the term in somewhat different ways, though the context generally makes what he means reasonably clear. But to get a first foothold we must make the following distinctions:[1]

1 The first concept to be distinguished is what Marx sometimes calls '*factors*' of production. These may be distinguished into:
(a) 'labour-power', that is, people's capacity to perform labour, and
(b) 'means of production', which may be further divided into:
(i) the objects on which labour-power works; and (ii) the instruments which work on these objects as used or supervised by labour-power.
2 Now, even considered just as such, in isolation from one another, these factors in general stand in certain relations to 'agents of production' (individual human beings, institutions, corporations, etc.) which control them. These, when legally legitimated and protected, may be called 'property' relations. Marx very often designates these relations simply as 'relations of production'. However, in order to distinguish this sense of 'relations of production' from another important concept which might be equally so-called, let us call them, when it is necessary to make a finer discrimination, '*social relations of production*'.
3 The necessity for a different but related concept becomes obvious once we reflect that in isolation from one another these factors of production cannot produce anything. To do so they have to be brought into connection with one another. We therefore distinguish what may be called '*technical relations of production*', which are the relations between 1 above in an

actual process of production. (For example, assembly-line type of organization of production is a technical relation of production.) If we now consider 1 above as combined in such technical relations we have...

4 '*productive forces*'.

Marx uses 'mode of production' in at least three different ways. Firstly, he occasionally uses it to designate approximately what I have marked out in 4 above, in abstraction from the determinate forms of 2 above in which they are embedded. A 'mode of production' in this sense is then simply a determinate way of producing goods considered simply in its technical aspect. Secondly, in a wider sense he uses it to include both this and also the social relations — 2 above — which are the matrix of the productive forces and from which the preceding sense is abstracted. Thirdly, Marx sometimes uses the term to designate a yet wider sense in which what is included in the concept is not merely the production of goods in the narrower sense (the first distinguished) and the relevant social relations of production (the second sense) but also the ways in which a society 'circulates' (exchanges, distributes and consumes) what it produces.

In speaking, in the passage cited previously, about 'the capitalist mode of production and the relations of production and forms of intercourse that correspond to it', Marx would seem to be referring successively to these three ideas. But for the sake of clarity and brevity I shall henceforth use the term 'capitalist mode of production' to refer to a mode of production in the widest (the third) sense, understanding this as synonymous with the passage cited just above.

3

What then is the character of the specifically *capitalist* mode of production ('CMP' for short) which Marx proposes to investigate and of which in particular he proposes to discover the 'economic law of motion'?

Marx answers this question towards the end of *Capital* when he writes that what differentiates the CMP from other modes of production is:

the fact that being a commodity is the dominant and determining characteristic of its product. This implies... that the labourer himself comes forward merely as a seller of commodities, and thus as a free wage-labourer, so that labour appears in general as wage-labour.... The relation between capital and wage-labour determines the entire character of the mode of production. (C 3:1019)

What then is a 'commodity'? Marx answers (C 1:125f) that it is in the first place what he calls a 'use-value', that is, something that is able to satisfy a human want or need. There is no normative accent here: bombs are use-values as much as the drugs that help heal the wounds they cause. Use-values are paradigmatically objects of various sorts in the usual sense, like sealing-wax and string; but they may be less palpable things like songs or services of instruction. Use-values are not inherently such: they generally come to be so (tobacco for example) and may cease to be so (perhaps tobacco some time in the future). But things are generally use-values on the basis of some inherent properties of the object. A commodity is, in the second place, a use-value that is produced on a more-or-less regular basis for exchange in the market, directly with other use-values (barter) or — in an in any way developed commodity-society — with money. In brief, it has an 'exchange-value'.

Now if being a commodity is the general character of use-values in the CMP then in particular 'labour-power' will be a commodity, the exchange-value of which is expressed in wages. Under what conditions is labour-power a commodity? Clearly, at a minimum, on the condition that the owners of the labour-power, the labourers, do not control the means of production (otherwise they would in general work them themselves). So the situation in which the commodity is the general form of use-values presupposes that one group owns the means of production and that by virtue of this those who work the means of production have to sell their labour-power to those who do own those means. And this is just to define the social relations of production characterizing the CMP.

If the general form of use-value is the commodity then the point of buying labour-power and putting it to work on means of production is to produce and sell commodities. What is the point of this? Clearly to increase the wealth laid out in buying the labour-power and the means of production on which it is put to work. This use of a sum of exchange-value — typically money — is a special case of the general concept of 'capital', namely, the concept of a sum of money which is increased by buying a commodity and then selling it (or its products) again.

This gives us the general concept of the CMP in its most schematic form.

4

Enough has been said to indicate that the idea of a 'mode of production' is 'abstract' in at least two ways.

First, it is 'abstract' in comparison with, say, the idea of the Australian economy on this particular day in July 1982, in much the same way in which the idea of 'mass' is abstract in comparison with the weight of this tea-cup. That is, it has no simple relation to realities more or less immediately accessible to the senses.

Second, it is 'abstract' in the way in which it abstracts from other features of the social totality for the study of which it is meant to be a tool. For example, no capitalist economy of the slightest degree of complexity is thinkable without a more-or-less complicated system of formalized legal contracts (wage-contracts, ones between capitalists for the supply of goods, etc.); but a consideration of it simply from the point of view of its being a specific mode of production prescinds from this aspect, or takes it into account only as regards its effects. Similarly, religion for instance is, amongst its other functions, an important agent of social control over many parts of the work-force, but religion as such does not belong to the 'mode of production' as an economic concept.

We can now begin to see how the two aspects of Marx's self-defined object belong together. He indicates that he is setting out to study a certain mode of production, the CMP, and that what he is seeking is thus an *economic* 'law of motion'; that is, he is seeking the key to the problem of the development of capitalist society insofar as this development proceeds in accordance with economic factors. This is not to claim that there are no other factors that contribute to that development but merely that these are being abstracted from in the inquiry to be undertaken.

Consider a parallel situation in another field. We may say that the basic *aim* of Newtonian mechanics is to serve as a means for explaining, predicting and controlling actual motions: those of planets, double stars, comets, missiles, rockets in deep space and so on. But Newtonian mechanics is not *about* these objects or their motions, though these are, in a sense, 'illustrations' of it. It is *about* abstract 'objects' like mass-points of zero diameter which travel along force-free paths and so on. Though these notions have no simple (or even complicated) correspondences (in any literal sense) to the real world of planets and rockets they can, by complex procedures of mediation, both theoretical and material-instrumental, help to accomplish the basic aim of the project. Of course, even though the system of pure mechanics can thus help people understand actual movements insofar as these are determined by mechanical forces like gravitation or the thrust of burning jet fuel, a finer-tuned understanding and control has to take account of factors which lie outside the field of mechanics and which are the subject-matters of other sciences using equally abstract notions — electrodynamics, thermodynamics, and so on.

All this having been said by way of preliminary, let us turn now to a tracing out of the more detailed parts of Marx's analyses, and in the first place to those in the first volume of *Capital*.

Notes

1 The principal sources for my presentation of the basic ideas of historical materialism as regards the domain of the economic here and later on are: the preface to the *Contribution to the Critique of Political Economy* (EW 425f); C 1:Chapter 7 (Chapter 5 of the German edition); C 2:120; C 3 927f, 957. See also for more details my paper '"Productive forces" and "relations of production" in Marx'. *Analyse und Kritik*, forthcoming 1983.

Chapter 8
The production and reproduction of capital (*Capital*, Volumes 1 and 2)

1

I have already said that for Marx a commodity is a use-value which is produced on a more-or-less regular basis for sale in the market, and thus has an 'exchange-value'. This is typically expressed in terms of a certain amount of money. But since the concept of money has not yet been formally introduced we may think in terms of a barter economy in which the exchange-value of a unit amount of one commodity is expressed in terms of the amounts of other commodities for which it is exchangeable.

Marx now asks the following question (C 1:127). In perfectly general terms, how can it be that use-values that are qualitatively different can stand in a quantitative relation, so that such and such an amount x of such and such a commodity A is exchangeable for amount y of commodity B? He answers that for this to be so there must be something in common between the commodities, something that may be expressed in homogeneous units. (Similarly, if a bag of sugar in one pan of a beam balance is balanced by a piece of gold in the other pan, we say that, despite the qualitative differences, they are equal with respect to the measure of a common property, weight — or, more accurately, mass.) This property that commodities share, despite other qualitative differences, and by virtue of which they can be equated in exchange, and expressed in exchange-values, Marx calls 'value'; and the magnitude of value is expressed by the magnitude of exchange-value.

2

Marx now asks (in effect): is it possible to identify the nature of value more exactly? Can we say more about it than simply that it is what is presupposed by the existence of exchange-values? (Compare the situation in the history of genetics. Mendel early formed the concept of a hypothetical factor responsible for the transmission of hereditary characteristics — later called the 'gene' — which was at that time not specified more concretely than this. This was then long afterwards identified as a particular complex organic substance, DNA.)

His suggestion is that the relevant factor which commodities have in common is that they are all (or at least for the over-whelmingly greater part) *products of labour*, and hence that labour is the key to the problem of value. It is very important to note here that there is no question of a 'proof' that value is to be identified in some way with labour; it is a matter of 'plausible reasoning' the significance of which can only be tested by the worth of the theory of which it is a point of departure.

At this point Marx makes a distinction which is, he says 'the pivot about which the understanding of political economy turns' (C 1:132), the 'whole secret' of his new conception of political economy as he wrote to Engels (6 January 1868). This is the distinction between 'concrete' labour on the one hand, and 'abstract' labour on the other.

Consider the labours which are involved in, say, making a chair, fixing a wheel on a vehicle chassis, plucking a chicken. Each of these may be looked at from the point of view of what is special to it, what makes it labour resulting in that particular type of product. But we can also consider these labours from the point of view of what is common to them, simply as purposeful expenditures of human energy. If we consider a specific instance of labour from the first point of view then we are considering it, in Marx's terminology, as 'concrete labour', if from the second as 'abstract labour'.

Notice here that Marx is not saying that there are two separable sorts of labour. It is just that one and the same actual instance of labour has two distinguishable aspects, or falls under two different descriptions, 'concrete' and 'abstract', according as we consider it as productive of a particular sort of use-value or simply as purposive labour in general. Marx's terminology here is unfortunate to the extent that it might mislead some into thinking that what he is saying is that 'concrete' labour is the actual instance of labour from which we abstract to produce the idea of 'abstract labour'. But in fact 'concrete labour' is just as 'abstract' as 'abstract labour'; each picks out or 'abstracts' certain aspects of actual instances of labour.

An analogy may help here. Accelerations can be imparted to objects in an immense number of different ways: through pushing and pulling, or striking, or heating, or the use of magnets, and so on. Now instances of each of these may be considered in one or other of two different ways. It may be considered as a specific sort of kinetic or thermal or whatever process; or it may be considered simply as a producer of accelerations. From this second, 'abstract' point of view we can speak of the action of a 'force' in general, and the latter given a general measure in terms of a certain function of the mass of the body accelerated and the acceleration produced.

Marx identifies 'value' with abstract labour, and the magnitude of the value of a certain sort of commodity (expressed in its exchange-value) at a certain place and time with the duration of expenditure of the abstract labour necessary to produce a commodity of that sort at that place and time. More accurately, he identifies the magnitude of value with an amount of 'socially necessary' abstract labour, that is, with the abstract labour-time required to produce the use-value 'under the conditions of production normal for a given society and with the average degree of skill and intensity of labour prevalent in that society' (C 1:129). So it is not the amount of abstract labour that actually went to produce a specific set of use-values that constitutes their exchange-values but the amount that is socially necessary at a certain place and time to *re*produce those use-values.

3

The simplest form of the exchange-relation that turns a simple use-value into a commodity is

amount x of commodity A = (is worth, exchanges for) amount y of commodity B

But this is an abstraction from the more realistic case in which the exchange-value of commodity A is expressed in terms of a *number* of other commodities:

$$x \text{ of } A = \begin{array}{l} y \text{ of commodity } B \\ z \text{ of commodity } C \\ w \text{ of commodity } D \end{array}$$

.

.

.

However this way of expressing the value of A is inadequate to the needs of a society which more-or-less generally produces its use-values as commodities, for there is no simple general standard in terms of which the values of all commodities may be expressed.

Such a general equivalent is arrived at just by reversing the above equation: then the indefinite list of commodities B, C, D, ... express their values in terms of A. The commodity A thus singled out is *money*. (Precisely which commodity is so privileged depends on various factors, and in particular its physical characteristics.) So according to Marx's theory of money the latter is essentially just an ordinary commodity which *functions* differently from other commodities insofar as these express their values in it. But money is able to function thus only because it has value as the representation of a certain amount of abstract labour, just like any other commodity.

4

Marx's notion of 'capital' (C 1:Chapter 4) can now be introduced more precisely than before. Consider a sum of value, represented in general by a sum of money M. Suppose it to be exchanged for another sum of value, represented by commodities C, which are in turn exchanged for another sum of value represented in general by a sum of money M', where M' is greater than M by an amount s. M has then performed a 'circuit' - M - C - M' ($M' = M + s$) insofar as the sum of value which it represents at last returns to the form of money. For Marx a 'capital' is any sum of value that goes through a circuit of this sort. (Note that the concept of capital is defined not in terms of any material properties of things but solely in terms of certain of their relational features, namely, the places which they have in a certain sort of 'circuit'.) The sum s Marx calls 'surplus-value'.

5

The following problem now arises: where does surplus-value come from? In other words: how is capital possible?

Marx rejects an obvious answer, namely, that it arises in general from 'buying cheap and selling dear'. His argument here is, very briefly, this. If it be allowed that commodity owner A can exchange his commodity with commodity owner B for a sum of money that represents more than the value of his commodity, then, since the situation is symmetrical, B can do the same to A so that each's surplus cancels out and there is no general solution to the problem of the origin of surplus. Certainly a merchant may by good luck or good management or both make a profit by buying cheap and selling dear. But this only redistributes an existing surplus: if he is to gain someone else must lose. The question thus remains: how is surplus produced in the first place in order later to be redistributed? As a result of the sort of reasoning just rehearsed Marx lays it down that a solution to this problem must be consistent with commodities' uniformly exchanging at their values. (This condition is relaxed in the third volume of *Capital* but not in such a way as to render the present level of abstraction superfluous.)

Marx's own solution (C 1:Chapter 6) involves the introduction of two further sets of concepts. The first is one that has been brought in already in the preceding chapter, namely, that between 'labour' and 'labour-power'. The latter is the aggregate of all those capacities (physical, intellectual, etc.) by virtue of which human beings can execute the former. In other words, labour is the result of the realization of labour-power. The second new set of concepts is a distinction between 'necessary' and 'surplus' labour. The 'necessary' labour of a society (it can be applied by extension to individuals too) is the amount of labour requisite for reproducing that society at a certain material and cultural level. This is, of course, different at different times and places; so what counts as necessary labour is, beyond a certain biologically determined point, a socially determined amount. 'Surplus' labour is whatever labour is performed over and above this.

The key to Marx's solution to the problem of the origin of surplus-value lies in the observation that after a certain level of productivity has been reached a person or group is able, by the consumption of certain use-values, to labour for a time longer than that necessary for the production of the use-values requisite for reproducing the labour-power thus realized as labour. So, for the sake of illustration, it might take — expressed in terms of labour-time — only two hours of social labour to produce the food, clothing, shelter and so on necessary for someone to work for eight hours. That is, the working day, the time during which labour-power is realized as labour, is divisible into 'necessary' and 'surplus' parts — specifically, in the imaginary case considered, two and six hours respectively. The first is the part of the working day equal in length to the labour-time required to produce the use-values which are necessary and sufficient to produce and reproduce the labour-power which is used up during the whole working day. The second is the difference between the latter and the necessary part.

Marx's actual solution to the problem of the origin of surplus-value is now straightforward. What the capitalist *buys* is the worker's labour-*power*. What he pays for it is equal to, or fluctuates around, the cost of the reproduction of that labour-power; in other words he pays an amount of money which represents the labour-time necessary to reproduce the labour-power which is equal to 'necessary' labour-time. This is the wage. So only equivalent values are exchanged. But when the capitalist *uses* the labour-power that he has bought it realizes itself in an amount of *labour*-time *greater* than the *necessary* labour-time. That is, the worker produces surplus labour-time that is appropriated by the capitalist gratis. (Of course, capitalists in fact appropriate the *whole* of workers' labour-time but — roughly speaking — pay them back as wages in one week the money which represents the necessary labour-time that they generated the week before. So workers produce not only a surplus for the capitalist but their own wages as well.) Since we are dealing with capitalism, in which labour-time is represented by the 'value' of the use-values it produces, the surplus *labour-time* is represented as surplus-*value*. Thus labour-power in being used adds to the value of the means of production an increment equal to the surplus part of the working day. The capitalist is able to sell the product at its value and still make a profit equal in amount to surplus-value. The condition that exchanges must be exchanges of equivalent values is still satisfied. This is the essence of Marx's theory of the origin of surplus, of the possibility of capital, of exploitation, put it how you will.

6

The concepts of capital and of surplus-value having been introduced it is now possible to make some further distinctions and extensions of Marx's conceptual apparatus.

To start with, he distinguishes between 'constant' and 'variable' capital — c and v as these forms are generally designated (C 1: Chapter 8). The first is capital represented by means of production (instruments of production and raw materials); the second is capital represented by labour-power purchased by the capitalist. The first is so-called because, on Marx's 'labour theory of value', its value is not changed in the process of production, being just transferred to the product, its being only the second which generates new value, and which therefore 'varies' in the process of production.

This process can now be represented thus:

$$(c + v) \longrightarrow (c + v + s)$$

Since on Marx's account surplus-value stems from the variable part of capital alone, the *rate* of surplus-value — usually designated by s' — is equal to the ratio between a given amount of surplus and the variable capital (as usual measured in value terms) necessary to produce it: $s' = s/v$. This is to be distinguished from the rate of *profit* — p' — which is equal to the ratio between a given amount of surplus and the *total*

87

amount of capital necessary to produce it: $p' = s / c+v$. Thus for Marx surplus-value and profit are equal in *magnitude*, but quite different *conceptually*. (Some consequences of this will be taken up in the next chapter.) But the *rates* of surplus-value and of profit are necessarily different since the denominators are different in all cases.

There is also a distinction between two forms of surplus-value which is vitally important for Marx's theory, namely, that between 'absolute' and 'relative' surplus-value (C 1: Chapter 12). 'Absolute' surplus-value changes if there is a change in surplus-value as a result of a change in the overall length of the working day. Thus if a working day of eight hours be lengthened to ten hours, then, assuming the necessary part to be constant, the surplus labour-time increases by two hours, which is represented as an increase in 'absolute' surplus-value. But the amount of surplus-value can also be changed by changing the length of necessary labour-time in a given working day. (This is done, in the final analysis, by increasing the productivity of branches engaged in producing the commodities necessary for reproducing labour-power.) Thus if the working day is eight hours and the necessary part two hours, the surplus-value represents six hours labour-time. But if the necessary part is cut in half then, everything else remaining the same, the surplus-value is increased to seven hours. Not only can (relative) surplus-value be increased without increasing the absolute length of the working day, but it can easily be seen that it is possible to increase it whilst actually decreasing the length of the working day as a whole.

7

So far I have been following the general lines of Marx's presentation in the first five parts of the first volume of *Capital*. Part VI is a fairly short but very important treatment of the topic of wages, the first and theoretically most fundamental chapter of which I shall return to in Chapter 11. Parts VII and VIII are concerned with the process of accumulation of capital. They treat three main themes. One of these is that of the *historical origins* of capitalism ('primitive' or 'original' accumulation) (Chapters 26-31). Marx here traces the process of the original installation of the capital-relation in the classical land of capitalism, England, with the expropriation of the land of the peasantry, showing how 'capital comes into the world dripping from head to toe, from every pore, with blood and dirt' (C 1:926). These are mainly historical dissertations which I shall not attempt to recapitulate. A second theme is that of the *developmental tendencies* of capitalist accumulation (Chapters 25 and 32). I shall say something about this topic towards the end of the next chapter.

The third main theme is that of the general *structure* of capital-accumulation (Chapters 23 and 24). Marx here distinguishes two types of reproduction of the capital-relation, namely, 'simple' reproduction and 'reproduction on an increasing scale' or 'expanded' reproduction. The first is just reproduction of the capital-relation in one cycle on the same scale as in the preceding cycle, the surplus expropriated in one cycle being simply siphoned off (hoarded, spent as revenue, or whatever) and the cycle repeated as before. For reasons built into its character capitalist reproduction is in general not of the simple but of the expanded type. That is, part of the surplus produced in one cycle is ploughed back into the process of production in the form of increased investment. (This means, of course, other things being equal, that at the end of each cycle a mass of surplus is produced which is greater than that produced at the end of the previous cycle.) Marx's account at this point is from the broadest possible point of view with no consideration of the micro-structure of the process of production, capital being treated as a totality. The process of reproduction is taken up again in the third and final part of the next, second volume of *Capital*, this time with some necessary distinctions within capital as a whole. So I now turn to this second volume.

8

We have seen that the most general way of conceiving capital is to consider it as a sum of value (in general, money: M) which is exchanged for commodities (C) and which, as a result of further exchanges of C (or its products), returns augmented by surplus-value as M'. In brief:

$$M - C - M'$$

We have also seen that, on Marx's view, the origins of surplus-value lie in the purchase and use of a unique type of commodity, namely, labour-power (L), to transform means of production (MP) into other commodities of a value greater than the sum of the values of the labour-power and means of production that went to produce them. So we can fill out the simplest formula for the circuit of capital, repeated above, by expanding the middle term thus:

$$M - (C \underset{\diagdown MP}{\overset{\diagup L}{}} \cdots P \cdots C') - M'$$

When means of production are precipitated into the actual process of production (that is, when they are activated by labour-power) they become 'productive capital' (P). The result of the process of production is a mass of other commodities which have a value in excess of that of the C which went to generate them, a value in fact equal to C', which is now 'commodity capital'. This latter is, when sold, realized in a sum of money M' greater than M. This money-capital is then ready to begin another circuit.

If the main subject of the first volume of *Capital* is the productive form of capital, P, the central subject of the second volume — subtitled *The Process of Circulation of Capital* — is in the parts of the above schema flanking P.

9

The volume is laid out in three major parts. The first is entitled 'The metamorphoses of capital and their circuits'. We have just seen that capital appears in various functional forms. It is important to be clear about the fact that throughout *Capital* Marx is talking basically about capital as a sum of value which is involved in a certain sort of circuit, so that from the point of view of *value* a handful of dollars and a pile of pig-iron are the *same* capital: it is just that the material representatives, the 'bearers' of value are different. So the very same capital appears now as money capital, then as productive capital and finally as commodity capital, before once more assuming the form of money capital, these being simply different functional forms of the same capital. As we have seen, a circuit of a form of capital is the trajectory it describes in passing through a series of other forms back to the same form. The expanded formula above is the circuit of money-capital and the emphasis in the first part of the second volume of *Capital* is on this circuit. But it embraces a study of the forms of the circuits of each type of capital, and of the inter-relations between them, every capital being simultaneously in each of the three circuits, some in the form of money for investment in new forces of production, some in the form of forces of production being fabricated into commodities, some in the form of commodities between production and sale.

The second part of the second volume is entitled 'The turnover of capital', a 'turnover' of a capital being 'the circuit of capital, when this is taken not as an isolated act but as a periodic process' (C 2:235). The turnover time is obviously equal to the sum of the times of production and of circulation. This part studies the conditions influencing the way in which a capital performs a circuit, the way the different components of capital interact, and the conditions influencing the amount of surplus-value attracted by capital. The emphasis in this part is on the circuit of the second form of capital, namely, productive capital.

The third part is on 'The reproduction and circulation of the aggregate social capital'. It has at its heart the third basic form of capital, namely, commodity capital. It picks up the thread dropped in Chapter 24 of the first volume, now treating reproduction not in terms of an undifferentiated whole of capital but as having an inner structure.

In sum, Marx's account here depends upon a distinction between two sectors of the social product, namely, what he calls Department I, comprising means of production (capital goods), and Department II, comprising articles of individual consumption. Marx argues that the fundamental economic condition for a capitalist economy to be in *equilibrium* is for there to be a reciprocal balance of supply and demand between Departments I and II; in other words, the relevant condition is that the production of capital goods gives rise to a demand for consumer goods equal to the demand for capital goods generated by the production of consumer goods. For there to be a *continuity* of capitalist production it is necessary that during a series of production cycles three conditions should be satisfied: that there be a production of the capital goods needed to replace those used up in the course of production, and the consumer goods needed to reconstitute labour-power; that purchasing power capable of realizing the value of those capital goods and consumer goods be created and actually used; and that this purchasing power be distributed in such a way that supply and demand balance as regards both capital goods and consumer goods. These principles are stated as conditions for the equilibrium and continuity of a capitalist economy — in brief, its stability. But their *import* is rather to suggest the almost inevitable instability of such an economy, given the complex balancing of conditions for stability on the one hand, and the unplanned character of capitalism on the other.

Chapter 9
The shaping of capital as a whole
(*Capital*, Volume 3)

1

Systematically speaking, the first two volumes of *Capital* are preliminaries to the third. The main subject of the first volume is the structure and mechanism of the *production* of capital; the main subject of the second the *circulation* of capital in respect of its different functional forms, the details of its turnover and the conditions for its being reproduced, particularly on an expanded scale. The main themes of each volume are treated in relative independence of those of the other. The third volume considers, to cite its subtitle, *The Process of Capitalist Production as a Whole*. The first two volumes treat capital predominantly from the point of view of 'capital in general'. In other words, they treat capital as such, abstracting from the ways in which it actually manifests itself from the point of view of 'many capitals', that is, the parcels in which capital actually exists; hence they largely abstract from competition between capitals. Volume 3 removes this restriction. It thus considers how surplus-value assumes the form of profit, how it is distributed to various individual capitals, the long-term behaviour of profit, how it is distributed to various sorts of capitals, and finally how the total revenue of capitalist production appears to the agents of this mode of production.

More specifically, the third volume is divided into seven parts. These may be broken up, to start with, into two main segments, namely, the first six on the one hand, and the seventh on the other. Most broadly conceived the first six parts form a study of the way that surplus-value manifests itself in the capitalist economy; the final part is a study of how newly created value as a whole (that is, the surplus plus the value which replaces the variable capital expended in the previous cycle) appears. This last part is concerned with a critique of the

93

received political economy as such and so belongs to the subject-matter of Chapter 11 below. I shall therefore concentrate here on the first six parts.

Within these we can distinguish between Parts I-III on the one hand and Parts IV-VI on the other.

Within Parts I-III Marx considers successively three topics:

1   Part I looks at the way in which surplus-value is represented as profit on the form of capital that is fundamental for the CMP, namely, industrial capital, or, more precisely, the productive form of industrial capital; it also examines the connections between rate of surplus-value and rate of profit.
2   Part II presents Marx's account of the way in which rates of profit in individual enterprises are converted into an average rate of profit, and, connected with this, the concept of 'surplus profit'.[1]
3   Part III presents what he regarded as one of the central parts of *Capital*, namely, the 'law of motion' (law of variation) of the average rate of profit, namely, its tendency to fall. He regarded this as absolutely fundamental for the understanding of the development of capitalism, and its clear presentation and theoretical grounding (the fact itself had been noted by, for example, Ricardo) as one of his main achievements.

Turning now to Parts IV-VI, in a letter to Engels (8 January 1868) written soon after the publication of the first volume of *Capital* he lists as one of the 'fundamentally new elements of the book' the fact that:

in contrast to *all* former political economy, which *from the very outset* treats the particular fragments of surplus-value with their fixed forms of rent, profit, and interest as already given, I first deal with the general form of surplus-value, in which all these fragments are still undifferentiated — in solution, as it were.

In Parts IV-VI Marx crystallizes out these particular forms of profit from the general pool of profit (surplus-value) generated by productive capital, showing how it is distributed not only to its parent capital but also to other forms of capital.

I shall now briefly outline the content of these chapters, keeping Marx's order of presentation except with regard to Part III which I shall reserve to the end, being as it is the main conclusion of the work from the point of view of the dynamics of capitalism.

2

Part I of the third volume of *Capital* studies the representation of surplus-value as 'profit'. As I have already outlined Marx's conception of the difference between the two (preceding chapter, Section 6) there is no need to go over it here, and we can pass straightaway to Part II in which Marx develops the crucial concept of 'average rate of profit' and traces some of its consequences.

In the first place it is necessary to have the notion of 'composition of capital'. The 'value-composition' of capital is determined by the proportion in which it is divided into its constant and variable components if these are considered just as amounts of *value*. The 'technical composition' of capital is determined by the proportion in which it is divided as regards the *mass* of labour necessary for their employment on the other. The 'organic' composition' (henceforth *OC*) of capital is 'the value-composition of capital, insofar as it is determined by its technical composition and mirrors changes in the latter' (C 1:762). $OC = c/v$: this is what Marx generally means by 'composition of capital' without further qualification.

Now, if two different branches of production have capitals of different *OC* then, from the point of view of the theory developed so far, the rates of profit in the two will be different. (This and similar points in the immediately following can be verified by a little elementary algebra.) Also different branches of production do in fact have capitals of different *OC*; but they also tend to have the same rates of profit. So there is an inconsistency between a consequence of the theory as developed so far and certain factual assumptions. Marx accepts the latter and modifies the theory by relaxing one of the basic assumptions of the theory so far, namely, that commodities are sold at their values. (Such a move, consisting in the modification of an assumption which defines the field of a theory when the latter shows itself to be no longer applicable is a standard one in the sciences.)

Marx's argument proceeds, in effect, in two steps. The first consists in the setting up of certain broad structural conditions for surplus-value's being distributed to individual capitals in such a way that, even though they have different *OC*s, they attract the same rate of profit. Basically, this happens if commodities tend to exchange, not at their value, but at 'prices of production', defined as equal to their 'cost-price', or total capital advanced for their production, plus an *average* rate of profit. It can easily be shown that insofar as the *OC*s of the various capitals differ the values of the commodities they generate differ. But this means only that though prices of production (henceforth just 'prices') differ from values, the deviations balance one another out by the uniform rate of distribution of surplus. A simple schematic example based on Marx's own presentation may help to make this clearer.

Consider just five capitals, and assume a uniform rate of surplus-value of 100 per cent. Then using the abbreviations introduced so far, plus the following:

   cc : constant capital assumed used up
   V : value of commodities
   cp : cost price
   pp : price of production
   d : deviation of *pp* from *V*

we have the following grid:

Capitals	*s*	*cc*	*V*	*cp*	*p'*	*pp*	*d*
I 60*c* + 40*v*	40	51	131	91	40%	113	- 18
II 70*c* + 30*v*	30	51	111	81	30%	103	- 8
III 80*c* + 20*v*	20	50	90	70	20%	92	+ 2
IV 85*c* + 15*v*	15	40	70	55	15%	77	+ 7
V 95*c* + 5*v*	5	10	20	15	5%	37	+ 17
390*c* + 110*v*	110					110	0 (Total)
78*c* + 22*v*	22					22	0 (Average)

To begin with, Marx considers the five capitals as a *single* capital with different component parts (as if the total social capital were like a single enterprise which included several

96

component companies). Then we have a total capital of 500, a surplus of 110, and an average OC equal to $78c + 22v$. If each of the capitals of 100 is regarded as simply one fifth of the total capital, irrespective of the OCs of its parts, its OC is just this $78c + 22v$ and an average surplus of 22 accrues to it. For this to occur it is only necessary for each individual capital to exchange its products at a price equal to the cost-price for that capital plus the average profit, that is, to exchange its products at 'prices of production'.

Thus Marx's point of departure is the general relations of production characteristic of the CMP, the situation defined by the existence of capital and wage-labour. At a first approximation capital is taken to be one unified whole which appropriates surplus from wage-labour. The question then concerns the way in which this total amount of expropriated labour is distributed to the various individual capitals that in fact make up this total capital. The *structural* conditions for the possibility of equal distribution have just been outlined: they consist basically in the cost-pricing of commodities by the individual capitals at magnitudes which systematically deviate from values, in such a way as to yield an average profit.

The *mechanism* by which the structural conditions for equal distribution of surplus are realized is competition. Consider our simple neo-Robinson Crusoe capitalist society of five capitals again. Suppose that capital I were to generate prices of production such that its rate of profit exceeded that of the other capitals. Then (assuming free mobility of capitals) capital would flow from these into branch of production I so as to make a higher than average profit also. But at a certain point the supply of commodities produced by these other capitals would, by virtue of the relative capital-shortage there, become sufficiently short for them to be sold at prices which would make the rate of profit there higher than that of I (and over-supply in branch I would decrease the rate there) so that capital would, by virtue of the relative capital-shortage there, become tends to be established in which prices within different lines of production tend to be such as to yield the average rate of profit to capitals of different OC.

3

Bypassing Part III of the third volume of *Capital* for the moment, let us turn to Parts IV-VI. Marx here traces the ways in which the surplus produced by industrial capital (in particular by the variable part) is distributed among various sorts of capitals.

Marx divides industrial capital into two types: 'productive capital' and 'capital of circulation' (also called 'merchants'', 'mercantile' or 'trading' capital). The first is capital as it actually occurs in the process of production. The second sort of industrial capital is itself of two types. First, there is capital represented by commodities in the interval between their emerging from the process of production and their being sold; this Marx calls 'commercial' or 'commodity-dealing' capital. Second, there is capital represented by money which is in circulation for the buying and selling of productive capital; this he calls 'money capital' or 'money-dealing capital'.

These are all just different functional forms of the same capital. But they become independent in the division of labour among capitalists. (This occurs, for one thing, because their functions are more efficiently carried out that way.) But Marx is emphatic that capital of circulation is unproductive in the sense that it does not create any *new* value. The circulation of capital which it expedites results in costs which must be deducted from the basic fund of surplus-value created by productive capital. It makes savings in circulation costs the source of its own share of the surplus. Wage-workers in the domain of circulation are exploited by extraction of surplus-*labour* rather than surplus-value: their labour permits their employers to take a share of already produced profits in excess of the wages they pay.

Money may be not only a use-value (for example, as means of payment) but also itself a commodity. As such it is 'interest-bearing' or 'financial' capital. As a commodity it has a use-value and an exchange-value like any other commodity. Its use-value is to serve as capital, to be a means for making a profit: in brief, the realization of its use-value is profit. Its exchange-value is the interest it earns, the interest being a part of the profit which its use as productive capital yields.

4

The final means for attracting a part of the surplus is land (including of course the sea and air). This is the fundamental means of production. In its pristine state it has (in Marx's terms) no value since it is not something which represents the expenditure of labour (unless it be God's, which possibility may be safely neglected here). Nevertheless, it may be used by its owners to attract revenue. The economically fundamental way in which this is done is through (ground-) rent.

Marx's general explanation of rent is in terms of the concept of 'surplus profit'. What we have been concerned with so far has been 'average profit', that is, profit generated under ordinary circumstances by equalization of rates of profit through free mobility of capital under pressure of competition. 'Surplus profit' is profit that accrues to an individual branch, or segment of a branch, in excess of the average profit, by virtue of special circumstances of some sort. According to Marx, rent is essentially the surplus profit paid to the owner of land by a capitalist.

He distinguishes between three basic forms of rent. First, in the case of 'differential' rent the *selling price* of the product of the land equals the *average* 'price of production', but the *individual* price of production is less than the average, because the individual cost-price is less than the average owing to higher than average productivity of the land due either to natural advantages like above average fertility or convenience of location ('differential rent I') or to different amounts of capital investment ('differential rent II'). Second, in the case of 'absolute' rent the selling price of the product is greater than the price of production, though not greater than value; this is because the OC in agriculture tends to be lower than the social average, hence the rate of profit higher than the average, and because the landowners' monopoly of land prevents the operation of the ordinary tendency towards an equalization of the rate of profit. Third, in the case of 'monopoly rent proper' the selling price of the product is greater than the price of production and also greater than value, by virtue of special characteristics of certain pieces of land (for example, land able to bear vines producing grapes of special wine-making quality).

The price is limited only by purchasers' ability and inclination to pay.

Marx's discussion of rent is of special importance because it is only a special case of a more general situation which is a great deal more relevant and important today than when Marx originally wrote, namely, the phenomenon of surplus profits generated by monopoly. In the case of natural resources necessary for production — including in the first place land — there is the possibility of what Mandel calls 'natural' monopoly just by virtue of the fact that such resources are in the nature of the case limited. But more generally there are what Mandel calls 'artificial' monopolies which 'are determined by limits in capital mobility related to conditions arising from the results of specific stages (forms) of the accumulation of capital itself'[2] like the minimum level (at a particular place and time) for entry into the capitalist arena, monopoly rights in patents old and new, restrictive trade practices, and so on.

5

Now that the more 'structural' chapters of Volume 3 of *Capital* have been briefly outlined I return to Part III in which Marx presents what he considers the basic law of capitalist development. Part II of Volume 3 has presented a theory of the process of *formation* of an average rate of profit. Part III presents the basic law of its *variation* which is, according to Marx, that there is a tendency for that average rate to fall.

The general idea is very simple. Let us suppose, as Marx does in the part of *Capital* under consideration, that there is a general tendency in a capitalist economy for the average OC to increase. (I shall look into this in a little more detail in the next chapter.) It is easy to show that if this ratio c/v increases, then since the rate of profit equals $s/(c+v)$, this must decrease (other things being equal).

Marx speaks of this law of variation of the rate of profit as a law of 'tendency'. There is nothing special about this: what are asserted as laws in *Capital* are, if seldom explicitly flagged in this manner, generally flanked with the appropriate qualification. (Indeed this is true of scientific laws in general: they are all 'tendential' in the sense that their operation depends on the occurrence of conditions the obtaining of which the law does not itself guarantee.[3])

One peculiarity of the present case however is that the structural conditions that give rise to it also produce tendencies which counteract it, so that it has, so to speak, in-built negative feedback. Marx devotes a whole chapter to these. An example is as follows. We have seen that the essence of the derivation of the law is that the ratios c/v and $s/(c+v)$ are so related that an increase in the first entails a decrease in the second. Now it must be remembered that we have been dealing here throughout in *value* terms, not in terms of the *mass* of commodities involved. But an increase in c/v in value terms means in general an increase in productivity; that is, roughly, a constant amount of money buys a greater amount of the commodity in question. Thus there tends to be a cheapening of the elements especially of c hence a relative decrease in c in the above ratios, a factor which tends to counteract a fall in the rate of profit. However it is clear that Marx believed that such counteracting tendencies only complicate the process of a fall in the rate of profit and do not do away with it.

There are also other factors not thus 'internally' related to the law itself which may interfere in the process of the fall in the rate of profit. For example, one way to counteract the fall is to increase the rate of surplus-value, that is, to increase the degree of exploitation of labour. (It can easily be shown that an increase in s' entails, other things being equal, an increase in p'.) Now whether it is feasible to increase s', and if so to what extent, is not a question that can be decided on the ground of economics alone; it is a matter of the ability of capital to impose this increase on the working class. And this is only to illustrate the point already made that the considerations in *Capital* largely abstract from factors that are not 'strictly' economic.

Marx does not tire, in the part of *Capital* we are looking at, of pointing up what he takes to be the significance of the tendency of the rate of profit to fall. He puts it in different ways. A favourite one is to say that what it shows is that capital has internal limits to its own possibility of development. For, though one tendency of capitalism is to develop the productive forces without limit, since capitalist production is for the sake not of need but of accumulation of surplus, the 'governor' of investment and hence of the actual growth of the forces of production is primarily rate of profit. So the very same economic structure that tends to develop the forces of production at the same time tends to inhibit that development: the very development of the productive forces which is synonymous with the growth in the *OC* of capital acts, through the entailed tendency of the rate of profit to fall, to produce 'negative feedback' on that development. The situation is further reinforced by the fact that the displacement of the labour-force in favour of improved technology means (in the absence of fresh fields of production to absorb the displaced labour) a decrease in disposable income to realize the surplus embodied in the commodities in fact produced by the improved technology.

Notes

1 This part of *Capital* is the location of what has been called 'the transformation problem', on which there is an immense literature. Discussion of this question would go well beyond the limits of the present exposition.
2 See Ernest Mandel's Introduction to the Penguin/New Left Review edition of *Capital*, Volume 3 (1981), p. 59. On the whole question see this introduction pp. 12f, 56ff.
3 On the interpretation of natural laws as laws of tendency see Bhaskar, R. *A Realist Theory of Science* (2nd ed., Brighton, Harvester, 1978).

Chapter 10
Capital — Some remaining questions

1

As we have seen, Marx's law of the tendency of the rate of profit to fall, as presented in the third volume of *Capital*, depends upon the assumption of a tendency for capital to accumulate. It is odd, but a fact, that though this tendency is regarded by Marx as quite fundamental to the CMP he nowhere explains, separately and clearly, *why* it occurs, though of course he does devote immense pains to showing *how* and *that* it does. This question of the rationale of capital-accumulation is one which we must now look at in more detail. And the best way to start is probably to go back to the chapters towards the end of the first volume of *Capital* that deal with the dynamics of capital-accumulation.

Chapter 25 of the first volume of *Capital* is entitled 'The general law of capitalist accumulation'. In the first section Marx argues that if accumulation of capital occurs and if the OC of capital remains the same then there must result a growing demand for labour-power. (For if capital is increasing in absolute amount and the proportion between the constant and the variable remains the same, the absolute amount of variable capital must increase, and that simply means that more labour-power must be purchased and thus become capital.) A consequence of this is, Marx goes on to point out, that the price of labour-power (the wage) tends to rise. But a rise in wages will occur only to the extent that it does not seriously interfere with the process of accumulation; if it does so then the consequence is that such a slackening weakens the demand for labour-power and thus causes a decline in wages, so restoring the conditions for accumulation.

In the next section Marx writes that at a certain point 'the development of the productivity of social labour becomes the

most powerful lever of accumulation' (C 1:772). This development of the productivity of social labour in general comes
about through improvements in the methods of production
and in particular through improvements in technology. This
has two consequences. On the side of capital the minimum
scale of viable capitalist production rises, which means that
individual capitals become larger ('concentration' of capital),
in the process absorbing smaller, increasingly less viable
capitals ('centralization' of capital). Thus there occurs a
decrease in the number but an increase in the size of individual
capitals. On the side of wage-labour, the fact that it becomes
more productive means that there arises a tendency for a
relative decrease in the variable part of capital. That is, there is
a progressive production of a relative surplus population or
industrial reserve army. What Marx calls 'the absolute general
law of capitalist accumulation' (C 1:798 — emphasized in the
original) is the development of social productivity on the one
hand, and, on the other, the development of an industrial
reserve army.

The considerations just indicated give a clear indication of
the direction in which Marx's basic explanation of the
tendency of capital to accumulate must be sought: the
development of social productivity made possible by the
accumulation of capital (and in turn making the latter
possible) makes possible a greater degree of control by capital
of the work-force of wage-labour. Increase in the OC —
increase in the proportion of constant to variable capital —
makes it possible to increase the scale of production without a
proportionate increase in the demand for labour and hence
without upward pressure on wages. In general, the existence of
an industrial reserve army is a potent source of social control
by capital over wage-labour.

The point is brought out in the course of the chapter I have
been partly summarizing:

Within the capitalist system [Marx writes] all means for the
development of production are transformed into means of
domination and exploitation of the producer...the law which
always holds the relative surplus population or industrial reserve
army in equilibrium with the extent and energy of accumulation

rivets the worker to capital more firmly than the wedges of Hephaestus held Prometheus to the rock. (C 1:799)

And this is in line with Marx's comment that 'the relation between capital and wage-labour determines the entire character of the capitalist mode of production' (C 3:1019). (I shall return to this topic in the next chapter.)

2

This anchoring in the process of *production* of the tendency of capital to accumulate is worth emphasizing, because a very common account ascribes to Marx the idea that it is primarily rooted in the process of *circulation* of capital — specifically in the fact of *competition* between capitals. Such an explanation goes somewhat as follows. Capitalists compete to sell their products. The battle of competition is fought by the cheapening of commodities. The latter is best achieved by increasing the productivity of labour, and this in turn is most efficiently attained, in the last resort, by improvements in the means of production and by economies of scale. But this requires access to increasingly large amounts of capital, at least a considerable amount of which must come from *accumulated* funds.

But that this cannot be Marx's view (unless he is inconsistent at this point) is evident from the fact that he holds both that capital-accumulation is a fundamental feature of capitalism and also that competition, as a phenomenon of circulation, cannot explain any basic feature of capitalism (for example, C 1:433): its efficacy consists in operating, so to speak, mechanisms which are in the sphere of production. We have already, in fact, had an example of this in the preceding chapter in tracing how competition works to realize an average rate of profit the conditions for the possibility of which are of other provenance.

3

At the end of this preliminary journey through *Capital* it is time to reflect for a moment on Marx's general procedure, thus returning to some themes indicated at the beginning of Chapter 7 above and developing them in a way that would not have been intelligible before the presentation of some of Marx's substantive rather than methodological ideas.

Marx set out his conception of method in the third section of the '1857 Introduction' (introduction to the *Grundrisse*) entitled 'The method of political economy' (G 10ff). He says here to begin with that the right method would seem to be to start with 'the real and the concrete', 'the real precondition', that is, the actual objective state of affairs which is the necessary condition for the inquiry's taking place at all. For example, economics might be thought properly to begin with the phenomenon of population as something completely concrete. But, he argues, this seemingly concrete starting-point is in fact highly *abstract* insofar as no mention is made of, say, the classes of which it is composed, the factors on which the existence of classes depend (capital, wage-labour, for example) and then what these factors presuppose (mechanisms of exchange, etc.). He goes on to say that the concrete, understood as the real objective situation, is concrete by virtue of its being the focus, the point of intersection of many different properties and relations. This concrete is what we *start from*, what is vouchsafed us, in the final analysis, by observation, furnishing us with our basic stock of representations. But when we seek to *understand* it we must find by theoretical analysis what these properties and relations which comprise it are and then, with the materials afforded by clear abstract concepts of them, build up a theoretical representation of the concrete starting-point.

Thus Marx is, in fact, distinguishing between two senses of 'concrete', which might be called 'the real concrete' and 'the theoretical concrete'. The first is the real objective situation that we are seeking to understand, whilst the second is a representation of that situation constructed from a number of abstract concepts. The first is given and independent of us, unchanged by our understanding of it; the second is produced by us as theorisers.[1]

This presentation in the *Grundrisse* of the method of theorizing thus represents it as two-fold: firstly, from the real concrete to the discovery of the abstractions which represent the factors that make the real concrete what it is, and then, secondly, a theoretical representation of that real concrete by a specific combination of these abstractions. (The method recalls Galileo's 'resolutive-compositive method'.[2]) It is repeated in all essentials, if more succinctly, in *Capital*, where he writes that 'in the analysis of economic forms neither microscopes nor chemical reagents are of assistance. The power of abstraction must replace both' (C 1:90). Later on he supplements this. He begins by distinguishing between 'the mode of presentation' and the 'mode of inquiry' and says that the two must differ in form. The second 'has to appropriate the material in detail, to analyze its different forms of development and to track down their inner connection. Only after this work has been done can the real movement be appropriately presented' (C 1:102).[3]

Capital is in fact constructed in accord with these methodological principles.

The first sentence of the first chapter of the first volume of *Capital* directs attention to the real concrete from which the inquiry is to begin: 'The wealth of societies in which the capitalist mode of production prevails appear as an "immense collection of commodities"' (C 1:125). The first move in the process of abstraction comes immediately: 'the individual commodity appears as its elementary form. Our investigation therefore begins with the analysis of the commodity'. In the study of the commodity further abstractions present themselves in succession: use-value, exchange-value, value, concrete and abstract labour. So the first volume proceeds, the entire book working for the most part at one over-arching level of abstraction, namely that of the process of capitalist production from the total economic system. Even within this, further abstractions are made. For example, the process of production is analysed prescinding from the fact that capital does not in fact exist as an aggregate mass, but in the form of 'many capitals'.

The second volume of *Capital* relaxes the assumptions underlying the first volume to the extent of bringing in the process of circulation of capital. The third volume brings the two together and begins the process of presentation of the real concrete in the form of the theoretical concrete. As Marx says at the end of his own incomparable summary of the structure of *Capital* as a whole in the opening paragraph of the third volume, for the latter:

it is a matter of discovering and presenting the concrete forms which grow out of the *process of the movement of capital considered as a whole*. In their real movement capitals confront each other in concrete forms which are such that the form of capital in the immediate process of production as well as the form in the process of circulation, appear only as particular aspects. The formations of capital as they are developed in this volume thus approach step by step the form which they assume on the surface of society. (C 3:117)

Notes

1 Marx comments that Hegel confused the two, identifying the theoretical process of production of a concrete *representation* with a real process of production of the concrete *real situation* which the theoretical concrete is meant to help us understand. This is essentially the same line of criticism of Hegel as those in Marx's 1843 analysis of Hegel's *Philosophy of Right*, in the *1844 Manuscripts*, and especially in the section on 'The mystery of speculative construction', in *The Holy Family* (CW 4:57ff).

2 Such a comparison of Galileo and Marx is a central theme of della Volpe's *Logic as a Positive Science* (London, NLB, 1980).

3 Marx goes on: 'If this is done successfully, if the life of the subject-matter is now reflected in the domain of ideas, then it may appear as if we have before us an a priori construction' (C 1:102). This would partly explain Hegel's confusion — see note 1 above.

Chapter 11
Productive forces, relations of production, classes

1

The past four chapters have been occupied with sketching the rough outlines of certain major parts of Marx's most important concrete analysis from the point of view of historical materialism. Some of the general categories of the latter have already been briefly introduced. I now want to consider some of the basic concepts of historical materialism in more detail.

If we look at the famous passage from the Preface to the *Contribution to the Critique of Political Economy* (1859) which for long has been widely regarded as the classical summary of historical materialism, we find the key concept to be one which is designated by Marx in various fairly clearly synonymous ways: 'the economic structure of society', 'the real base', 'the mode of production of material life', the 'economic foundation', and so on. For the sake of brevity I shall refer to this simply as 'the base'.

Now the base is said to be identical with 'relations of production' and these to 'correspond' to 'productive forces'. I have already introduced the concepts of 'relations of production' and 'productive forces' in Chapter 7 above. But it is now necessary to look at them more closely, in particular as regards their relations and specifically the idea of 'correspondence' between the two.

The relation may be spelled out as follows. To begin with, specific social relations of production have a certain range of sorts of factors of production as necessary conditions of existence: not any old factors can serve as the terms for being combined according to certain relations of production. For example, handicraft is as little compatible with the social relations of production characteristic of modern capitalism as the productive powers of the latter are compatible with guild organization of production. In that sense social relations of production 'correspond' to productive powers.

Nevertheless, it is the social relations of production which determine the mode of combination of the factors of production (the technical relations of production) though of course within the constraints set by the objective character of these factors. For example, in a process of producing petrol from oil there is a range of ways in which the operation can be organized in ways largely determined by social relations, but these have to respect the naturally determined sequence of steps. Using Marx's own terminology we may speak in this way of 'the material conditions of the labour process' as distinct from 'its social form' (C 2:434).

So according to Marx it is the social relations of production that determine the state of development of the productive forces. Nevertheless, at least in the case of progress in the development of the productive powers, it may come about that the latter develop to a point at which the social relations of production of which these powers have been the terms hitherto are no longer adequate to the new powers, and different social relations of production are necessary if further progress is to be achieved or even if regression is not to occur. So it is clear, for this reason alone, there is no simple answer to the question: 'which is primarily determining, productive powers or relations of production?' since changes in the former may turn out to be indispensable necessary conditions for changes in the latter.

2

What has been said may be illuminated and the next part of the discussion introduced by a sketch of Marx's study of the history of Western European capitalism, the only period of economic history that he treated in detail.

Marx periodized the history of capitalism in different ways. But for present purposes we can restrict ourselves to two broad and overlapping forms. In the first the distinction is between the period of 'formal subsumption of labour under capital' on the one hand, and 'real subsumption of labour under capital' on the other (C 1:1019ff). The one embraces the period from the emergence of capitalism to the Industrial Revolution, or what Marx calls 'manufacture'. As regards the emergence of capitalism Marx shows how capitalist relations of production presupposed a growth of productive power in the countryside as well as in the city, a growth that could not be encompassed by pre-capitalist relations of production (C 1:1064); insofar, there was a lack of 'correspondence' between those powers and those relations. Thus a development of the productive forces was, in Marx's view, a clearly necessary condition for the emergence of capitalist relations of production. Marx also emphasizes (C 1:439) that early capitalism had a technological base virtually indistinguishable from the economic structure it was replacing. This is, in fact, the clue to the meaning of the phrase 'formal subsumption of labour under capital'. Labourers are 'subsumed' under capital insofar as they are legally separated from the means of production and hence have to sell their labour-power in order to live. But the subsumption is only 'formal' because, whilst they are *legally* dispossessed they are not strictly *technically* dispossessed, since they still have a large degree of actual control over the labour-process by virtue of the fact that the instruments of production depend for their use on their skill and strength: *they use* the instruments of labour. Thus at this stage capitalist relations of production have not acquired a technical basis appropriate to it, insofar as capital still does not have effective control over the labour-process and insofar as the accumulation of surplus has limits imposed on it both by the physical constitution of labourers and by the power they have to resist exploitation stemming from the technical relation which they have to the instruments they use. We can say then, in the language of the 1859 Preface, that forces of production (using the usual terminology) and relations of production here fail to 'correspond': the former, having provided the original technical basis for capitalist relations of production to get a foothold, are now inadequate to the latter.

The 'real subsumption of labour under capital' begins with the Industrial Revolution and lies in the *creation* by capital of a technical base adequate to it. It consists essentially in the introduction of the machine proper in place of the tool. Now the *workers* do not *use tools*: *machines use workers*. The accumulation of surplus is now not restricted by the physical constitution of workers and they become dispossessed not merely legally but also technically.

Marx distinguishes, effectively, two sub-periods within this overall period of real subsumption of labour under capital. During the first (the exact dating is unimportant here) there was a 'correspondence' between the forces and relations of production insofar as the latter actually fostered the development of the former; during the second the latter has formed an obstacle to the development of the former and hence there has been a lack of 'correspondence' between the two, formally similar to that which obtained at the beginning of the epoch of capitalism but with the source of non-correspondence reversed, its being now the productive forces which are in advance of the relations of production.

This brief sketch fills out the thesis that it is capitalist social relations of production that have encouraged the development of productive powers, and, particularly, technology, and supplements the earlier considerations about the roots of capital-accumulation (in the preceding chapter). In sum, the development of the productive forces is forwarded in the first place by the struggle between capitals for a share of the surplus: better technology means (other things being equal) cheaper products and hence competitive advantage. But it is forwarded in the second place by the exigency of extracting the surplus in the first place: again other things being equal, the more advanced the technology the less control the individual worker has over the labour-process and hence the less power in the struggle with capital.[1] So one of the most crucial keys to the development of the productive forces under capitalism (as shown in the example sketched above) is the state of the struggle between capital and labour. And this is extensible backwards into the first period and forward to the present. In words I have already quoted Marx wrote that 'capital comes into the world dripping from head to toe, from every pore, with blood and dirt' (C 1:926). And late capitalist crises have their outcomes determined — hence in particular the possibilities of productive development — by, amongst other things, the outcome of the struggle between capital and labour (e.g. the capacity of the working-class to resist attacks on real wages).

A more general point that emerges from this is the fact that social relations of production are, over large portions of history anyway, a matter not just of *control* over the factors of production but a matter of *differential* control: by virtue of certain agents of production owning some or all of them others do not. But this is in fact just to say that social relations of production are in general bound up with the notion of *class* and hence, as may quickly be seen, with the notion of *class-struggle*.

3

Marx explicitly disclaimed any merit for having discovered the existence of classes or of class-struggle. 'Long before me bourgeois historians had described the historical development of . . . class-struggle and bourgeois economists the economic anatomy of the classes' (letter to J. Weydemeyer, 5 March 1852). But what, amongst other things, is peculiar to Marx is the *centrality* of the concept of class in his thinking from the very beginnings of the formulation of what is recognisably historical materialism. Unfortunately his use of the idea of class did not achieve a corresponding theorization, so that for a general understanding of the concepts we have to depend upon scattered statements and what can be inferred from particular analyses.

Marx's most compendious formulation is doubtless a few lines from *The Eighteenth Brumaire of Louis Bonaparte*. Here, in the course of discussion of the small-holding peasantry in contemporary France, Marx writes:

Insofar as millions of families live under economic conditions of existence that separate their mode of life, their interests and their culture from those of other classes and put them in hostile opposition to the latter, they form a class. (CW 11:187)

There are a number of points here that need to be signalled:

1 A perhaps obvious point, but one which, as such, is likely to be missed, is that the concept of '(a) class' is here introduced via that of 'classes'. This does not, as might be thought at first glance, introduce any circularity into the characterisation, any more than defining '(a) twin' via that of 'twins'.

2   It is a specific set of 'economic conditions of existence' that is fundaɪ.ɪental for the demarcation of a class.

3   It is the conditions mentioned in 2 above that separate the 'mode of life...interests...and customs' of one class from another.

4   These conditions also put one class 'in hostile opposition' to another class.

Indeed the clear import of the passage is that 2 above is only class-determining *insofar as* it has the effects 3 and 4 above. The crucial character of 4 above in particular is emphasized in *The German Ideology*: 'Separate individuals form a class only insofar as they have to carry on a common struggle against another class' (CW 5:77. Cf. also G 597.) Thus *class-struggle* is not, in Marx's view, something *subsequent* to the existence of classes, but *constitutive* of them. Classes do not form up and only then engage in struggle like a football team first assembling and then playing another team: it is in the struggle itself that the classes are formed. (Again there is no circularity here. Someone is not first a swimmer, say, and then enters the water: he becomes a swimmer by swimming. And of course someone can be a swimmer without forever swimming.)

What, more specifically, are the 'economic conditions of existence' which generate differential forms of life and class-struggle? They are, of course, in the final analysis, differential relations to the means of production as regards control/ownership, and to the product of the use of those means, by virtue of which one group extracts surplus product from another. In general it is by virtue of control/ownership of the means of production that one group is able to extract surplus from another group. This differential control/ownership is in general naturally contested — hence the fact of class-struggle.

Thus in its simplest and most general form Marx's class-theory holds that in any class-society there are two basic classes: the one which produces surplus, directly or indirectly, and the one that extracts it. Of course, as the theory becomes less abstract complexities enter. Just the following may be noted here:

1   Besides the two basic classes there are what may be called 'transitional classes'. These are of two general kinds. One

comprises groupings which are in process of formation, the other groupings in process of dissolution, within a society whose basic class-division is otherwise. The clearest example of the first is the bourgeoisie within feudalism; an example of the second is the simple commodity production of small family farms in an advanced capitalist society.

2   There are what may be called, using a much over-used word, 'middle classes'. This term is used here to designate precisely what its name suggests, namely, groupings which stand between the two basic classes. They are of a very diverse character. Thus bank employees may be regarded as members of the middle class insofar as, on Marx's account, they do not, strictly speaking, produce surplus but live off part of the surplus produced by others and are paid in the form of wages; but they enable capital to realize what has been produced and are exploited insofar as (to reiterate a point already made) they are paid wages less than the profit which the use of their labour enables capital to extract. Such a grouping is thus Janus-faced. The factor of class struggle is particularly important here in 'locating' such a part of the middle class: it is in the arena of class-struggle that such a grouping shows to which basic class it inclines at a particular time.

3   Finally, there are 'fractions' of classes marked out in various ways. Thus capital is fractured along the lines of its industrial, rural, financial, etc. forms, and also along national divisions. Labour too tends to be split along various lines, for example that between skilled and unskilled workers. Both sorts of divisions are sites of possible and often actual conflicts.

What is distinctive about Marx's class-theory? As we have seen it is not that it marks the recognition of the existence of classes or of class-conflict. In the letter already cited in this connection Marx himself states his own view of that in which his originality consists:

What I did that was new was to prove: 1) that the *existence of classes* is only bound up with *particular historical phases in the development of production*, 2) that the class-struggle necessarily leads to the *dictatorship of the proletariat*, 3) that this dictatorship itself only constitutes the transition to the *abolition of all classes* and to a *classless society*.

115

According to the first point, classes are historically specific phenomena with determinate conditions of existence, and not a necessary feature of all forms of human society; furthermore, these conditions are said to be determined by the nature of *production*. As to the second point, numerous bourgeois theorists have foreseen an end to the class-struggle but within the terms of the continued existence of classes, through arriving at some sort of reconciliation of class-interests. Marx on the contrary sees the most historically significant next phase as being that of the supremacy of the working class (rather than that of capital); but this is still seen as a phase of the class-struggle and not its end, which — so the third point says — is only possible with an end to the existence of all classes. But this points ahead to the subject-matter of later chapters. For the moment we must take up the thread dropped at the end of the preceding section.

4

What the considerations of the preceding section make plain is that something has been left out of explicit consideration thus far in the discussion of the relation between productive forces and relations of production, namely, the fact(or) of class-struggle. It must be brought clearly into view that the combination of the productive powers into productive forces by virtue of social relations of production is, when these are class-relations, seldom if ever the sort of more or less automatic process that the ways of talking so far could have suggested, but rather a matter which is fundamentally contested. And it must be remembered that the generation of new social relations of production in the case where the old ones have forwarded the development of productive powers to a point incompatible with them is by no means an automatically occurring process, but once more a matter of struggle between classes. All this is, indeed, just to spell out what Marx says when he writes in a fundamental passage that 'it is always the direct relation of the owners of the conditions of production to the direct producers . . . in which we find the innermost secret, the hidden foundation of the whole social structure' (C 3:927).

In sum I am ascribing to Marx the view:

116

1   That the social relations of production in general determine the productive forces to the extent that they determine —
within certain independent technical constraints — the way in
which the productive powers are combined.

2   However, that a definite type of social relations of
production has a definite range of types of productive powers
as a necessary condition of existence.

3   That the socal relations of production are brought into
existence and sustained, to the extent that they are, and in the
cases with which Marx was centrally concerned, namely, class-
societies, through class-struggle.

So the correct answer to the question 'Do productive forces
determine the character of the relations of production or
conversely?' is 'Neither, since the ultimate determinant of both
(subject to the qualifications of scope already made) is the
class-struggle, the nature and course of which has, naturally,
its own determinants (on the one hand, the state of development of the productive powers, on the other, the political and
ideological situation).'

Finally it must be emphasized, at the risk of underlining the
obvious, that this explanatory reference to class-struggle is
obviously applicable only to class-societies. Marx has no
special theory about the economies of pre-class societies, nor
about the origin of class, and only fragmentary remarks about
post-class societies. It would be wholly contrary to the spirit of
historical materialism to posit universal mechanisms of particular historical developments, historically unspecific springs
of all social change (as, for example, accounts in terms of
'human nature' do).

Notes

1   Cf. *The Poverty of Philosophy:*

In England, strikes have regularly given rise to the invention and
application of new machines. Machines were ... the weapon employed
by the capitalists to quell the revolt of specialised labour. The *self-acting
mule*, the greatest invention of modern industry, put out of action the
spinners who were in revolt ... combinations and strikes had ... [the] ...
effect of making the efforts of mechanical genius react against them.
(CW 6:207)

Chapter 12
The primacy of practice

1

I suggested in the preceding chapter that both Marx's own concrete analyses and a great many of his explicit statements point to the centrality of the notion of class for socio-historical analysis of at least the most significant portions of human history so far, and that whoever says class (in Marx's sense anyway) says class-struggle.

An index of the fact that the famous statement in the 1859 Preface is quite misleading and inadequate if it is considered, as it has been by more writers on Marx than anyone can usefully list, to be an outline statement of historical materialism as such is that the term 'class' is not so much as mentioned. The closest that text comes to it is when, towards the end of the passage, Marx speaks of capitalism as

the last antagonistic form of the process of social production, antagonistic not in the sense of individual antagonism, but in that of an antagonism that grows out of individuals' conditions of social life. (EW 426)

For the rest there is just rather bland 'evolutionist' language to the effect that 'at a certain stage of development' productive forces come into contradiction with the relations of production 'within which they have moved hitherto' and so on. Of course, if the reader remembers that the productive forces include the direct producers, that relations of production involve property relations which are in general contested in the arena of the class-struggle then all is, if not well, at least a good deal better. But then this can hardly be assumed if what we are dealing with is supposed to be an introductory statement.

2

Of course there is no question of any change in Marx's quite fundamental view, expressed in the opening of the first chapter of the *Communist Manifesto*: 'The history of all hitherto existing society is the history of class struggles' (CW 6:482) (except to restrict the statement to post-primitive communist societies). It is reaffirmed as late as 1879 by Marx and Engels:

For almost forty years we have stressed the class struggle as the most immediate driving power in history and, in particular, the class struggle between the bourgeoisie and the proletariat as the great lever of the modern social upheavals. (PW 3:374f)

But the absence of a clear notion of class and class-struggle in the 1859 Preface may be an index of a lack of explicitness and centrality in Marx's later writings of a concept crucial in the earlier presentations of historical materialism, that is, *practice*. The first of the 'Theses on Feuerbach', the founding document of historical materialism, opened by saying that 'the chief defect of all previous materialism ... is that ... reality ... [is] conceived only in the form of the *object*, ... not as ... practice', and the eighth asserted that 'all social life is essentially *practical*' (CW 5:3, 5), that is, a matter of practices — more-or-less regular ways of transforming a given subject-matter by the use of certain material-instrumental means applied to it by labour-power. This insight into the centrality of practice for theorizing about social and historical matters later tends to be pushed to some extent into the background, and the idea of society as a matter of *relations* comes more to the fore. Thus in the *Grundrisse* we read (265) that 'society does not consist of individuals but expresses the sum of connections, the relations within which these individuals stand'. Now it is true of course that bourgeois social theory typically takes individuals as primary, relations being then superadded and regarded either as grounded in the individuals or as merely accidental with regard to them. But the fundamental framework of this conception is not done away with simply by taking instead the relations as fundamental and regarding the individuals as in some sense constituted by or mere accidental 'supports' for the relations. To do this is simply to reverse the

119

order of primacy of the elements within the same fundamental framework.

The only way to escape this entirely is to cease setting things up in terms of individuals on the one hand, and relations on the other, and to make fundamental the idea of modes of transformation as articulated in the notion of a practice. What is determinant about the character of a practice is neither the objective material which is transformed nor the executor of the transformation, but the means by which the transformation is effected, means which determine both what sorts of materials may be transformed and also the nature of the activity of the executor of the practice. Thus a central intent of the relational conception, namely, the demotion of the individual as a primary explanatory factor is preserved. Again, practices are structured by relations (in particular relations of production), but it is the practice which is fundamental and it is ultimately changes which come about by virtue of the on-going practice that lead to changes in those relations. It is hard to see how a set of relations — in particular relations of production — could, just considered as relations, ever change, even when taken together with productive forces, unless indeed the latter are seen as ways of considering certain aspects of a certain set of practices, namely, economic ones.

3

This recuperation of the primacy of practice suggests a re-examination of the idea of what the materialism of historical materialism consists in.[1]

The answer to this question, in general terms at least, may well seem to be fairly obvious, and indeed to have been partly answered already in terms first of the distinction between economic 'base' and 'superstructure', and second of a thesis asserting the determination of the second by the first. As Marx writes in the 1859 Preface:

The mode of production of material life conditions the general process of social, political and mental life. It is not the consciousness of people that determines their being, but, on the contrary, their social being that determines their consciousness. (EW 425)

In the terms introduced earlier in this chapter we may say that Marx's thesis here is that, within the network of practices that constitutes a society, one group, namely, the economic practices, are the most important in determining the character of the others. Marx gives many paradigmatic examples, like his derivation of the bourgois ideology of equality and freedom from the material conditions of the exchange-relations (G 240ff), or his treatment of the relation between exchange-practices and certain legal structures and practices in his late 'Marginalia to Adolph Wagner's *Textbook'* (*Texts on Method*, 210).

It is certainly this which has been historically taken to be what is distinctively materialist about historical materialism. And there is no doubt that it is at least a central thesis of that doctrine as it appears in Marx's writings — indeed, most probably, what Marx had primarily in mind. But is it the only sense in which historical materialism is a *materialism*?

To give some purchase to this question let us look, for example, at the initial couple of chapters of the first volume of *Capital*. For example, in the first chapter he writes thus:

People do not ... bring the products of their labour into relation with each other as values because they see these objects merely as the material embodiments of homogeneous human labour. The reverse is true. By equating their different products to each other in exchange as values, they equate their different kinds of labour as human labour. *They do not know it, but they do it*. Value, therefore, does not have what it is written on its forehead. Rather, it transforms every product of labour into a social hieroglyphic. Later on, people try to decipher the hieroglyphic, to get behind the secret of their own social product, for the characteristic which objects of utility have of being values is as much people's social product as is their language. (C 1:166f). (Emphasis added.)

Thus, to start with, the economic practice is carried on in accordance with principles about which the executors of the practice are unaware. It just happens that way, like a child's speaking a language. (Marx's analogy with language at the end of the passage is not a mere accidental flourish.) 'They do not know it, but they do it.' At a later stage the executors of the practice may form theories about the functioning of the practice but it is the objective character of the practice itself

121

that will be decisive here, not least in determining mis-apprehensions about the practice. (See the discussion of 'the fetishism of commodities' in the next chapter.)

Or, again, consider Marx's derivation of money in the second chapter on 'The process of exchange'. At the beginning of this chapter he traces, in a passage of great inspissation and subtlety, the way in which money arises as a necessary condition for the operation of a ramified commodity-producing economy. The actual argument cannot even be summarized here, but is in any case unnecessary for present purposes. All that it is essential to note is the gloss that Marx adds. 'In their difficulties', he writes — their difficulties that is of being in the situation of a ramifying commodity-producing economy before the invention of money — 'our commodity-owners think like Faust: "In the beginning was the act." They have already acted before thinking. The natural laws of the commodity have manifested themselves in the natural instinct of the owners of commodities' (C 1:180).

Once more, as in the previous case, a certain practice — that of commodity-exchange — extends itself in accordance with the objective tendencies of its functioning, the executors of the practice conforming themselves to these tendencies. Again, it is not a matter of a relation between a mode of production on the one hand, and a 'superstructural' feature on the other, but between the objective structure of a practice and the way in which it is carried on, in particular the ideas in terms of which it is carried on.

This idea of the primacy of material practices with respect to the explanation of social life and its changes, and in particular with regard to thought about the latter, is different from the earlier thesis which asserts that one of the social practices, namely the economic, is primary with regard to the determination of the other practices which go to constitute a society. Indeed the two sorts of materialism are logically independent of one another.

This distinction between the two theses regarding materialism in the field of society and history is not made explicitly by Marx. Perhaps the closest he comes to it is in writing in *The German Ideology* that the materialist conception of history is demarcated from the idealist conception in respect simply of the fact that the former 'does not explain practice from the idea but explains the formation of ideas from material practice' (CW 5:54). But if Marx does, in fact, actually work with this sense of materialism without making it explicit or even being specially aware of it — as I have suggested may well be the case — then this is itself an example of the situation to which this sense of materialism points.

Notes

1 For a discussion of the general question of materialism in the context of Marx's thought see W. Suchting, 'On Materialism' *Radical Philosophy*, No. 31, Summer 1982.

Chapter 13
Capital as *Critique of Political Economy*

1

I have so far been discussing *Capital* as political economy. But in introducing this work in Chapter 7 I remarked that its sub-title is *Critique of Political Economy*. What does it mean to describe *Capital* as a 'critique' of political economy? And how does this sub-title connect with the main title?

We have already met the term 'critique' in Marx's work on several occasions: his early journalism was done in the name of 'critique' and his 1843 confrontation with Hegel's theory of the state was a 'critique'. In this context the term signified for Marx not just a criticism of a position that revealed its internal difficulties but also one that traced the origins of these difficulties.

The idea of 'critique' in the context of Marx's political economy is related to this but goes beyond it. It is, in the first place, an exhibition of internal difficulties in a certain systematically and historically delimited body of theory — 'political economy'. In the second place, 'critique' exhibits the ways in which these difficulties come about. This is done first, by showing how they are generated by the basic framework of the theory, and second, by showing how this general framework itself comes about by virtue of the very economic practices that constitute the capitalist mode of production. Thus these practices generate not only capital but also the basis of certain misleading representations of itself which are formulated and systematized to varying extents in the theories of the system, that is, in 'political economy'. This explains the connection between the main and sub-title of the work.

There is obviously no question of presenting Marx's critique of political economy as a whole, even in outline. Instead I shall say something about just two major themes, namely, 'fetishism' and 'the wage-form', and conclude by looking at the relation of politics to the 'critique of political economy'.

2

'Fetishism', like 'alienation', is one of those words which have almost passed into ordinary language. As so used it generally has either no specifiable meaning or one with little or no relation to Marx's. So it is important to tie down more closely the sense that Marx gives to it.

The first major use of the term in *Capital* occurs in the long section which concludes the first chapter of Volume 1, that entitled 'The fetishism of commodities and its secret'. To start with then, what does Marx mean by 'the fetishism of commodities'? He certainly does not mean what people often seem to think he does, namely, something like being excessively preoccupied with consumer goods or material possessions in general. Rather it consists:

simply in the fact that the commodity reflects the social characteristics of people's own labour as objective characteristics of the products of labour themselves, as socio-natural properties of these things, hence also the social relations of the producers to the sum total of labour as a social relation between objects which exists apart from the producers ... It is just the definite social relation between people themselves which assumes here, for them, the phantasmagoric form of a relation between things. (C 1:164f)

Thus the 'fetishism of commodities', as Marx uses the term, signifies the representation of characteristics of things which they in fact have by virtue of their being the terms of social relations as intrinsic, natural properties of those things. And Marx lists here two main sorts of cases of this. One is where (to cite an earlier passage):

the equality of the kinds of human labour takes on a material form in the equality of the products of labour considered as objective values and the measure of the expenditure of human labour-power by its duration takes on the form of the magnitude of the value of the objects of labour. (C 1:164)

The other is where

the relations between the producers, in which these social characteristics of their labours are manifested, take on the form of a social
relation between the products of labour.

In brief, the fetishism of commodities consists first in the fact
that the social labour that produces use-values is represented
as an intrinsic property of them (a mode of representation
which is particularly clear in the case of money); it consists
second in the fact that the behaviour of commodities (in
particular their market-behaviour), which stems from a relation between different individual labours (mediated by objects),
is represented as stemming from the relation between the
objects themselves.

If this is what Marx means by 'the fetishism of commodities',
what is its 'secret', what explains it? How is it that one state of
affairs is (misleadingly) represented as another? The answer
is in terms of what makes a commodity a commodity. This is
that it is a use-value, produced by concrete, private labour,
which is exchanged with similar use-values, by virtue of which
the labour expended in its production comes under the
description social labour and the relation of the private labour
to the sum total of labour becomes manifest.

Specifically, with regard to the first aspect of fetishism, we
have to start with the exchange-relation between two use-
values, the simplest form of which is (as we have already seen)

amount x of commodity A = (is worth, exchanges for)
amount y of commodity B

Here a certain amount of labour, represented as the *value* of A
is expressed in terms of a certain amount of B *considered simply
as a use-value*, as something having certain physical properties
which make it apt for satisfying certain wants or needs. Insofar
as we are dealing with a pure commodity economy there is no
way of expressing the amount of labour which produced a
certain thing except by putting it into relation with something
else in exchange. So in the simplest case, that of barter, the
value of something (the proportion of the total social labour
that went to produce it) can only be expressed in terms of how
many or how much of different other things are exchangeable
for it. That is, value, a social and relational property, has its
sole 'form of appearance' in the natural and intrinsic proper-

ties of things, and is thus treated as itself a natural and intrinsic property.

Now — and here we come to the second aspect of 'the fetishism of commodities' — by virtue of the fact that private labours are not brought into relation directly but only via the products of such labours as they exchange (or fail to do so) in the market-place, the relation between these labours (for example, the proportions in which concrete labours of different types have been expended in different branches of production) is only known about via the relation between commodities at the market-place (whether and if so in what proportions they exchange). The priority of the latter relation as regards knowledge is then represented as priority as regards causation. Furthermore, the fact that the expenditures of private labours is *regulated* by the relation of commodities to one another at the market-place suggests that the whole situation is *determined* simply by the relations between objects rather than by the relations between people's labours as *mediated* by these objects. The overall effect is thus a thoroughgoing obfuscation of the real situation.

Marx himself applied the notion of fetishism to other economic phenomena. It is the basis of his critique, especially in the final part of the third volume of *Capital*, of what he called 'The trinity formula'. This is the idea that wages, profit and rent, the three main sorts of revenue in capitalism, are derived from three sorts of *objects,* physical states of affairs, namely, labour, capital and land, rather than being simply representations of different amounts of labour-time, which are commanded by certain objective states of affairs by virtue of those things standing in certain relationships. (He presents interest-bearing capital conceived as money having inherent powers of self-expansion as the final expression of fetishism.[1])

3

By contrast with what others have made of it Marx himself did not place great emphasis on his treatment of the fetishism of commodities; at least he did not treat it like 'the wage-form', that is the representation of the value (or price) of labour-power as wages. This is, he says, the basis of 'all the

127

mystifications of the capitalist mode of production' (C 1:680), and he lists his analysis of it as one of 'the three fundamentally new elements' in the first volume of *Capital* (letter to Engels 8 January 1868).[2] So it will clearly pay us to look with some care at the chapter in *Capital* in which the wage-form is treated (C 1:Chapter 19).

Marx begins by saying that 'on the surface of bourgeois society the worker's wage appears as the price of labour' (C 1:675). He goes on immediately to give reasons for thinking that there must be something radically wrong with this. For one thing, assuming that the magnitude of the value of a commodity is the amount of labour expended on its production, the value of, say, an eight-hour working day is the eight working hours contained in it. So the idea of the worker's wage as the price of labour reduces to a tautology. For another thing, a direct exchange of money with living labour would either violate the principle that it is equal values that are exchanged, or, if not, render it unintelligible how surplus is produced by the worker for his employer. Furthermore (continuing to assume a labour theory of value as did, in one form at least, those against whom Marx was arguing, namely, the classical economists) 'in the expression "value of labour", the concept of value is twisted into its opposite. It is an imaginary expression' (C 1:677). Marx does not spell this out but his meaning is reasonably easy to fathom. For whilst (on the labour theory of value) value is explained in terms of (abstract) labour, and hence it is permissible to speak of the labour-content of value, here what is spoken of is the value-content of labour, which, on the assumptions made, is as incoherent as to speak of the length of length. So the idea of wages as expressing the value of labour suffers from internal inadequacies.

But, he goes on, imaginary expressions like 'value of labour', 'arise . . . from the relations of production themselves. They are categories for the forms of appearance of essential relations' (C 1:677). Towards the end of the chapter Marx returns to this question of 'the necessity, the *raison d'être* of this form of appearance' (C 1:681). First, he says, since production is carried on with cotton, iron, labour, and so on, and since these are bought and sold in the ordinary way, it is natural to think that 'labour' is too. The buyer gives a certain sum of money, the seller an article other than the money. Second, since exchange-value (value, price) on the one hand, and use-value on the other, are incommensurable expressions in general (one belonging to the domain of society, the other to that of nature), 'value (or price) of labour' does not seem to differ in principle from 'value (or price) of cotton'.

Third, since the worker in general receives his wage *after* what he has actually sold (his labour-*power*) has been used, that is, consumed as labour, it appears as though what he has been paid for is in fact *labour*.

Fourth, what is immediately present is the specific, concrete, use-value-creating function of the labour-power that is sold, and not its power to generate abstract labour, the value-creating function.

Finally, 'the actual movement of wages presents phenomena which seem to prove that it is not the value of labour-power which is paid for, but the value of its function of labour itself'. These phenomena may be reduced to two broad classes.

To the first belong changes in wages which result from changes in the length of the working day. Here it appears to be obvious that the wage is payment for the labour and not for the labour-power purchased at the beginning of the working-day. Marx comments: 'One might as well conclude that it is not the value of a machine which is paid for, but that of its operation, because it costs more to hire a machine for a week than a day' (C 1:682). Thus it will obviously cost more to hire a machine for two hours than for one, but this is because the machine's working-life is decreased more in two hours than in one; in other words, its capacity to function is decreased more, and its original exchange-value stems from the production of that ability to function. So what is being paid for is not the actual functioning of the machine but a part of its original capacity to function. Similarly, assuming a constant rate of intensity of labour, more labour-power is required to work a ten-hour day than an eight-hour day, so it is obvious that the price paid for someone to work the first will be greater than that paid for someone to work the second.

The second class of cases of misleading phenomena stemming from the actual movement of wages embraces those where there are individual differences between the wages of different workers who perform the same function. Marx comments that this just means that there are differences in the productivity of different labour-powers: if one worker can make ten commodity-units in the same time as another can make five such units, then the first worker is functionally equivalent to two of the second sort and hence his labour power is worth more.

In addition to these general features of the practice of paying for labour-power in the form of wages there are special ones which stem from the specific locations of capital and of wage-labour in the practice and which generate misleading representations of what is really going on.

In the first place, consider the matter from the point of view of the worker. Suppose a working day of constant length. The value of a worker's labour-power may vary according to variations in the value of the usual means for reproducing that labour-power; or, if the value of the labour-power remains constant the price may still vary due to changes in the relation of supply and demand. But all that is apparent is the fact that he works the same number of hours per day. Therefore every change in the amount of the money-equivalent that he receives for what he sells labour-power appears to him as a change in the value or price of his constant number of hours of *labour*.

In the second place, the capitalist simply wants to obtain as much labour as possible for a given (or smaller) amount of money. In practice therefore the only relevant factor is the difference between the price of labour (-power) and the value which it creates when it is put to work. So the distinction between labour and labour-power is a matter of indifference.

The consequences of conceiving wages as the price of labour rather than of labour-power are far-reaching. In general its effect is to obliterate 'every trace of the division of the working-day into necessary and surplus labour, into paid labour and unpaid labour. All labour appears as paid labour' (C 1:680). Thus the fact and mechanism of exploitation is concealed.[3]

4

I have been tracing the way in which, according to Marx,

certain economic practices in the CMP generate their own forms of obfuscating representation. Early in the chapter on the wage-form Marx says that classical political economy failed to produce a correct theory of this head, precisely because it simply took over these misleading misrepresentations at face-value. 'Classical political economy borrowed the category "price of labour" from everyday life without further criticism, and then simply asked the question, how is this price determined?' (C 1:677). In the very last paragraph Marx return to the question. He begins by repeating the point made in the passage just quoted:

What is true of all forms of appearance and their hidden background is also true of the forms of appearance 'value and price of labour', or 'wages', as contrasted with the essential relation manifested in it, namely the value and price of labour-power. The forms of appearance are reproduced directly and spontaneously, as customary forms of thought, the essential relation must be discovered by science.

Marx concludes:

Classical political economy stumbles very near to the true state of affairs, but without consciously formulating it. It is unable to do this as long as it is stuck within its bourgeois skin. (C 1:682)

Classical political economy almost got it right in the following way. In taking up the question: how is the price of labour determined? it rejected the answer that it is a matter of supply and demand. Holding to the principle that the price of labour is its value expressed in money, as with all other comodities, it further held that, as with all other commodities, this value is its cost of production. Its answer to the above question was that the value of labour is the cost of production of the worker who supplies the labour. But this is, in fact, an answer (and indeed a correct answer) to a *different* question, namely: how is the price of labour-*power* determined? For the worker is a bearer not of labour but of labour-power. Hence it failed to answer the explicit question, but answered an implicit one — correctly — though it failed consciously to formulate that new question, involving as it did a quite new concept; hence it landed up in 'inextricable confusions and contradictions'.

Thus Marx gives two explanations of why classical political economy did not succeed in getting the answer to the problem in question right: first, because it took certain common-sense conceptions for granted, and second, because it was, in the final analysis, a *bourgeois* discipline. How, if at all, are these two explanations related? (It is tempting to suppose straight off that the first is the case because of the second.) This problem may be compounded — but again perhaps its solution facilitated — by another. The implication is that Marx's working-class, communist standpoint gave him certain corresponding theoretical advantages. If so, what and why? To answer these questions is to complete the task of 'critique' posed at the beginning of the chapter.

5

A certain sort of answer can be rejected at once. Marx was always very insistent on the necessity for genuinely scientific inquirers to keep separate their own prior political commitments on the one hand, from their theoretical work on the other, at least as regards the process of arriving at theoretical results. Thus he never tires of pillorying Malthus for his having derived from the interests of the bourgeoisie and the landed classes what he gave out as the conclusions of his unprejudiced research — for having given a 'scientific' gloss to results already given from outside the field of theory. 'When a man seeks to *accommodate* science to as viewpoint which is derived not from science itself...but from *outside, from alien, external interests*, then I call him "low"' (*Theories of Surplus Value*, 2:119). Now Marx certainly did not think of classical political economy as being the product of 'low' theorists. So what is in question here in asking about the significance of class-'standpoint' for the formation of theory is not how pre-determined results are mirrored or justified in that work but how that standpoint bears upon the process of production of theory.

6

The clues for an answer to this question are to be found in the early pages of the first volume of *Capital.* In the course of the first chapter Marx locates the fundamental defect of the received political economy in its not having analysed the value-*form*, that is to say, the nature of the relations which bring it about that labour-time is represented not directly as such but as (exchange-) value, a quasi-property of objects (C 1:173f).

In a footnote at this point he enlarges on what is said in the main text. Even classical political economy's

... best representatives, Adam Smith and Ricardo, treat the form of value as something of indifference... The explanation for this is ... that ... the value-form of the product of labour is the most abstract, but also the most universal form of the bourgeois mode of production; by that fact it stamps the bourgeois mode of production as a particular kind of social production of a historical and transitory character. If then we make the mistake of treating it as the eternal natural form of social production, we necessarily overlook the specificity of the value-form, and consequently of the commodity-form together with its further developments, the money-form, the capital form, etc.

Thus the root of the theoretical errors of classical political economy is represented in these passages as being, in the first place, a failure to analyse — indeed even to *see* the *problem* of analysing — the value-form, that is, the relations within which a use-value is a commodity. This in turn is explained in terms of the failure to see the commodity as a special, historically specific form of production of use-values, a failure indeed to pose the question of the specificity of capitalism and hence a failure to form the concept of a 'mode of production'. Conversely (Marx is saying implicitly) it is precisely the seeing of the commodity as an historically specific form that permits not only the posing of the question of the value-form and the subsequent construction of the theory of money, and capital etc., but also the construction of the general concept of a mode of production.

What is in question then are the social conditions for both the failure to pose the question at issue, and for the successful posing of the question. The problem concerns not so much what *concealed* the question as what *revealed* it.

Marx gives us a clear answer to this if we turn back some dozens of pages:

In so far as political economy is bourgeois, i.e. in so far as it views the

133

capitalist order as the absolute and ultimate form of social production, instead of as a historically transient stage of development, it can
only remain a science while the class struggle remains latent or
manifests itself only in isolated and sporadic phenomena. (C 1:96)

Marx is saying that the specificity of the capitalist mode of
production can only be overlooked whilst the rule of the
bourgeoisie goes unchallenged, that is, whilst there is no
posing, on the social scale of class-conflict, of the question of
an alternative mode of social organization. After this has
happened only two roads remain open. One leads towards a
theory of the capitalist mode of production conceived as an
historically specific and transitory one. The other leads to a
more or less conscious concealment of this fact which has been
made manifest by the class-struggle. In the passage referred to
and just quoted from, Marx locates this decisive watershed at
1830 with the first major class-struggles in Paris: 1848
definitively confirmed the development. This period represents the watershed between what Marx calls 'classical' and
'vulgar' political economy.

So, in sum, Marx's answer to our question is that the social
conditions within which classical political economy was
nurtured did not put the nature of capitalism in question, did
not occasion the asking of questions as to the specificity of
capitalism, and hence did not provide the appropriate context
for the formation of the concept of a mode of production.
Marx stood on the ground of the working class 'whose
historical task is the overthrow of the capitalist mode of
production and the final abolition of all classes' (C 1:98). This
did not provide him with ready-made answers to questions of
political economy. What it did was to provide the *practical*
occasion for calling capitalism into question in the light of an
alternative model of social organisation and thus to provide
the *theoretical* occasion for the construction of the concept of a
mode of production. It was the new *theoretical* framework
that generated the theory of capitalism, but it was the *social*
developments (and Marx's participation in them) that provided the conditions for the emergence of the new theoretical
framework.[4]

Notes

1 Marx himself uses the notion of fetishism only with respect to strictly economic phenomena. The relation of this to 'reification' and how far Marx's concept of fetishism can be generalized beyond the economic context (for example, so that femininity or negritude becomes a form of fetishism) in a separate question.

2 The other two 'elements' which he lists are the distinction between concrete and abstract labour, and the treatment of surplus-value independently of its particular forms of distribution, both of which I have already considered.

3 The mystification of the wage-form has, according to Marx, profound consequences throughout the system of political economy. There is no opportunity to go into the matter here. However, see for example in Volume 2 of *Capital* (especially Chapters 8, 10 and 11) Marx's treatment of the fixed / circulating capital distinction and how it conceals the exploitation that the constant / variable capital distinction reveals, and in Volume 3 (especially Chapter 2) the origin of the concept of profit and its obfuscating effects compared with that of surplus-value.

4 It is in the light of this that we can understand throwaway remarks like 'the antithesis to political economy — namely socialism and communism' (G 884). Cf. also below text to Chapter 19, note 2.

Chapter 14
Ideology

1

Marx's 'critique of political economy' in *Capital* is to a large extent a critique of a certain body of 'ideology'. That is why I have looked at certain aspects of this critique of a certain particular body of subject matter before attempting to consider Marx's account of ideology in its general form.

Unfortunately there is virtually nothing of a general *theory* of ideology in Marx's writings; it is not even clear that there is a quite homogeneous doctrine underlying his various remarks about it. So what he says about the subject has to be pieced together from indications here and there, with careful regard to the period in his work to which reference is being made. I shall essay a chronological sketch in the following, tracing out continuities and discontinuities where necessary.

2

The most comprehensive founding text of historical materialism, *The German Ideology*, shows by its very title the important place held by the notion of ideology in Marx's thinking at that time; the idea, though not the term itself, is also clearly evident in its pendant, the 'Theses on Feuerbach'. Among the main features of Marx's conception of ideology at this stage are the following:

1   Ideologies are forms of consciousness, ways of seeing the world, world-outlooks, 'phantoms formed in the people's brains' (CW 5:36).
2   Ideologies involve the idea of self-subsistent domains of ideas independent of the material world.
3   The distinctive feature about ideology at the stage of *The*

German Ideology is what is called in one place (CW 5:36) the 'camera oscura' effect; that is, to be in the grip of ideology or to have an ideological consciousness is to have a conception of the relation between ideas, consciousness on the one hand and social reality on the other the inverse of what Marx held is the real one, the ideologist thinking that the first is primary and produces the second. It is the idea that the world is

dominated by ideas, ideas and concepts as the determining principles ...ideologists...put things upside down and regard...ideology both as the creative force and as the aim of all social relations.... (CW 5:24, 420)

This is of course continuous with the fundamental 1843 criticism of Hegel and later variants thereof. Thus an ideological approach entails *idealism*, the opposite of materialism. When Marx wrote a dozen years later, in a famous passage, that 'it is not the consciousness of people that determines their existence' (EW 425), he was in effect rejecting what he called 'ideology' at the time of *The German Ideology*. It is a consequence of all this that ideologies 'have no history, no development' (CW 5:37), that is, no autonomous history. 4 Though ideologies are forms of consciousness, involve commitments to the existence of independently existing domains of ideas which have ultimate causal efficacy, they are not simply errors, even widespread ones, errors that might be expected to disappear with the advent of scientific understanding, like dreams when we awake. Ideologies are non-veridical forms of consciousness all right, illusions if you like, but, like illusions, they have their own determinate material conditions of existence:

Ideas are the conscious expression — real or illusory — of people's real relations and activities, of their production, of their intercourse, of their social and political conduct. (CW 5:36)

In *The German Ideology*, the 'camera oscura' is attributed to the division of labour (in a way which it is not possible to go into here). And in the fourth of the 'Theses on Feuerbach' it is emphasized that it is necessary to trace out the origins of religious ideology to the material character of the society in which it functions:

Feuerbach starts out from the fact of religious self-estrangement, of the duplication of the world into a religious, imaginary world and a real one. His work consists in resolving the religious world into its secular basis. He overlooks the fact that after completing this work the chief thing still remains to be done. For the fact that the secular basis lifts off from itself and establishes itself in the clouds as an independent realm can only be explained by the inner strife and intrinsic contradictoriness of this secular basis...(CW 5:7)

This is, of course, in the direct line of development of the thought in 'On the Jewish question' and the 'Introduction' to the critique of Hegel's philosophy of right. Both religion and the state are illusory representations of aspects of humanity's 'species-being', of its universal character, which is denied in the everyday life of civil society where particularity, separation, division is the norm. It is important to go beyond a mere tracing of correspondences between religious conceptions and features of the social world and to list the *mechanisms* by which the one *generates* the other, for the existence of mere correspondences is of course consistent with (indeed required by) a thoroughly *idealist* conception of the relation between the two. (After all Hegel had given a superb explanation of the origins of religion within the framework of a thoroughly idealist philosophy.[1])

5   It is because ideological conceptions are generated by material conditions and are not just random errors that a necessary condition for removing them is a change in these material conditions. As Marx goes on in the fourth of the Feuerbach-theses just quoted in part: '...this secular basis ...must itself, therefore, first be understood in its contradiction and then, by the removal of the contradiction, revolutionized in practice'. And this is the real import of the famous last thesis on Feuerbach: 'The philosophers have only *interpreted* the world in various ways; the point is to *change* it (CW 5:5). The philosophers have only interpreted the world in various ways: they have treated the situation that (for example, includes religion) like a given text the meaning of which has to be spelled out and the import of which assessed; the point is to change the world because only by doing so can the ideological conceptions *generated* by it be exposed.

6   As to the *effects*, the *social functions* of ideology, the *The*

German Ideology it is represented as basically obfuscatory, though this is a contradictory matter. On the one hand, it mystifies in general the relation between reality and ideas and hence interferes with attempts to change the prevailing situation. But, on the other, it can act as a means for social change. For people may and do conceive themselves as having — despite their really diffrent and conflicting interests — a general interest; and a class (in fact representing basically just another particular interest) which aspires to domination must represent its own particular interest and life-situation as a general one in order to gain the allegiance of other groups, and indeed to have an appropriate self-image (CW 5:420). Marx adds that in fact, to start with, the particular interest of a class may indeed represent a general interest insofar as the realisation of its particular interests may advance humanity as a whole in certain ways. In general the immediate effect of ideology is to blur certain conflicts, contradictions and to promote certain unities, harmonies. And of course to the extent that such a picture gains allegiance it becomes an implicit criticism of the actual. This complex character of ideology, making it the site both of adaptation and accommodation but also the opposite is well brought out in the great rhetorical passage at the beginning of 'A contribution to the critique of Hegel's philosophy of right. Introduction' which, though of course somewhat earlier than *The German Ideology*, is, in this respect at least, in the spirit of it:

Religion is ... [society's] general basis of consolation and justification ... *Religious* misery is at once the *expression* of real misery and a *protest* against real misery. Religion is the sigh of the distressed creature, the heart of a heartless world, the spirit of spiritless conditions. It is the *opium* of the people. (CW 3:175)

7 'The ideas of the ruling class are in every epoch the ruling ideas' (CW 5:59). Marx grounds this as follows:

The class which has the means of material production at its disposal, consequently also controls the means of mental production, so that the ideas of those who lack the means of mental production are on the whole subject to it. The ruling ideas are nothing more than the dominant material relations, the dominant material relations grasped as ideas; hence of the relations that make the one class the ruling one, therefore the ideas of its dominance. (CW 5:59)

4

After *The German Ideology* the notion of ideology continues to be used, but with one or two exceptions it is not explicitly characterized until we come to the 1859 Preface. This is the main source, however exiguous, for the later Marx's explicit remarks on ideology. The relevant indications are contained in the following passages:

> ... the economic structure of society [is] the real base on which arises a legal and political superstructure and to which correspond specific forms of social consciousness. The mode of production of material life conditions the general process of social, political and mental life ... People's social existence determines their consciousness. At a certain stage of their development the material productive forces of society come into contradiction with the existing relations of production ... In the consideration of such transformations it is always necessary to distinguish between the material transformation of the economic conditions of production, which can be ascertained with the precision of natural science, and the legal, political, religious, artistic or philosophical, in short ideological forms in which people become conscious of this conflict and fight it out. (EW 425, 426)

There is, to begin with, what is at the very least a terminological point in the interpretation of this passage. (I think that in fact it is much more than that.) Amongst others the following phrases are used:

1 'legal and political superstructure';
2 'specific forms of social consciousness';
3 'the general process of social, political and mental life';
4 'legal, political, religious, artistic or philosophical, in short ideological forms'.

What are the relations between these? In particular, which, if any, are meant to be synonymous?

Broadly speaking the 'orthodox' Marxist tradition has, on the basis of the 1859 Preface, distinguished in the first place between 'base' and 'superstructure' and then made a further distinction, within the latter, between the 'legal and political' superstructure on the one hand and the 'ideological' superstructure on the other. But just the sentences cited above suffice to show that this traditional reading does not have a completely uncontroversial textual basis. What is called the 'superstructure' here is explicitly designated as 'legal and political' and 'specific forms of social consciousness' are as explicitly *distinguished* from it. That 'legal' and 'political' ones are listed among other 'ideological forms' is not directly to the point, since Marx would certainly want to say (cf. above, Chapter 12) that legal and political practices and institutions are to be distinguished from views about them, from representations of them.

If we turn for help to the only other relevant passage that uses the 'superstructure' terminology — one from *The Eighteenth Brumaire of Louis Bonaparte* (1852) — we find the following:

Upon the different forms of property, upon the social conditions of existence, rises an entire superstructure of different and distinctly formed sentiments, illusions, modes of thought and views of life. The entire class creates and forms them out of its material foundations and out of the corresponding social relations. (CW 11:128)

Here 'superstructure' seems clearly meant to include (whether or not it is exhausted by) what in the previous passage was called 'ideological forms' and perhaps even 'specific forms of social consciousness'.

The analysis of texts could proceed further but almost certainly without much hope of achieving a greater degree of determinateness about Marx's terminology. So it may be best to proceed on the basis of a mixture of textual reference and stipulation and agree on the following:

1 From the base is to be distinguished at least 'a legal and political superstructure' on the one hand and certain 'ideological forms' on the other.
2 There is textual evidence to support the view that Marx thought of both as parts of a 'superstructure'. (Hence the traditional view will be followed though with reservations.)
3 At a minimum it is left open whether 'base' and 'superstructure' exhaustively dichotomize the social whole, though, less cautiously, the reference to natural science suggests that they do not.

With this as a foothold we can make the following points about the general idea of ideology in the 1859 Preface:

1   Ideological forms pertain to the way in which people are aware of their real conditions of existence, and serve as a basis of action.

2   Such forms are non-veridical.

3   They are 'conditioned', 'determined' by the economic base and 'correspond' to it.

4   Because of 3 above and because their real conditions of existence can be known about with the exactitude of natural science, it is scientific knowledge of the relevant sort that reveals the nature of the real situation about which the ideological forms vouchsafe only non-veridical information.

4

This characterization relates closely to the examples of ideology presented and criticized in *Capital*, as surveyed in the preceding chapter:

1   Both fetishism and the wage-form are presented as ways in which people become aware of their real conditions of existence. In the first the real situation is the structure of the exchange-relation between commodities, and in the second the particular exchange-relation between labour-power and money.

2   These forms are presented as structured by the economic base: the one is explained by the nature of an exchange-economy and the other by the special character of the exchange of labour-power and money, itself determined in the same way as the first.

3   These forms are non-veridical: fetishism represents social characteristics of commodities as intrinsic ones and the wage-form represents the exchange in question as what it is not, namely, one between labour and money.

4   In both cases knowledge of the real situation of which the ideological forms are non-veridical representations is vouchsafed (and can be vouchsafed) only by science, which breaks with everyday conceptions and forms the concepts of 'mode of production' and of 'labour-power'.

In addition however there are some features of ideological forms in *Capital* not noted, explicitly at least, in the statement in the 1859 Preface. I shall mention three of them:

1   With regard to the ideological forms in *Capital* Marx generally emphasizes their significance for the class-struggle resulting from the fact that they mystify and obscure class-relations and exploitation and hence serve to help maintain class-domination.

2   Ideological forms in *Capital* tend to involve a (not very well defined) idea of 'inversion (*Verkehrung)*'. Thus in fetishism an allegedly intrinsic property (value) is held to determine (exchange-) relations between commodities, whereas in fact it is relations between commodities (as representatives of the abstract labour which went to produce them) which determine their 'values'. In the case of the wage-form, whilst in reality labour is predicated of value, here value is predicated of labour. (It will be noted that this is a quite different type of 'inversion' from that referred to by the 'camera oscura' effect in *The German Ideology*.[2])

3   *Capital* has a more developed conception of the 'non-veridical' character of ideology. Specifically, Marx uses three related groups of terms in this context: 'essence' or 'essential relation' (or 'true relation'); 'appearance (*Erscheinung)*' or 'form of appearance'; 'semblance' ('*Schein*': sometimes translated as 'illusion'). Here is a passage in which they all occur:

Exchange value appears [*erscheint*] first of all as the quantitative relation, the proportion, in which use-values of one kind exchange for use-values of another kind, a relation that changes constantly with time and place. Hence exchange-value seems [*scheint*] to be something accidental and purely relative .... Ricardo ... has reduced the seeming relativity which ... diamonds, pearls, etc., possess as exchange-values, to the true relation hidden behind the semblance to their relativity as mere expressions of human labour. (C 1:126, 177 n.38)

This conceptual panoply is heavily influenced by Hegel. Marx nowhere gives any explanation of his usages. But they can be understood as follows.

Consider the simple case of an optical illusion — say the case of a straight stick semi-immersed in water and appearing to be bent where it enters the water. Now the situation may be described in terms of the above concepts thus. The stick is in fact straight: that is the 'true relation' between its parts, the 'essence' of the matter (or part of it anyway). However, in the relational circumstances which in fact obtain (rays of light reflected from the stick through a liquid with a certain refractive index) the stick appears to be bent. This is a fact about the situation as objective as the straightness of the stick itself. It has nothing essential to do with perception (a photo would show the same as the eye). Thus a 'bent stick' is an 'appearance' or 'form of appearance' of a straight stick, and necessarily so in those circumstances. Understanding the situation does not make the stick look any less bent but it stands in the way of false judgments about the real shape of the stick. But if all the mediations involved in the situation — those by virtue of which the straight stick appears bent — are left out of account, and the appearance is taken in isolation from the conditions of its generation, then we have the 'semblance' of a bent stick. As Marx says of profit, wages and rent considered as generated by capital (understood as certain *things*), labour, and land, this is the form of existence of the relations of capitalist production 'divorced from the hidden connections and the intermediate connecting links' (*Theories of Surplus-Value*, 3:453).

Applied to the cases cited in the passage quoted above this comes out as follows. Exchange-values are, in the first place, proportions in which use-values exchange. This Marx claims to have shown to be determined by the socially necessary abstract labour-time they represent. Exchange-value is an adequate 'appearance' of this; at least so long as the mediations are understood, nothing illusory enters the situation. Semblance or illusion arises only when these mediations are not taken into account and exchange-values are taken to be merely accidental and totally relative.

Notes

1 See Hegel's *Phenomenology of Spirit*, especially the section on 'Faith and pure insight' (Chapter VI, B, Ib), pp. 321ff of the

A. V. Miller translation (Oxford University Press, 1977). There is a good discussion of the ultimately idealist character of Hegel's account in Norman, R. *Hegel's Phenomenology. A Philosophical Introduction* (Brighton, Sussex University Press, 1976), pp. 94ff.

2 This earlier sense is preserved in the sentence which follows the passage already cited from *The Eighteenth Brumaire*:

> The single individual, to whom they are transmitted through tradition and upbringing, may imagine that they form the real motives and the starting-point of his activity. (CW 11:128)

Chapter 15
Politics and law

1

In the case of the 'legal and political superstructure', as in that of ideology, it must be said to start with that there is no worked-out theory in Marx's writings. The topic of the state — the chief concept of the political — was, as we have seen, one major part of the 1857 plan for a comprehensive treatise on political economy; but this was not so much as even sketched. So once more we have to piece together his views as best we can from occasional general comments and concrete analyses. I shall concentrate here on the sphere of the political and in particular on the state, saying something about law at the end.

2

I have already surveyed Marx's views on the state in his earliest writings. In its broadest outlines his position there was the following:

1   The state is tied to civil society as its necessary complement. It is only because there is a sphere in which human beings are totally separated, pursue their purely individual aims, that there has to be one which claims to represent the common character of those individuals as members of the human species.
2   But in the form of the state the species-being of human beings is represented as actually separate from their real, empirical, individual lives. It is 'estranged' from real people. In fact, it is just another sphere of particularity. The communal being of people exists only in the sphere of the *imaginary*.
3   Insofar as civil society is the presupposition of the state (as what makes necessary a complement that claims to be

146

universal), and insofar as private property is the foundation of civil society, it is private property that is the secret of the existence of the state.

In the earliest writings then the state is primarily related to private property through the idea that the latter generates a sphere of pure particularity in which everyday life is actually lived, a *real* sphere which requires an *ideal* sphere of complementary universality to satisfy humanity's need for a representation of its universal character as a species. This might be called the view of the state as 'imaginary universal'.

I have already noted also that in the 1844 article against Ruge another conception made its appearance. This is that civil society is a sphere of reciprocal plundering, of 'slavery', and that the state rests on this. The idea is vague and rhetorical at this stage. But a full blown view emerges not long after in *The German Ideology*, once Marx broke through to the concept of class. It is not merely that private property, the principle of civil society, generates the state as the bearer of an imaginary universality, but that the state has a reciprocal effect: the actual state as a set of practices and institutions has the function of helping to assure the existence of private property. Thus we read in *The German Ideology* that 'the state is the form in which the individuals of the ruling class assert their common interests', the form in which 'the ruling class establishes its joint domination as public power' (CW 5:90, 355). This is in all essentials the view expressed in the *Manifesto of the Communist Party* little more than a year later: 'The executive of the modern State is but a committee for managing the common affairs of the whole bourgeoisie' (CW 6:486). This might be called the 'class-power' view of the state.

3

A first thing to be said about these two conceptions is that, in appropriate formulations at least, there is no contradiction between them. Indeed in a sense they are complementary. The end of assuring class-power is served very well indeed by people's identifying their common interests with those of an imaginary organization which is, in fact, dominated by one class, in finding forms of false unity in the state, the nation, rather than for the exploited to identify themselves as belonging fundamentally to a distinct class.

In fact the two different conceptions can be reduced to a common denominator which may be called, borrowing a term from Engels, the factor of 'cohesion' (SW 3:332). The sphere of private interest, which involves not merely *difference* but *conflict* (in the final analysis *class*-conflict) is held together, on the one hand, by the state as the bearer of imaginary universality, and, on the other, by the state as a set of institutions and practices which are more-or-less directly dominated by the ruling class for its own ends. Moreover, it is arguable that in general it can do the second only insofar as the first is in place.

Indeed the two views of the state coexist in *The German Ideology* cheek by jowl. To cite just one passage among many:

The illusory community in which individuals have up till now combined always took on an independent existence in relation to them, and since it was the combination of one class over against another, it was at the same time for the oppressed class not only a completely illusory community, but a new fetter as well. (CW 5:78)

Certainly there can be no doubt whatever that with time the second conception becomes dominant. The transition to this as the main focus of attention is marked by the famous *Manifesto* passage already cited. And of course there are perfectly intelligible reasons why this should have been so, stemming in the final analysis from the political centrality of the coercive aspect of the state in the nineteenth century. But it is also true that this theme does not entirely disappear from Marx's thought. It is seen particularly in his reflections on the Paris Commune in *The Civil War in France* written a quarter of a century after *The German Ideology*. Thus in the course of exemplifying the Commune's project for a federal structure of local governments for all of France, he writes that:

the unity of the nation was ... to become a reality by the destruction of the State power which claimed to be the embodiment of that unity independent of, and superior to, the nation itself. (PW 3:210)

Again, in the first of the preliminary drafts he describes the state as a 'parasitical [excrescence upon] civil society, pretending to be its ideal counterpart', as a 'supernaturalist abortion of society' (PW 3:247, 249); the Commune is said to have been 'the reabsorption of the state power by society as its living forces instead of as forces controlling and subduing it, by the popular masses themselves' (PW 3:250). Finally, in the second of the preliminary drafts:

The state power ... had always been the power for the maintenance of order, i.e. the existing order of society.... But as long as this order was accepted as an uncontrovertible and uncontested necessity, the state power could assume an aspect of impartiality ... . With the entrance of society itself into ... the phase of class-struggle, ... the state-power ... could not but change also ... and more and more develop its character as the instrument of class-despotism. (*Writings on the Paris Commune*, ed. H. Draper, 197.)

Nevertheless, this does not alter the basic fact that the conception of the state as an embodiment of common interest is recessive in Marx's thinking after about 1846. It only began to return to some degree in the work of Gramsci on the 'hegemonic' (consensus) versus the coercive view of the state in the present century. The failure to ask questions regarding the anchorage of the more 'instrumental' aspects of the State in the ground of people's lived experience has made possible very mechanistic views of the state where even within these limits questions about the conditions for the possibility of coercion have not been asked. (Why do people tend to accept coercion so readily? Why is it so generally easy to find among the exploited themselves means for the exercise of coercion of other parts of the exploited?)[1]

4

Let us turn now from these general considerations to some more detailed remarks on Marx's thinking about the state.

Taking a point of departure from the *Manifesto* passage already cited, three points are worth signalling in what is said there:

1 The statement specifies only a certain *function* of 'the executive of the modern State': it does not say anything about the particular modalities by and through which this function is exercised. In particular it is consistent with this that the function can be exercised through a variety of state *forms* (dictatorship, representative democracy, and so on) — just as

the function of transmitting a message can be taken care of by a telex, a telephone, a smoke signal, semaphore, and so on — and by a variety of *mechanisms* (coercion, production of consensus, etc.).

2   The function in question is referred to the *executive* of the modern state, which leaves it open that, for example, a different account may be given of the legislature.

3   The passage says that the function of the executive of the modern state is to manage 'the common affairs of the whole bourgeoisie'. Now this way of putting it suggests at least two things, namely, that the bourgeoisie is not homogeneous, and that the parts have different and perhaps even conflicting interests.

With regard to the first point, the simple picture of the *Manifesto*, according to which capitalist society more and more approximates to a two-class model is, in the later concrete analyses at least, replaced by a more complex picture of class-(in particular ruling class-) structure, recognizing a variety of classes or at least segments of classes. This fact is reconciled with the thesis of the unity of the function of the state through the idea that whilst the ruling group is structurally complex it may be dominated by a single group. (Marx analyses the financial aristocracy in France between 1830 and 1848 from this point of view.) Related to this is his distinction, made in concrete analyses, between the class or group that *rules* — in the sense that it is the class whose economic interests are the dominant ones — and the class, group or individual that *governs* — in sense of actually operating the levers of power. (Marx's paradigm is the relation between the English bourgeoisie, and particularly the industrial bourgeoisie, on the one hand, and the English landed aristocracy on the other.[2])

With regard to the second point, this function of minding the common affairs of the whole bourgeoisie is not only perfectly consistent with its acting in a way which is incompatible with the particular interests of a segment of the bourgeoisie, where these particular interests are inconsistent with the common interests of the class, but indeed presupposes it. That is, in order to do its job the state must have a certain room to move independently of the immediate interests of the class. Engels later referred to the 'relative autonomy' of the state, the 'relative' signalling that the 'autonomy' has limits given by the long-run interests of the ruling class. That is (other things being equal) the state can act against the short-run interests of the whole ruling class, and against the long-term interests of some parts of the ruling class, though not against long-term interests of the whole ruling class.

This idea of 'relative autonomy' is developed further in Marx's close analysis of the rule of Louis Bonaparte (and also to some extent Bismarck). Marx found here what he took to be a general phenomenon of the modern state — what he called 'Bonapartism'. By this is meant what to all appearances is the phenomenon of a state as the organized rule not of a class or even dominant group but of an individual who 'stands above' the whole of society, including the contending classes that constitute it, and regulates the relations between them. In his analysis Marx traces in detail how Louis Napoleon, using the politically headless and unorganized peasantry as a base, was able to rule to some extent independently of either the bourgeoisie or the working class. He emphasizes, however, that there was no contradiction with bourgeois interests involved in this as Napoleon maintained the conditions of capitalist exploitation and hence the economic basis of his own power.

5

I have spoken so far exclusively about the political part of the 'legal and political superstructure', and indeed only about the state. To conclude, I want to touch upon just one question concerning the other theme, that of the law. This question is relevant both to the substantive particular theme and also throws light on the general character of historical materialism.

It may be introduced in the form of a criticism which has been made by a number of writers on historical materialism and which is designed to question the very coherence of that theory. It may be put as follows. We have seen that in the 1859 Preface Marx speaks of 'relations of production, or, what is only a legal expression for the same thing ... property relations'. Now it has been urged that there is a contradiction between, on the one hand, the thesis that the law is part of the superstructure, and the superstructure determined by the economic base (which is constituted by relations of product-ion), and, on the other hand, the thesis that relations of production are legal — specifically property — relations. In brief the objection is that on Marx's view legal relations are supposed to help constitute what is supposed to determine them.

But the objection is based on an inadequate understanding of Marx's position. With regard to relations of production and property Marx distinguishes between 'possession (*Besitz*)' and 'ownership' or 'property (*Eigentum*)'. The first consists in an actual capacity to put means of production into operation, the second in relations to the means of production which confer power to direct them to certain ends and to dispose of the product. (For example, if I put someone on an already stocked farm in order to run it in return for a part of the product, then that person has 'possession' of the land, tools and so on, but does not 'own' these things, which are not his 'property'.)

The property-relation or relation of ownership may be codified in formal legal terms; but then again it may not, as it may simply be a matter of non-formal though generally recognized entitlements. In either case the rights, in so far as they are real, effective rights, depend on some sanctions outside the field of mere claims to entitlement. Of course there is a tendency for the second sort of property to be transformed into the first, especially within the context of the capitalist mode of production. But Marx's historical materialist thesis is that what is primary, in terms of what makes a property right 'real' rather than merely formal, is the material power to assert the claim in question. And this is perfectly consistent with recognizing that the legal recognition and codification of the 'real' right may — and in general does — serve to reinforce that right. This is no more difficult to understand than is the case of, say, a flagpole whose stability is reinforced by supports which would not themselves have the necessary anchorage were the flagpole not there.[3]

Thus, when Marx speaks of 'property relations' as being 'only a legal expression for . . . relations of production' he must be understood to be saying that in certain circumstances a description drawn from the sphere of law can be used to *pick out* a situation which is not essentially *constituted* legally or

152

which does not depend ultimately on merely legal claims. In a similar way 'the only second son in the room now' may be used to pick out young Bill Smith, if he is in fact the only second son in the room now — the phrase in question is 'only a kinship expression' for the person — without the characteristic of being a second son being at all constitutive of Bill Smith.

More generally, Marx's historical materialist thesis is that what are primary, with regard to the legal superstructure, are certain social practices proceeding in more or less regular ways. These may be codified in part or as a whole (insofar as this is practicable) in legal terms, which may then help to regulate the practices from which the legal formulations sprang. So, for example, Marx describes the legal forms of contract with respect to the fundamental relation of capitalism, namely, the exchange-relation (C. 1:178, and *Texts on Method*, 210).

Notes

1 Furthermore it may be suggested that in the idea of the state as the expression of illusory community is to be found one of the main clues for the solution of a problem not solved and hardly posed by Marxists to this day, namely, that of the persistence and force of nationalism, something quite at odds with Marx's own expectations. If something like this is fruitful then it may also be necessary to return to the treatment of religion initiated by Hegel and by Feuerbach in order to generate a programme for explaining the tenacity of the grip of religion and its immense continuing power to shape people's consciousness and behaviour.

2 See his article in the *New York Herald Tribune* of 6 April 1857 entitled 'The Elections in Britain'. This important article should be contained in CW 15, not available at the time of writing. It is, however, reprinted in *Marx and Engels on Britain* (Moscow, Foreign Languages Publishing House, 1953) and in German translation in W 12:156ff.

3 On all this see especially Marx's discussion of 'The Genesis of capitalist ground rent', in *Capital*, Volume 3, especially p. 929. E. P. Thompson's perfectly just strictures on the idea of law as epiphenomenal in his *Whigs and Hunters. The Origin of the Black Act* (New York, Pantheon Books, 1975), pp. 258ff, apply to certain sorts of 'vulgar Marxism' but certainly not to Marx's own work.

Chapter 16
'Base' and 'superstructure' and their relations

1

The immediately preceding chapters have considered in general terms Marx's conception of 'base' and 'superstructure'. Now that these ideas have been introduced we must look a little more closely at them and then at the relations between what they designate.

The base-superstructure model in the 1859 Preface (and in one or two other places in Marx's writings) is obviously derived from the relation of a building to its foundations. In considering how adequate it is to Marx's theoretical intentions it must be said to begin with that it brings out very clearly at least one necessary feature of Marx's conception, namely, the view that there is a quite fundamental asymmetry between the two parts: the economic is held to determine the character of the whole in a way that the legal-political/ideological does not. It is necessary, however, to express the matter in this fairly vague way because to put it any more strongly would be to speak quite falsely: to say that the base is necessary for the superstructure but not conversely would be quite incorrect.

And this immediately brings out one fundamental weakness of the model: for the foundations of a building can exist without the building whilst the building cannot exist (as such anyway) without the foundations. But, of course, if the superstructure cannot exist without the base, the converse is also true. Even though the economic domain in capitalism, of all modes of production that we know of, is most free of involvement with the other sectors, it obviously could not exist without such superstructural features as a legal system (for example, regulating transactions between labour and capital on the one hand, and between capitals on the other), means of state coercion, an educational system, certain value-systems (produced and reproduced in various practices and institutions such as the family, church, school, etc.), and so on. And if we consider other modes of production where the economic is nowhere near as autonomous as in capitalism (for example, in societies where religious rituals permeate material producttion) the base-superstructure model taken fairly literally is even more obviously inadequate.

In sum, what is needed is a way of conceiving the situation which Marx theorized in terms of the base-superstructure model in such a way that an appropriate analytical-theoretical *distinction* can be made without any implication of a *separation* in reality between the elements that the distinction in question points to.

2

For a way of doing this which both captures the main thrust of Marx's model and has some continuity with his own formulations, whilst being also free of the weakness of that model pointed out above, a paradigm is afforded by Marx's presentation of the capitalist production process as being simultaneously a process of production of use-values and of surplus-value (C 1:Chapter 7, Section 2). That is, the very same material process at the very same time both produces use-values and exploits labour-power. We can put this by saying that one and same process has different *functions*. Something may be said to have a function in this sense if it typically generates certain sorts of outcomes which are necessary in the circumstances for the maintenance of a certain type of system. Then we can apply the idea to the base-superstructure problem and speak of, say, 'base functions' and 'superstructural functions'.[1]

Thus an on-going society must not only produce its means of material life at any one time but must also reproduce itself. This reproduction involves all the features which characterize it as a mode of production (or combination of such). Specifically it must reproduce both the forces of production and also the relations of production. That is, it must reproduce both raw materials, instruments of production and labour-power in all its aspects (purely physical, but also aptitudes, skills, attitudes, and so on), as well as patterns of control over the means of production. In general we can say that the 'base function' is that of producing and reproducing the material elements which go to form the productive forces and which are the objects of control with respect to the relations of production, whilst the 'superstructural function' is the reproduction of the social conditions for the optimally smooth functioning of the economic.

This way of conceiving the matter is free of the difficulties which beset the topographical, 'layer cake' model, pointed out earlier. One and the same thing (structure, process) may at one and the same time have, in principle at least, any number of functions, which are analytically distinguishable but not in fact separable. One and the same practice may have both 'base functions' and 'superstructural functions' at the same time. For example, the factory floor is the site of a practice which is economic in so far as it results in the production of use-values and indeed of surplus-value, but which is at the same time political (for example, constant trials of strength between capital and labour), and also ideological (for example, production of the 'right' attitudes in the labour-force). Again the police force (for argument's sake) involves practices which are political insofar as they are directed to preserving the existing property relations, but which are also economic (the police as consumers of equipment of various sorts as well as parts of the distribution process of certain commodities like drugs) and ideological (production of certain sorts of attitudes among the members of the police force and among the general public). And, of course, the question of relations of determination between functions can be posed just as it can on the topographical model.

However, in general one will be of more consequence than the others (at least at a certain place and time) and to that extent the practice may be regarded as exercising a *predominantly* base-function or a *predominantly* superstructural function. Nevertheless the different functions coexist, and whilst being distinguishable are not separable, except where a certain practice ceases to have a certain function.

Again, the functions are not tied to any particular material structures or processes in an essentialist way. Thus a religious

156

order might cease to play a basically superstructural role and begin to serve a mainly economic function, in the same way as an ash-tray may become a paper-weight, or the same semantic content of a message may be carried now by sound-waves, now by electromagnetic waves.

All this having been said, no harm is done if we continue to speak of 'base' and 'superstructure', these being understood in terms of the qualifications just made.

Let us now look at the relations between the two.

3

What we have on this in Marx's texts by way of explicit doctrine is very exiguous indeed. In the 1859 Preface it is simply said to start with that the superstructure 'corresponds' to the base, then that the latter 'conditions' or 'determines'[2] the former, and finally that changes in the base lead sooner or later to corresponding changes in the superstructure (EW 425).

Now this statement is inadequate both to Marx's own practice and also to the elementary factual requirements which any such theory would have to meet. What can be distilled from it and affirmed for both concepts is something like the following:

1   The base exercises some ultimately determining influence on the superstructure such that the latter 'corresponds' to the former, at least in the long run. If this condition is not met then the theory loses its distinctiveness and we have just another pluralist, many-factor theory. But to this must be added a further condition which is not mentioned in the Preface account though not inconsistent with it. This may be put as follows.

2   A specific base does not determine a specific corresponding superstructure in such a way that, in principle at least, a unique base could be inferred from a given superstructure or conversely. This thesis is clearly implied by, for example, Marx's many analyses of the different state-forms which 'fit' with the same general type of capitalist base. Finally it is necessary to add a third condition.

3   The superstructure must in some way exercise an influence on the base. This condition is certainly at least obscured by

some of Marx's formulations, but it is in line with Marx's own concrete treatments. So, for example, regarding the political dimension of the superstructure, we have seen that Marx (and Engels) wrote already in the programmatic part of the *Manifesto of the Communist Party* that:

the first step in the revolution of the working class is to raise the proletariat to the position of ruling class .... The proletariat will use its political supremacy to wrest ... all capital from the bourgeoisie. (CW 6:504)

That is, political change is envisaged as preceding change in the economic.[3] Again, as regards 'forms of consciousness', ideology, Marx writes of the working class:

The recognition of products as its own, and the judgement that its separation from the conditions of its realisation is improper, forcibly imposed — is an enormous [advance in] consciousness, ... and as such the death-knell [of capitalism] as, with the slave's consciousness that he *cannot be the property of another*, with his consciousness of himself as a person, the existence of slavery becomes a merely artificial, vegetative one, and ceases to be able to continue as the basis of production. (G 463)

Putting these together we get from 2 and 3 above together the thesis that the superstructure must have an 'autonomy' with respect to the base, but from 1 above the thesis that this autonomy is limited by or is so only 'relatively' to the base. So, in sum, the three criteria of adequacy amount to the 'relative autonomy' of the superstructure with respect to the base.

Fairly clearly 1 above is the key thesis. About this further questions arise: Is it possible to say anything more definite (anchored of course in Marx's own texts) about this relation of 'correspondence' between base and superstructure where the former is 'ultimately' the determining factor? More specifically still, can we say anything (again subject to the condition of being identifiably Marx's view) about the *mechanisms* by which the one 'ultimately' determines the other?

4

An answer to the first question is suggested by a couple of things that Marx says. One occurs in the first volume of

Capital. This quotes, *à propos* of a criticism of it, a segment of the 1859 Preface on the relation between base and super-structure to which I have already referred. Marx cites his critic as conceding that what was said in the Preface passage

is all very true for our own times, in which material interests are preponderant, but not for the Middle Ages, dominated by Catholicism, nor for Athens and Rome, dominated by politics.

He goes on:

One thing is clear: the Middle Ages could not live on Catholicism, nor could the ancient world on politics. On the contrary, it is the manner in which they gained their livelihood which explains why in the one case politics, in the other Catholicism, played the chief role. (C 1:175f)

This may be supplemented, as a textual basis for an account, by another from *Capital*, this time from the third volume:

... in all forms in which the direct labourer remains the 'possessor' of the means of production and conditions of labour necessary for the production of his own means of subsistence, ... [he] conducts his agricultural activity and the rural home industries connected with it independently .... Under such conditions the surplus-labour for the nominal owner of the land can only be extorted ... by other than economic pressure, whatever the form assumed may be. (C 3:926)

Thus in the form of production which is referred to here the direct producer 'possesses' — that is, has immediate control over — though he does not own — his means of production. So the work he does for his own subsistence is clearly demarcated in space and time from the extra work he has to do for the 'nominal' or formal owner of the means of production (the landlord). This is quite different from the case of capitalism where necessary labour and surplus labour are extracted within one spatio-temporal segment (for example, the working day) without any perceptible distinction between them, by virtue of workers' total separation from the means of production. Thus within capitalism the production of surplus is, in principle at least, an automatic product of the labour-process: the capitalist buys workers' labour-power for a definite time and appropriates all of the produce, normally returning the equivalent of the necessary part as wages. This

159

cannot be the case in the feudal example in question. So the direct producer has to be brought by other than economic means to perform surplus labour or yield surplus product. If we now add to this what Marx says in the first passage cited above, the extra-economic force can be identified with religion and specifically with Catholicism, an effect of which is to help assure the delivery of surplus.

Using a terminology first introduced by Althusser and Balibar, religion may be said to be the 'dominant' element in the situation insofar as it is the principal factor responsible for reproduction of the mode of production in question. But the economic is 'determinant', insofar as it is what determines which is to be the 'dominant' element.[4] In the specific case of capitalism the 'determinant' and 'dominant' elements coincide in general.

This satisfies the three criteria of adequacy for an account of the base-superstructure relation along Marx's own lines. For the dominant superstructural form is in the first place constrained within certain definite limits by the base. But, second, it is not uniquely determined in the same way (presumably the functions performed by Catholicism could in principle have been exercised by other forms of religion or even other superstructural forms entirely). Finally, it has its own causal efficacy with regard to the base.

5

The above account pertains more to the first of the two questions posed at the end of Section 4 above. One which relates more to the second — that concerning the specific *mechanisms* by which the base exercises its determining role — must now be sought. Let us again begin by looking at a couple of texts.

At one point in *The Eighteenth Brumaire of Louis Bonaparte* Marx discusses Social Democracy, and puts forward the view that it is essentially a political movement of the petty bourgeoisie. But he goes on to caution that this does not mean that

the democratic representatives are indeed all shopkeepers or enthu-siastic supporters of shopkeepers. In their education and individual position they may be as far apart from them as heaven from earth.

He goes on:

What makes them representatives of the petty bourgeoisie is the fact that in their minds they do not get beyond the limits which the latter do not get beyond in life, that they are consequently driven, theoretically, to the same problems and solutions to which material interest and social position drive the latter in practice.

Marx concludes:

This is, in general, the relationship between the *political* and *literary representatives* of a class and the class they represent. (CW 11:130f)

The thrust of this text is in the direction not of an explanation of the superstructural form in terms of its *creation* by the base but rather in terms of the way in which the base *selects* such forms as are appropriate for certain functions, quite independently of the origins of the forms. In other words, the superstructural form does not exist by virtue of a teleology exercised by the base generating such forms, but by virtue of the effectiveness of the base in limiting the sorts of viable ones.

Such an account looks very like a Darwinian one applied to the domain in question; and it is not accidental that Marx was from the beginning very sensitive to the significance of the idea of natural selection. Thus he writes to Lassalle about *The Origin of Species*, not long after its publication (in the same year as his *Contribution to the Critique of Political Economy*), that 'not only is the death-blow dealt here for the first time to "teleology" in the natural sciences but its rational meaning is empirically explained' (16 January 1861).

Darwin worked, it will be remembered, with two main ideas, namely that of a pool of variations within a species and that of natural selection. He simply assumed the first. (He was indeed in no position to do anything else at the time he was working.) Some of these variations are better adapted than others to the environment in which the species finds itself. These rather than the less-adapted members of the species tend to survive and reproduce, the environment performing the process of selection involved. The environment is not assumed to produce the variations, but to determine the species that exist at a time, to

161

the extent that it limits the number and sort of variations that are reproduced.

The analogy for the social case is fairly obvious. Corresponding to the pool of species variations is a pool of superstructural forms — legal and political institutions and practices, ideas, religions, and so on — which are not necessarily produced by the base (not in any direct way at least) and whose existence cannot in general be explained by it. The base performs its determining role by specifying the limits of variation of those superstructural forms which find conditions for reproduction, the conditions being ones that promote the reproduction of the base. (This explains in particular what may be called 'sleeper' forms, that is, those which, like Roman law — cf. G 109 — may remain dormant for a long time until they find a base for the reproduction of which they are functional.)

This account is consistent with the three criteria of adequacy already set up. The base is determinant by prescribing the ultimate limits for possible variation of the superstructure; it leaves room for variation in the superstructure with respect to one and the same base; and it allows for independent efficacy of the superstructure with respect to the base. It is also consistent with the account in terms of 'dominant' and 'determinant' and can quite well supplement it.

Notes

1   For a functional interpretation of base and superstructure see Godelier, M. 'Infrastructures, societies and history' *New Left Review*, No. 112, November-December 1978.
2   Some writers on Marx have made much of the fact that in the 1859 Preface Marx says both that the base 'conditions (*bedingt*)' and 'determines (*bestimmt*)' the superstructure, arguing that the first is a less 'strong' mode of determination than the second, and that hence Marx is either ambiguous or meant a 'weaker' mode of connection than is suggested by 'determines'. I do not think that anything of systematic significance hangs on this linguistic point. Marx was a sensitive stylist and often used different words to make the same point for one or other literary reason. It would be very surprising indeed if he were to show by this different choice of verbs that he could not make up his mind on an important point in the course of a few lines. And even if

there were something to all this, why not interpret 'conditions' in the light of 'determines' rather than conversely? For what the point is worth, in the French translation (which Marx recommended to readers) the passage from the 1859 Preface, cited in a footnote, is rendered using the French verb *domine* for what is translated as 'conditions' in English. See the reprint by Garnier-Flammarion (Paris, 1969), p. 590.

3   Cf. what was said on the idea of 'permanent revolution', transitional demands' and 'dual power' in Chapter 5, Section 5 above, and also the much later statement of a similar point in the Inaugural Address to the International Working Men's Association (PW 3:80).

4   See Althusser, L. and Balibar, E. *Reading Capital* (London, NLB, 1970), especially pp. 216ff.

Chapter 17
Social change

1

There is sometimes a danger of forgetting that historical materialism is a materialist conception of *history*, of social *change*. Marx's basic theoretical interest was in understanding how this occurs, in the first instance as an aid to intervening in the course of human affairs. If he studies 'static', 'structural', 'synchronic' factors it is in order to understand this dynamic the better, and in the final analysis the first is explained in terms of the second.

I have already suggested at different places that Marx's treatment of change in what has most often been taken as the canonical statement of historical materialism, namely, the 1859 Preface to *A Contribution to the Critique of Political Economy*, is inadequate as a presentation of Marx's thinking about the nature of social change as we can read it out of other statements and out of concrete analyses. This inadequacy is of at least two sorts which I shall not recapitulate here beyond reminding the reader of them. First, the Preface passage in question gives the impression — or can do so — that the base has a more or less in-built tendency to change; second, it suggests that there is a simple one-way relation between changes in the base and those in the superstructure. Without losing grip of the fundamental point regarding the primacy in some appropriate sense of conflict between productive forces and relations of production we have to look elsewhere in Marx's writings for his most suggestive views about social change in general.

2

Traditional accounts of social change, of history, and in

164

particular the ones with which Marx was mainly concerned, have been of two broad sorts. One locates the mainspring of change in factors of a type which may be called in very general terms 'ideas', be these thought of as existing in the minds of individuals or as having some transindividual locus. The other locates it in various factors such as the nature of human beings conceived of as mechanical systems, or in geography, or the like. The first comprise idealist theories, the second traditional materialist doctrines.

Idealist theories are exemplified by the Hegelian philosophy, according to which the course of history is really the temporal unfolding of the implicit nature of Absolute Spirit. The motor of the development is, in the final analysis, the tendencies inherent in the supraindividual consciousness. (In the work of the Young Hegelian epigones this consciousness became identified with individual self-consciousness, but the idealist character of the view was of course not diminished thereby; indeed on the contrary.)

Marx made a number of criticisms of such a view in the period 1843-1846, as we have seen already. One of the most central was that the transitions which Hegel allegedly exhibited as being within the sphere of Spirit were in fact consequences of a covert importation of facts about the material reality of history into the realm of the ideal. Hegel's philosophical legerdemain consisted in representing developments which could only be explained by reference to the non-ideal world as explicable in terms of immanent changes in that ideal world. Concepts as such, Marx insists, have no inner principles of development, and hence the problem of social change cannot be explained by an idealist account: either it simply remains unsolved or the solution can only be achieved by going outside the idealist standpoint and taking up a materialist one.

3

But Marx was no less critical of traditional materialist treatments of history. The crux of his criticism of such accounts is presented with lapidary brevity in the first of the two paragraphs that form the third of the 'Theses on Feuer-bach' (CW 5:4).

What he is criticizing, he says, is 'the materialist doctrine about change of circumstances and education'. Marx is referring here in the first place to the sort of Enlightenment (especially French Enlightenment) view — which formed the basis of much Utopian Socialism — that people are a product of their external circumstances (geography, social situation, etc.) and education, so that the problem of changing people reduces to the problem of changing their circumstances and education.

This doctrine, he goes on, 'forgets that circumstances are changed by people and the educator himself must be educa-ted'. That is, if the account in question is true in general, then since circumstances do not change themselves, but are changed by people, how does it come about that people who are themselves conditioned by these circumstanmces can come to change them? And, if education forms people, how can it eventuate that people can be educated in ways different from those in which they have so far been? Marx is pointing up a fundamental problem in the sort of materialist determinism he is dealing with: if at a certain time people are determined in their characteristics by a given sort of natural and social environment, and by a given sort of upbringing, how can they ever change either? Change seems impossible in such a case, for the possible initiators of change (people) are locked, according to the theory itself, into a rigidly self-reproducing system.

Hence, Marx concludes, this sort of account 'must sunder society into two parts — of which one is superior to society'. That is, such views end up in effect exempting certain people from the general system of determination; and as such they are 'superior' to the rest of society which is the object of their benevolent emancipatory endeavours. These people instruct and exhort their fellows about the nature of their condition and the possibilities of changing it. Of course, this move in fact involves going outside the original account in the direction of idealism, for here, as in idealisms of all stripes, social change is ultimately accounted for by reference to the alleged effects of certain ideas, themselves left unaccounted for.

166

4

So the two traditional sorts of accounts can be seen as working within a common theoretical framework, even though they seem at first sight diametrically opposed: each passes into the other when pressed hard enough. From another direction too it can be seen how this common framework holds together incompatible approaches as a way of trying to solve the basic problem. So, in the Hegelian view, the pre-determined march of the Absolute Spirit must be supplemented (if the historical facts are to be accounted for) by taking into consideration the field of absolute contingency, of the rationally undetermined factors through which the march takes place; and in the traditional materialist view the deterministic, indeed fatalistic force of circumstances and of upbringing has to be qualified by the influence of free actions, of the purely voluntarist aspect.

These antinomistic but profoundly interconnected couples may be and often are associated with others. Thus, if the majority of people are, in fact, meshed into a deterministic system, then the only appropriate way of drawing them out of this and into action that will change it, is to bring to bear forces of a non-material sort, ones which are not subject to the determinism of the rest of the system. These are typically moral forces. So there live together, like Siamese twins, the determinism of the *facts* on the one hand, and freely posited and adopted *values* on the other. (This is chiefly for the materialist variant; there are mirror-images of the situation for idealisms.)

Again, in a situation of thoroughgoing determinism on the one hand, and free intervention on the other, the strategy of change must ultimately consist in the voluntary projection by individuals or groups of certain *ends* (the nature of which is determined by a particular critique — particularly moral critique — of the prevailing state of affairs) and then a casting about for means which are appropriate — given the deterministic character of the situation — for the bringing about of such ends.

The list could be continued, but what has been said is sufficient to exhibit the profoundly problematic character of traditional accounts of social change riven as they are by dichotomies such as idealism/(traditional) materialism, free will/

determinism, values/facts, means/ends, and so on, which they cannot transcend.

5

In the second and final paragraph of the third of the 'Theses on Feuerbach'—on the first paragraph of which I have been freely commenting so far — Marx sets out his solution to the problem which he has just sketched, and does so in an even more succinct way than he did the criticism: 'The coincidence of the changing of circumstances and of human activity or self-change can be conceived and rationally understood only as *revolutionary practice*'.

The relation between 'the changing of circumstances and ... self-change' had been precisely the problem of the traditional materialist view of social change pointed to by Marx in the first part of the third thesis: circumstances could be changed only by people, but this required changed people which in turn presupposed (on that account) changed circumstances. This chicken-and-egg problem can be avoided only if the change in circumstances and the change in people are simultaneous.

This condition is satisfied, Marx goes on to say, if we focus on *practice* — specifically *revolutionary* practice — as the central concept. As we saw when I moved this idea centre-stage in Chapter 12 above, a practice is a regular way of transforming some sort of subject matter by means of material techniques applied by labour of certain sorts. The subject matter and the labour aspects of the practice on the one hand correspond to the circumstances and the people on the other, in the earlier way of setting up the problem. So the crucially new factor is the means of transformation, the material techniques. This institutes a 'coincidence of the changing of circumstances and ... self-change', because new techniques require people adequate to the use of those techniques, so, if necessary, new skills, knowledge, dispositions of all sorts have to be generated, and this is precisely 'self-change'. Thus a new means of transformation not only changes circumstances but requires changed people also.

6

But does this really solve the original problem? What it does do — it might be said — is to show how, assuming a tendency to change, changed circumstances and changed people are generated simultaneously, both as a result of the transforming power of the material means employed. But what about the tendency to change itself?

The answer to this is, I think, that Marx simply takes it as a fact, for which there is no *global* explanation though there are *particular* ones, that practices in general tend to run into difficulties sooner or later, that is, come to a point when the goal of the practice can no longer be attained by the practice as it is, or at least cannot be carried on in as trouble-free a way as before. This might be for reasons more or less wholly accidental with respect to the practice (like a radical change in climate caused by changes in the temperature of the centre of the earth, effectively beyond human influence). Or it might be because of the impinging on the practice of the effects of another, where the overall effect is partly due to the specificities of the first (as perhaps the result of a military occupation). Or — and most significantly by far — the difficulties may be generated by the very operation of the practice itself over a period of time, like the feed-back on the practice of slash-and-burn agriculture by the soil erosion that results, or the long-term results of capitalist accumulation on the rate of growth (on which cf. Chapter 9 above).

We can call these difficulties in the way of the continuance of a practice by the comprehensive name 'problems'. These do not, of course, exist in and for themselves like stones on the street: that a situation constitutes a problem and if so what it is (how it is to be described) is a highly contextual matter. Problems require and in general call up a range of possible solutions. The 'realistic' ones will comprise those that have a grip on the real problematic situation by virtue of their using the materials which are to hand, and which form indeed the terms of the problem. What solutions are tried out at a time, and what adopted, however provisionally, will be determined by a large number of different factors which it is impossible to enumerate in advance, far less predict for a given situation. But in general the trying out and the adoption of a particular solution will involve some conflict: historically and in the case of fundamental problems the conflicts will, in class-societies, involve class-struggle.

7

This displacement of the various couples of the traditional accounts of social change (in particular the ends/means couple) by the problems/solutions framework deserves emphasis and textual exemplification, for it is a crucial feature of Marx's thought. What is in question then is no longer the free positing of an end or goal, on the basis of what is thought desirable in the abstract, more or less independently of what the actual tendencies in the situation are, and then the casting about for instrumental means to that end. It is rather the necessarily highly contextual delineation of concrete problems which are given rise to by the concrete character of the situation and which require specific solutions whose elements stem from that problematic situation. This is the profoundly immanentist, the radically 'anti-Utopian' character of Marx's thought, which is one of its most permanent features.

It is there even in Marx's letter to his father written in 1837, whilst he was an undergraduate;[1] and I have pointed to it in his final letter to Ruge in the exchange of 1842-1843. It is expressed with crystalline clarity in a passage such as this from *The German Ideology*:

Communism is for us not ... an *ideal* to which reality will have to adjust itself. We call communism the *real* movement which abolishes the present state of affairs. The conditions of this movement result from the now existing premise. (CW 5:49)

It emerges very clearly in the argumentation of the major political writing of the immediately following period, namely, the *Manifesto of the Communist Party*. The work begins with a rapid sketch of the origins and development of the modern bourgeoisie and contains many oft-cited paeans to capitalism: on account of its immense development of the social productive forces, its rationalization and demystification of nature and of social relations, its development of the capacities of humanity through its constant calling up of new needs and of the abilities to satisfy them. But, the authors go on, modern bourgeois society is gripped by a conflict between the product- ive forces which it has developed and its constitutive relations of production which are no longer adequate to them. This is manifested in crises of over-production which are temporarily moderated by enforced destruction of some of the productive forces, by the winning of new markets and more intensive exploitation of old ones 'that is to say, by paving the way for more extensive and more destructive crises, and by diminish- ing the means whereby crises are prevented' (CW 6:490). After a parallel sketch of the origins, development and current conditions of the proletariat they conclude:

... the bourgeoisie is unfit any longer to be the ruling class in society ... because it is incompetent to assure an existence to its slave within his slavery, because it cannot help letting him sink into such a state, that it has to feed him, instead of being fed by him. (CW 6:495f)

Thus the crux of the critique of capitalism here is that it has involved itself, through the development of its own character- istic practices, in problems which it cannot solve in its own terms: the goals of its own practices cannot be realized through those practices. The bourgeoisie is condemned as a ruling class not in terms of some general moral principle, but because, through the problems into which the mode of production that it dominates has run, it provokes its own replacement by the working class. If capitalism has embroiled itself in problems of its own making, then the very conditions which, from the point of view of the bourgeoisie *are* problems (a high level of development of the productive forces and an organized working class) and indeed insoluble ones, are conditions which form the materials for a *solution* of problems from the point of view of the working class. Thus the party of the working class does not represent a set of ideal ends and programmatic means to those ends drawn up in the abstract, but simply formulate the possible solution given rise to by the real tendencies in the situation:

The theoretical conclusions of the Communists are in no way based on ideas or principles that have been invented, or discovered by this or that would-be universal reformer. They merely express, in general

171

terms, actual relations springing from an existing class struggle, from a historical movement going on under our very eyes. (CW 6:498)

Such ideas formed the guide-lines for Marx's thinking during the revolutionary years 1848-1849, when it was a matter not of abstract thinking about change but about quite specific political questions. For example, in an early article of the period:

We do not make the utopian demand that at the outset a *united indivisible German republic* should be proclaimed ... The final act of constitution cannot be *decreed*, it coincides with the movement we have to go through. It is therefore not a question of putting into practice this or that view, this or that political idea, but of understanding the course of development. The National Assembly has to take only such steps as are practicable in the first instance. ('The programmes of the Radical-Democratic Party and of the Left at Frankfurt', 7 June 1848, CW 7:51)

After the defeat of the revolution — in the March 1850 address to the Central Committee of the Communist League (already put into context in Chapter 5 above) — Marx (and Engels) affirmed that 'the German workers are not able to attain power and achieve their own class interests without completely going through a lengthy revolutionary development' (CW 10:286). And the minutes of the September meeting, which resulted in a split in the League (again already mentioned) report Marx as saying that in the views put forward by the opposing faction:

The materialist standpoint of the *Manifesto* has given way to idealism. The revolution is seen not as the product of the realities of the situation but as the result of an effort of the *will* ... we say to the workers: You have 15,20,50 years of civil war to go through in order to alter the situation and to train yourselves for the exercise of power .... We are devoted to a party which, most fortunately for it, cannot yet come to power. If the proletariat were to come to power the measures it would introduce would be petty-bourgeois and not directly proletarian .... (CW 10:626, 628)

In *The Eighteenth Brumaire of Louis Bonaparte*, published a couple of years later, Marx describes how, after the defeat of June 1848, part of the French proletariat became involved in 'doctrinaire experiments ... hence into a movement in which it

172

renounces *the revolutionising of the old world by means of the latter's own great, combined resources*, and seeks rather to achieve its salvation behind society's back, in private fashion, with its limited conditions of existence, and hence necessarily suffers shipwreck' (CW 11:110f — the whole passage is emphasized in the original).

Just two decades later Marx was writing of the Paris Commune, in words that recalled his much earlier ones:

The working class ... have no ready-made utopias to introduce *par décret du peuple*. They know that in order to work out their own emancipation ... they will have to pass through long struggles, through a series of historic processes, transforming circumstances and people. They have no ideals to realise, but to set free the elements of the new society with which old collapsing bourgeois society itself is pregnant. (PW 3:213)

It was in this spirit that about the same time he referred in *Capital* to those who had criticised him for confining himself 'merely to the critical analysis of the actual facts, instead of writing recipes ... for the kitchens of the future' (C 1:99).

Finally, in a letter towards the end of his life he replied to a Dutch comrade (F. Domela-Nieuwenhuis) who had informed him that at its impending Zurich congress the Dutch Social Democratic Workers' Party would put up for discussion the question of what legislative measures the socialists, if they should seize power, were to take first to ensure the victory of socialism. Marx answered (22 February 1881) that this question is mistakenly posed:

What is to be done at any definite, given moment in the future, what is *immediately* to be done, depends of course entirely on the given historical conditions in which one is to act. But this question is posed in cloud-cuckoo land, and is therefore really a pseudo-question, to which the only answer must be — *a critique of the question itself. No equation can be solved unless the elements of its solution are involved in its terms.* (Emphasis of last sentence added.)

And he goes on a little later in the letter:

The doctrinaire and necessarily imaginary anticipation of the program of action for a revolution of the future only diverts people from the struggle of the present ... the moment a real proletarian revolution breaks out the conditions (even if certainly not idyllic) of its immediate, next modus operandi will be in existence.

8

This central feature about Marx' view of history, its radically immanent standpoint, can be related to a number of issues which are both illuminated by, and themselves illuminate, that standpoint. I shall close this chapter by mentioning a couple of them.

One concerns the sense in which a certain period of history may be said to create *obstacles* to human development. Thus it is often said that capitalism is to be condemned and is apt for replacement by another form of social organization because it is inadequate to satisfy human needs, because it obstructs possible human development.

Now Marx clearly thinks that this is both true and important. But it is not unimportant to be careful as to how it is understood. It is often put forward as though what is in question is the inability of capitalism to provide conditions for the satisfaction of a set of pre-given needs which are then customarily located in a 'human nature'. This view can be read out of the *1844 Manuscripts*. But the later Marx's way of interpreting the situation was rather as follows. A form of economic and social organization, by virtue of its distinctive practices, *brings forth* a set of needs and wants, a set of *potentialities* for action which at a certain point it cannot satisfy or satisfy fully basically for reasons internal to the practices which go to constitute it. For example, capitalism, by virtue of the facts of its development and structure, creates a form of human being with strivings and potentialities for a high degree of individual personal development. But the very developments of advanced capitalism are such as to come into conflict with those needs. Thus the very structures which give rise to the needs and potentialities also obstruct their fulfilment. This is the real sense in which the mode of production is 'limited': not by comparison with some ideal circumstances outside it but by virtue of a conflict between potentialities and actualities *within* it.

Marx insists on this internality of the idea of the limitedness of a mode of production at several places. In *Capital* Marx writes that 'the *real barrier* for capitalist production is *capital itself* (C 3:358), an idea repeated several times. That is, capitalism is limited, inadequate, when measured by its *own* standards.(Cf. earlier remarks above on some parts of the *Manifesto*.) and in the *Grundrisse* there is a passage which illuminates the same theme. Marx is discussing the transition from feudalism to capitalism, and writes that each of the circumstances that was a 'barrier (*Schranke*)' to free competition (compulsory guild membership, government regulation, internal tariffs, etc.)

was immanent limit (*Grenze*) for earlier modes of production, within which they spontaneously developed and moved. These limits became barriers only after the forces of production and the relations of intercourse had developed sufficiently to enable capital as such to emerge as the dominant principle of production. The limits which it tore down were barriers to its motion, its development and realisation. It is by no means the case that it thereby suspended all limits, nor all barriers; but rather only the limits not corresponding to it, which were barriers to it. Within its own limits — however much they may appear as barriers from a higher standpoint, and are posited as such by its own historic development — it feels free, and free of barriers, i.e. as limited only by itself, only by its own conditions of life. (G 649f)

Thus something is not a barrier in and of itself, though to be a definite something it must have limits. Something is a barrier when it stands in the way of the possibilities of development of something with the corresponding limits.

9

The considerations presented in the preceding sections also cast some light upon an enigmatic sentence in the 1859 Preface:

... new, higher relations of production never appear before the material conditions for their existence have matured in the womb of the old society. Hence *mankind always sets itself only such problems as it can solve*, since, on closer consideration, it will always be found that the problem itself arises only when the material conditions for its solution already exist or are at least in the process of formation. (EW 426 — emphases added)

The clue to the understanding of this lies in a reflection of the notion of a problem. A situation is not seen as presenting a problem until it is seen as one which may be changed in a way which removes the obstruction. That is, a situation may constitute say a source of interference with happiness but not be thought of as 'problematic'. (A problem may be involved but not rooted in the situation in itself; the problem may be for example, how to adapt to the situation.) Now what Marx is saying is that it is only when a social situation is such *both* that preceding developments create potentialities in it which turn some at least of the limits which define the situation into barriers, *and* that conditions exist for realising those potentialities, that the situation is conceived as posing a problem which as such admits or is thought to admit of a solution.[2]

Notes

1 In his letter Marx writes how his endeavours to unite his studies of law and philosophy in a work on the philosophy of law were vitiated by the 'opposition between what is and what ought to be, which is characteristic of idealism'. He sets up as a requirement that:

in the concrete expression of a living world of ideas ... the object itself must be studied in its development ... the rational character of the object itself must develop as something imbued with contradictions in itself and find its unity in itself.

He goes on to say that:

from the idealism which ... I had compared and nourished with the idealism of Kant and Fichte, I arrived at the point of seeking the idea in reality itself. If previously the gods had dwelt above the earth now they became its centre. (CW 1:12, 18).

The previous two sentences recall an epigram which he had already included in a handwritten volume containing a selection of his writings and presented to his father on the occasion of his birthday in March 1837. (See CW 1:577, the quatrain beginning 'Kant and Fichte ...' Remember that the speaker is Hegel.)

2 I think that this is related to Paulo Freire's concept of 'problematization'. See, for example, *The Pedagogy of the Oppressed* (New York, Herder and Herder, 1971).

Chapter 18
Dialectics

1

Consideration of Marx's ideas about social change inevitably leads at some point to the topic of 'dialectics'. In the second edition of the first volume of *Capital* Marx cites a long extract from a Russian reviewer of the first edition. The passage quoted begins by saying that Marx's principal concern in *Capital* is to find

the law of...the...development...of the phenomenon...with whose investigation he is concerned....i.e. the law of their transition from one form into another...the necessity of definite successive orders of social relations ...

and it continues by sketching what the reviewer takes to be Marx's manner of tackling such problems. Marx himself concludes the quotation of the whole passage thus: 'When the writer depicts so aptly what he calls my real method...what else is he depicting but the dialectical method?' (C 1:102). Marx thus considers the study of social change to be the province of 'the dialectical method'; and it is clear from other things he says that he thought of this as connected with a 'dialectic' at work in the real world (though neither he nor Engels ever used the term 'dialectical materialism').

But what did he mean by such expressions? Unfortunately he never provided much by way of explanation. He several times indicated his intention of writing a brief outline of the subject; but this he never did. Engels did write a fair amount on the subject and this is what has mainly been the theme of later discussion both by adherents of the idea of a dialectic and by its opponents. However it may be said that 'dialectics' has been widely regarded as a rather arcane aspect of classical Marxism — where the term has not been almost entirely denuded of

177

specifiable meaning. It has tended to be regarded by many who would otherwise consider themselves 'Marxists' as being, from a systematic point of view, adventitious frippery or rhetorical device in Marx's work, its presence to be explained historically, rather than as a systematically and theoretically important part of his thinking.

My own view is that it is thus important. But even if it were of mainly only historical interest no serious introduction to Marx's work can avoid an attempt to understand what he understood by 'dialectics'. In this chapter I shall put together what I take to be the essential elements of Marx's thinking in this regard, based upon the fragmentary remarks of a general nature that he has left upon the theme and upon what fairly clearly amount to exemplifications of 'dialectics'.

2

In trying to reconstruct Marx's views on dialectics we may start from a couple of passages in *Capital*. First, in an oft-quoted passage, Marx writes that his dialectical method is fundamentally the 'direct opposite' of that to be found in Hegel for whom

the process of thinking ... is the creator of the real world, which is only its external appearance. With me, on the contrary, the world of ideas is nothing but the material world transposed and translated into the human head.

He goes on:

... in Hegel's hands the dialectic suffers a mystification.... With him it is standing on its head. It must be inverted in order to discover the rational kernel in the mystical shell. (C 1:102, 103)

And second, much later in the work, Marx comments in passing that

... the Hegelian 'contradiction' ... is the source of all dialectics. (C 1:744n)

What then is the nature of 'the Hegelian "contradiction"'? (The scare-quotes about the last word is an obvious indication of Marx's intended critical distance from the Hegelian form of the concept thus alluded to.) Hegel himself gives us the answer when he writes in his major presentation of his system of logic that the essence of dialectics is 'the grasping of opposites in their unity'.[1] We shall have gained a foothold on Marx's conception if, in accordance with the first of the two passages just cited, we can give a materialist interpretation of this idea of a 'unity of opposites', as it may be called for short.

3

To do this let us start with an example. In *Capital* (C 1:420) Mark writes about

the tendency of capital to reduce as much as possible the number of workers employed, i.e. the amount of its variable component, the part which is changed into labour-power...which stands in contradiction with its other tendency to produce the greatest possible mass of surplus-value.

Here Marx identifies two tendencies in the capitalist mode of production. The first is the tendency towards a maximum possible decrease in the number of workers employed, or, what is the same thing, for a maximum possible decrease in the amount of variable capital (that represented by purchased labour-power) in relation to constant capital (that represented by means of production). The second is the tendency towards a maximum possible increase in the surplus-value produced.

Now in terms of Marx's political economy of capitalism, these two tendencies work towards reciprocally annulling effects. For if it is the case, as Marx holds, that surplus-value is simply a way of representing a certain portion of the labour which a worker expends when employed by capital, then any decrease in the amount of labour-power bought and used by capital will, other things being equal, mean a decrease in the mass of surplus-value produced. Thus the two tendencies identified work towards opposite outcomes.

But in the passage cited, Marx locates these two opposing tendencies as having the very same root, the structure of capital. He does not spell this out here, but we are already familiar enough with it from earlier discussions. In brief, we have seen how the first tendency stems, amongst other things, from the need by capital for the greatest possible degree of

179

control over the process of production and for constant cheapening of commodities; and we have seen how the second tendency arises basically from the need to accumulate capital in order to increase the constant capital component which is the complement to the decrease in the variable capital component. So the two 'opposites' have their 'unity' in the nature of capital.

What has just been pointed to is in fact a specification of what Marx regards as the fundamental contradiction of capitalism. He describes this in various ways, but it is generically the manner in which the relations of production characteristic of capitalism (private ownership of the means of production, and hence the existence of labour-power as a commodity) leads both to the development of the forces of production and also to the opposite of this (obstruction in maximization of surplus, tendency of the rate of profit to fall, underconsumption, and so on).

4

Let us try to list some general features of dialectical contradiction as conceived by Marx insofar as they emerge from a consideration of this example.

First, the whole situation is a real material one: the opposing aspects of the contradiction are actual forces and the unity constituted by that of concrete practices which produce and are reproduced (to the extent they are) by those forces. Second, the opposing aspects are 'tendencies', and thus both they and their unity are to be understood in a conditional manner, that is, as dependent upon a complex interaction of dispersed centres of causal efficacy. And since this is so, the interaction of all these various factors does not have any foregone conclusion, any outcome determined outside the process of their working together. Third, it flows in turn from the last point that the social development conditioned in this way does not have a pre-determined state of equilibrium as an immanent goal and thus the dialectic is 'critical and revolutionary' (C 1:103). Finally, in the light of all of the above — and flowing in the final analysis from the first point — there can be no question of knowledge of the field of the dialectic being

180

vouchsafed *a priori*; such knowledge will, to the extent that it is available at all, be found by whatever methods are appropriate for gaining knowledge about the real world.[2]

5

These features of Marx's conception of the dialectic may be illuminated and better understood by briefly contrasting them with the Hegelian dialectic from which (together with other materials) Marx produced his own views. In fact the Hegelian dialectic contrasts with Marx's on each and all of the points listed.

First, for Hegel the field of the dialectic is, in the final analysis, that of ideas, of essences. The unities in question are the unity of the aspects of an essence. Second, since development is basically the unfolding of the nature of these essences, it is necessary and characterized by an immanent goal or *telos*. So, in Hegel, Spirit is essentially rational freedom and the source of the dialectical development the conflict between the necessity for Spirit to attain its *telos* and the various successive inadequate conditions for this to occur. Third, insofar as the system has an immanent *telos* the development envisaged is one towards reconciliation of conflicts in a larger harmony; hence the Hegelian dialectic is conservative in its very foundations and not merely as a consequence of certain historical and personal factors. (This conservatism also stems from the first-mentioned aspect of the dialectic, namely, its idealism, as pointed out by Marx in some of his earlier work. Cf. above, Chapter 3, Section 7.) Fourth, since the field of the dialectic is that of essences, knowledge of the field can be achieved *a priori* as regards basics if not as regards all empirical details.

The point of Marx's much-discussed remark, quoted earlier, about the necessity to 'invert' the Hegelian dialectic in order to discover 'the rational kernel in the mystical shell' should now be clearer. For it can be seen from what has just been said that all the features of the Hegelian dialectic depend upon the idealist starting point: it is in the position that what is fundamental is ideas that the necessary, teleological, conservative and *a priori* features are grounded. Hence to avoid these it is necessary to reject their common foundation. However inappropriate Marx's metaphor of kernel and shell may be — it is certainly not a question of taking from Hegel something pre-formed in any sense — the necessity for the preliminary operation of inversion, that is, rejection of an idealist in favour of a materialist standpoint, is correct.

6

But is there not also a dialectic of concepts as well as of real forces and structures in Marx? I think there is here and there, but not where it has generally been looked for. I am thinking here in the first place of the analysis of the concept of the commodity in the opening part of the first volume of *Capital*, regarding which he speaks of 'flirtation' with Hegel's 'special mode of expression' (C 1: 103). I believe that we must take this description quite seriously and see the traces of Hegel here — as distinct from a mode of thought indebted to Hegel but quite different from it — as merely terminological. Let us briefly review the matter. (This discussion can be omitted at a first reading.)

It will be remembered that Marx presents the commodity as having two characteristics: use-value and (exchange-) value. These may in turn be regarded as the representations of, respectively, concrete labour and abstract labour, or of private labour and social labour. Now the terms in each pair of these characterizations — concrete/abstract, individual/social — are each exclusive of the other, as are the original pair (something's being a use-value for me excludes its being something to be exchanged, and conversely). Also each of these characterizations must simultaneously apply to something for it to be a commodity: to take just the original pair, something can only have an exchange-value if it has a use-value for the person who is to exchange something else for it, and its having a use-value is shown by its being able to be exchanged. So we have a case, it would seem, of a concept defined in terms of a unity of opposing determinations. And the development of the 'value-form' in the first chapter of *Capital* may be seen as the development of this internal contradiction in the concept.

A full discussion of this case would take us too far afield. But some points sufficient to settle the matter in essentials can be made fairly briefly.

First, the sense in which we have here a conceptual characterization in terms of a unity of opposites must be carefully specified. Strictly speaking there can be no such thing as a single commodity (any more than there can be a single sibling): a commodity is a use-value an exchange-relation with another use-value. Let us call the two use-values in the simplest case *A* and *B*. Then to be commodities *A* and *B* must be exchanged for one another. In this case, insofar as *A* is exchanged for *B*, from the point of view of *A* what is in question is only its (exchange-) value and *B*'s use-value. The situation is the symmetrical converse from the point of view of *B*. So, though in the total situation of exchange both *A* and *B* have, *qua* commodities, both use-value and (exchange-) value, they do not possess these characteristics in the same practical relations, and the situation is not at all parallel to saying that, for example, something is both red and not-red all over at the same time.

Second, whether an object possesses both these characteristics, and so counts as a commodity, is of course something that is dependent upon external conditions. If the object does not find another to exchange with (including money) then it has no exchange-value and, to the extent that all objects are produced as values, it has no use-value either. So the existence of an object as a commodity is a contingent matter, and there can be no immanent, internal-conceptual dialectic of the commodity. Put another way, the theory of the commodity permits the enunciation of certain conditional statements, but whether the antecedents of these conditionals are satisfied is contingent. So once more the dialectical unity of opposites is a matter of real tendencies in the (social) world and not a merely conceptual one.[3]

7

In this chapter I have concentrated upon the notion of contradiction, of the 'unity of opposites', as the key one for an understanding of Marx's conception of dialectics, in line with Marx's own statement on the matter cited at the beginning of

Section 2 above. I have not treated many other questions which would have to be taken up in a fuller discussion. In particular I have not remarked upon Marx's use of other principles, the origins of which are to be found in Hegel, and which occupied quite an important place in Engels' writings on dialectics: I refer to the idea of the 'transformation of quantity into quality' and that of the 'negation of the negation'.[4] These notions, particularly the second, play a comparatively peripheral role in Marx's conception of dialectics and any useful discussion of them would take up more space than can be spared in this introductory survey. I have also not remarked upon the fact that Marx clearly held that dialectical thinking applies to nature as well as to social affairs[5] (a point overlooked by those who wish to drive a wedge between him and Engels).

8

I conclude with two general points. The first is that the presentation has, I hope, shown that no special 'dialectical' logic is required by Marx's conception of dialectical contradiction. In particular it in no way requires the rejection of the ordinary logical principle that it is true either that a certain statement is true or that it is false (law of excluded middle); indeed the coherent presentation of Marx's conceptions on dialectics presupposes that principle.

The second is that dialectics or dialectical method in Marx's understanding of it is not some sort of super-science or super-method, superior to others in particular through being more general and permitting someone who has mastered it to gain results in special fields more or less automatically. It is rather a matter of certain general principles of procedure, the concrete use of which depends upon the special features of the particular field being studied; it is a question, so to speak, of strategies rather than recipes. In this respect it is worth recalling what Marx wrote on one occasion to Engels (1 February 1858) regarding a project of Lassalle's for a work on political economy to be produced by applying the principles of Hegelian logic to that field:

He will learn to his cost that to bring a science ... to the point where it can be dialectically presented is an altogether different thing from applying an abstract ready-made system of logic to mere inklings of such a system.

Notes

1 *Science of Logic*, trans. A. V. Miller (London, Allen and Unwin, 1969), p. 56.
2 For discussions of general questions about knowledge based on Marx's texts, see the paper by J. Curthoys and W. Suchting in *Inquiry*, *20* (1977), 243-397, and my paper on 'Knowledge and Practice' *Science and Society*, forthcoming 1983.
3 Cf. also W. Suchting, 'Marx on the Dialectics of Production and Consumption in the Introduction to the *Grundrisse*' *Social Praxis, 3* (1975), 291-313.
4 On the first see, for example, C 1:423, and on the second C 1:929.
5 See the clear evidence of C 1:423 and note thereto.

Chapter 19
Political economy and communism
1857-1864

1

We have seen that Marx's main theoretical preoccupation during the period we have been concerned with in this part was political economy. Since Marx's central political concern was the programme of communism it is obvious enough that his thinking about the latter should have developed in the light of this work in political economy. This is indeed the case. If the earlier philosophical communism soon gave place to more directly historical and political conceptions in the subsequent years leading up to his removal to England, these in turn lacked a sound political-economic foundation. We have seen that, programmatically at least, Marx very early tied the goal of communism to the existence of certain trends in the actual movement of capitalist society. But as of, say, 1850, this was still pretty much *only* programmatic, and it was the work of the following years to make this more concrete with a study of the real tendencies of capitalism.

The two chief works in which this proceeded were, of course, the *Grundrisse* and *Capital*. As regards the first, though it is basically a set of notebooks on political economy in the strict sense, it also, as I have already noted, touches upon many other topics which are not treated at all or at the same length in Marx's other writings or are treated in a very distinctive way. The discussions of communism in particular connect the basic themes of the political economy of capitalism with wider issues. As regards *Capital* there is much less direct comment on communism than in the *Grundrisse* but much more systematic treatment of the tendencies of capitalism that are relevant to the politics of communism. As I have considered the political economic doctrines of *Capital* already I shall not treat them here again. Instead I shall just briefly comment on their political implications as Marx saw them and conclude with some remarks on one of the main passages directly bearing on Marx's thinking about communism (Sections 5 & 6).

2

Marx writes in the *Grundrisse*[1] that 'the great historic aspect of capital is to *create ... surplus labour*' (325), that is (as explained in Chapter 8 above) labour over and above what is necessary for mere subsistence. This 'historic destiny' is fulfilled when three things have happened. The first is the situation where 'there has been such a development of needs that surplus labour above and beyond necessity has itself become a general need arising out of individual needs themselves'. This in turn involves two themes, namely, the development of individual needs and the development of labour as a 'general need' arising therefrom. With regard to the first, the development of general needs, we have seen that the 'normal' path for the expansion of capital is, according to Marx, the expansion of relative (rather than absolute) surplus-value, and that this means, in the final analysis, an increase in the productivity of labour. This in turn means, if available labour and means of production are to be fully utilized, an increase in productive power. And the results of the use of this can be sold and hence release profit for capital only if consumption is increased. This can occur either by quantitative expansion of existing consumption (two cars instead of one), or by creating new needs by expanding ones in a wider circle (more people buying their first car), or by the production of new sorts of needs through the production of new sorts of use-values. It is this last that Marx emphasizes. It amounts to the creation of more complex human beings, ones with more many-sided needs. It also means the production and extension of a general 'utilitarianism' in which human beings become the measure of all things:

Thus ... production founded upon capital creates ... a system of general exploitation of things natural and human, a system of general utility ... Hence the great civilising influence of capital ... capital drives beyond natural barriers and prejudices as much as beyond nature-worship, as well as all traditional, confined, complacent, encrusted satisfactions of present needs, and reproductions of old

187

ways of life. It is destructive to all of this, and constantly revolution-
ises it, tearing down all the barriers which hem in the development of
the forces of production, the expansion of needs, the all-sided
development of production, and the exploitation and exchange of
natural and mental forces. (409f)

So much for capitalism's development of individual needs.
Marx also says — and this was the second half of the first point
— that as a result 'surplus labour above and beyond necessity
has itself become a general need', something which merges into
the second condition for the fulfilling of capitalism's 'historic
destiny, namely, 'when the severe discipline of capital, acting
on succeeding generations has developed general industriousness as the general property of the new species' (325). I take it
that he means here in the first place, that to satisfy 'surplus'
individual needs generated in the way already explained,
surplus labour is necessary, this itself becoming a need which,
stemming as it does from the very development of individual
needs themselves, is not experienced as coercive. But in the
second place, capitalism as such, in its relentless pursuit of
surplus, forces people to work as hard as they can. This cause,
acting over generations, produces a general disposition to
work — 'industriousness' — as a new characteristic property
of the species.

Marx very clearly regards this development of an aptness for
labour as a progressive step in the evolution of humanity. Why
does he think this? He does not spell out his train of thought
but it may be somewhat as follows: First, whilst necessarily
labour is always externally constrained by the aim to which it is
directed and the obstacles to overcome in attaining it, 'this
overcoming of obstacles is in itself a liberating activity' (611).
This is so, presumably, for one thing because it requires an
increase in knowledge about a new portion of the world and
hence, insofar as knowledge is power, increases to that extent
the margin of unconstrained activity in the world; and it is also
because it increases actors' knowledge of their own powers,
develops new ones and thus increases the capacity to act. The
development of a disposition to labour is emancipatory for a
second reason, and this is in fact the one that Marx stresses.
Humanity begins with various needs of a mainly purely
biological provenance — in a state of what he calls at one place

'natural indigence' (325). As such they are simply 'given' for human beings. But the development of new needs generated by new ways of producing means that needs stemming more or less directly from nature, more or less unmediated by human beings themselves, give place to needs that are historically produced by human beings themselves. Insofar, the activity which goes to produce things to satisfy them is not determined by anything that lies outside of human activity itself. That is, humanity's freedom is increased to the extent that the aims of labour are self-posited by humanity rather than simply met with in nature.

3

The third and last of the three conditions that Marx lists for the fulfilling of capitalism's 'historic destiny' is that the development of the productive powers of labour has reached a stage where 'the possession and preservation of general wealth require a lesser labour-time of society as a whole', and where

the labouring society relates scientifically to the process of its progressive reproduction, its reproduction in a constantly greater abundance; hence where labour in which a human being does what things by themselves can do has ceased. (325)

This point relates to Marx's account in the *Grundrisse* of the general character of the specifically capitalist process of production. In this regard Marx distinguishes between two periods in the history of capitalist production. These are already familiar to us from the presentation in Chapter 10 of the concepts of 'formal' and 'real' 'subsumption of labour under capital'. It will be remembered that the first stage is characterized by labour-power's being put to work with technological means that are not generated by capitalism specifically. What characterizes the second period is the introduction of machinery (rather than tools). Here 'means of labour' cease to be such in the traditional sense of means for the transmission of the worker's labour to a raw material. Rather, what is transmitted to the raw material is the activity, the 'labour' of the machine itself, human labour-power being necessary only to supervise a process which in general takes its

189

own course (585, 692f). This is the system of production which is fully adequate to capital as such: here capital dominates labour not only by appropriating part of it as surplus but also by governing it technically through relegated living labour to a marginal place in the system of production. Marx describes the situation as a thoroughly alienated one for the worker. Here skill, strength, activity belong to the thing, machinery, whilst the workers themselves need no special skills or strength passively to tend the machines. Knowledge, science itself, insofar as it is embodied in machinery and helps oppress the labour-power which tends it, is an alien force.

4

Now the situation as sketched is, according to Marx, a contradictory one for capital. He sets this out in different ways at different places. One way is substantially that which I have already rehearsed in the preceding chapter. Briefly, capital seeks to maximize surplus-value, which can only be done by maximizing the appropriation of surplus labour-time. But the attempt to do this involves decreasing the proportion of labour-power used in the process of production. This also shows that embodied labour-time is no longer the appropriate criterion of wealth, since the amount of labour-time which must be expended to produce the basic means for society's reproduction constantly diminishes, something which shows indeed that the very labour theory of value itself is appropriate only to the period of human history marked by a comparatively low level of development of the productive forces (705, 708).[2]

Marx presents communism as the solution to the contradictions of advanced capitalism. If the productive powers of capitalism are taken over by the direct producers and utilized within new relations of production then the surplus labour-time which those productive powers made possible can be used directly as such, as surplus time: there is no longer the need to turn the surplus labour-time into surplus-value which places capitalism in a contradictory impasse. Surplus labour-time becomes disposable time for the whole of society, a time which can be used for the development of the individual and social powers and needs also developed by capitalism. Marx further writes that though the increase of generally available disposable time made possible by higher productivity will increase social needs by virtue of the developments made possible by that disposable time, these developments of human capacities will themselves make possible further developments of human productive powers. In the use of free time individuals become different from what they were before, and, as such, enter into production as different sorts of agents. Conversely, production itself is a context for the development of human powers, a point of view inconsistent with the idea, characteristic of capitalism, of an antithesis between labour time and free time (711f).

5

I have already sketched (in Chapter 10) Marx's general conception of the long-run tendencies of capitalism in *Capital*, namely, first, an increasing centralization and concentration of capital and, second, the formation of an industrial reserve army coexisting with a work-force which exists under increasingly oppressive conditions. Marx's own summing up of the situation from the point of view of the working class, though often quoted from, cannot be omitted from an introduction to his work:

... within the capitalist system all methods for raising the social productivity of labour are put into effect at the cost of the individual worker; all means for the development of production ... mutilate the worker into a fragment of a human being, degrade him to the level of an appendage of a machine, destroy the content of his labour by turning it into a torment, estrange from him the intellectual potentialities of the labour process in the same proportion as science in incorporated in it as an independent power; they deform the conditions under which he works, subject him during the labour process to a despotism the more hateful for its pettiness, turn his lifetime into labour-time... . But all methods for the production of surplus-value are at the same time methods of accumulation, and every extension of accumulation becomes, conversely, a means for the development of those methods. It follows therefore that in proportion as capital accumulates, the situation of the worker, whatever his payment, high or low, must grow worse. (C 1:799)

Amongst other things this passage makes it quite clear that Marx is not suggesting here that there is a tendency towards an absolute worsening of the economic conditions of the working class — he is not putting forward what has so often been ascribed to him, namely, a so-called 'immiseration theory'. What he says here is meant to apply to the worker 'whatever his payment, high or low'. His prediction of an increasing worsening of conditions for the working class is of a much more general sort.

In the penultimate chapter of the first volume of *Capital* he emphasizes the objectively co-operative character of the tendency towards the centralization of capital, its increasingly social character (*Vergesellschaftung*):

... there is a development of the co-operative form of the labour-process to an ever increasing degree ... the transformation of means of labour into ones which can only be used in common, the economising of all means of production by their use as the means of production of combined, social labour, the entanglement of all peoples in the net of the world market and thereby the international character of the capitalist regime. (C 1:929)

That is, the economy itself assumes, from its technical or material side, features apt for transformation into a properly socialist economy.[3] And at the same time the agents of such transformation are generated: with this economic development 'there also grows the revolt of the working class, constantly swelling and trained, united and organized by the mechanism of the capitalist process of production itself' (*loc. cit.*).

And a famous conclusion:

The monopoly of capital becomes a fetter upon the mode of production which has flourished with and under it. The centralisation and socialising of labour reach a point at which they become incompatible with their capitalist integument. It is burst asunder. The knell of capitalist private property sounds. The expropriators are expropriated. (*loc. cit.*)

6

I conclude this brief survey of the theme of communism in

Capital with a consideration of a passage near the end of the third volume. Like all of the treatments of communism in that work it is a aside from other more strictly political economic discussions, but it is one of the most significant such passages. Marx writes:

In fact, the realm of freedom only begins where labouring which is determined by neediness and purposes external to it ceases; thus in the nature of things it lies beyond the sphere of material production proper. Just as the savage must wrestle with nature to satisfy his wants, to maintain and reproduce his life, so must civilised man, and he must do so in all forms of society and under all possible modes of production. With his development this realm of necessity which pertains to nature expands because his wants do; but at the same time the productive forces which satisfy these wants also expand. Freedom in this domain can only consist in socialised man, the associated producers, rationally regulating their metabolism with nature, bringing it under their communal control, instead of being dominated by it as by a blind power; and achieving this with the least expenditure of energy and under conditions most worthy of and adequate to their human nature. But it nonetheless still remains a realm of necessity. Beyond it begins that development of human powers which is an end in itself, the true realm of freedom, which can however only blossom forth with this realm of necessity as its basis. The shortening of the working day is its basic condition. (C 3:958f)

The passage utilizes several distinctions:

1 between 'the realm of freedom' and 'the realm of necessity';
2 between 'that development of human energy which is an end in itself' and 'labouring which is determined by neediness and purposes external to it';
3 between material production in a wide sense and 'material production proper'.

It would seem that these distinctions are meant to be coincident.

The 'realm of necessity' is the domain of work which is done not for its own sake but because of the fact that human beings are a part of nature and have needs stemming from the conditions of reproduction as such: the aims of such labour are set by circumstances over which humanity has no control. Within this domain the only freedom which is possible consists in communal control over the process of production and its conditions, and its carrying through in a way that is maximally economical of time and as benign as possible. The realm of true freedom is one where what is carried on is activity directed towards goals which are posited by the actors themselves — this activity is not non-material, but is nevertheless not 'material production proper'. Put otherwise, the 'realm of necessity' is that of activity which is directed towards ends which are instrumental to achieving other ends, and not engaged in for its own sake, as is activity in the domain of freedom. This is once more the contrast, already met with in the *1844 Manuscripts*, between labour as forced and labour as self-realization. The contrast is also between pre-communist modes of production and communism. Capitalism in particular belongs to the realm of necessity because the product dominates the producers, because it is prodigal of time (except to the extent that it influences the production of surplus-value), and because everyone, directly or indirectly, is determined by the fundamental exigency of accumulating surplus-value.

Marx's characterization of communism here is worth remarking upon in at least two respects. First, the passage makes clear that communal control of the productive forces is not of the essence of communism as Marx conceives it — insofar as this is equated with the realm of freedom — but merely a necessary condition for it. Second, Marx prescinds from any positive characterization of communism: he rejects the various pictures of communist life which abound in Utopian communist literature — and even some 'Marxist' literature: communism is characterized as a state of things in which certain historically specific constraints on activity are absent, but what this makes concretely possible is left quite open.

Notes

1 For a more detailed discussion of this theme see my paper 'Capitalism and communism in the *Grundrisse*' *Social Praxis*, 8 (1981), 99-123.
2 With this last point cf. above Chapter 13, note 4.
3 See also his treatment of credit in advanced capitalism in Volume 3 of *Capital*, especially Chapter 27.

PART IV: 1864-1875

Chapter 20
Marx and the International Working Men's Association

1

In the early 1860s the Western European labour movement began to revive after an essentially defensive period following the defeats of 1848-1849. In the first place, the English working-class showed increasingly internationalist attitudes. For example, the British government's forcing of Garibaldi, one of the leaders of the Italian Risorgimento, to leave England after only a short stay led to workers' demonstrations and consequent clashes with the police. Again, despite the ill effects on the working-class of the Civil War in the United States, as a result of disturbances in the supply of cotton for the mills, the English workers were strongly on the side of the North. Further, the Polish insurrection of 1863 had the firm support of the working-class. In the second place, there was a movement for electoral reform. The Trade Union Manhood Suffrage Association was founded at the end of 1862, and a campaign of public meetings took place the following year.

As regards the French connection, a visit in 1862 by a delegation of workers from France to the London International Exhibition made possible a revival of contacts between various leaders of the English and French working-classes. In mid-1863 another French delegation came to London to speak at a meeting in support of Poland organized by the London Trades Council (formed in 1860). At this meeting the importation into England of Continental strike-breakers was discussed and it was proposed to keep up regular and systematic communications between the workers of the two countries. The International Working Men's Association (IWMA) — often called, with pardonable anachronism, 'the First International' — was founded at a meeting in London on 28 September 1864.

2

Marx thus had nothing to do with the actual founding of the IWMA which was to begin with a purely trade union affair, though with a political orientation. But at the inaugural meeting he was elected to its Provisional Committee and became a member of the commission appointed by it to draw up the Association's programme documents. Thus Marx was once more drawn into day to day politics after an absence of nearly fifteen years.

In the event, Marx himself wrote an 'Inaugural Address' and the 'Provisional Rules', both of which were adopted in November by the Provisional Committee as the leading body of the Association. The composition of these documents was a matter of no little delicacy, considering the diversity and indeed conflict of trends within the Association: the English trade unionists were in general not even socialist, and the socialists, mainly from the Continent, represented a great variety of views. The writing with which it is natural to compare these documents — especially the 'Inaugural Address' — is of course the *Manifesto of the Communist Party*. The differences are indeed striking: the one formulated in high rhetoric, the other in comparatively muted tones, the one with a ringing proclamation of a programme of communism, the other with only a very cautious reference to it.

Marx's care was to keep the IWMA as unified as possible, even at the expense of playing down real differences, where this did not seriously affect the policy and action of the organiz- ation. In a letter to Engels (4 November 1864) in which he expressed himself semi-apologetically for inserting some moralistic phrases in the general rules of the Association, he justified them as being in line with 'the present standpoint of the workers' movement'. 'It will take time', he went on, 'before the awakened movement allows the old boldness of speech. It will be necessary to be *fortiter in re, suaviter in modo* [firm in content, moderate in manner]'. This is why Marx's writings in connection with the IWMA have to be read very carefully: often between the lines as well as along them.

What was Marx's strategic perspective for the Association?

We cannot be sure of this, but D. D. H. Cole has put a very plausible view:

What he [Marx] wanted to do in founding the International was to take the workers' movement as it was and to build up its strength in the day-to-day struggle, in the belief that it could then be led into the right courses and develop, under ideological leadership, a revolutionary outlook arising out of the experience of the struggle for partial reforms, economic and political. ... In effect, Marx in 1864 saw revolution again approaching in Europe, and especially in France, but was less concerned to foment it than to do all he could to build up the power of the working-class movement in readiness for the situations to which it would give rise.[1]

3

Marx began the 'Inaugural Address' with a survey of the period from 1848 to 1864. Its main theme is the contradiction between two facts about this period: on the one hand, the unprecedented growth of industry and commerce, and on the other, the increasing misery of the working classes both in England and the Continent. Moreover:

in all countries of Europe it has now become a truth demonstrable to every unprejudiced mind ... that, on the present false base, every fresh development of the productive powers of labour must tend to deepen social contrasts and point social antagonisms. (PW 3:77)

If this is the economic scene the political picture has been one of roll-back for the cause of the working class: forcible destruction of workers' organizations, destruction or migration of their members, triumphant reaction, buying off of segments of the working class, and, in England in particular, the decline of Chartism. However, he continues, there have been two partly compensating developments: the carrying of the Ten Hours' Bill, and the co-operative movement. But in regard to the second, Marx warned that unless this were to have national dimensions it could do nothing to lighten the burdens of the working class, and any threat to their privileges would be met 'by the lords of land and the lords of capital' with all the means at their disposal. Thus suavely does Marx

199

introduce the idea of a communist reorganization of society, and the workers' first duty, in order to resist the attempts by the 'lords' to prevent their emancipation, the duty, that is, 'to conquer political power' (PW 3:80). Workers can succeed in this only if they combine their numerical superiority with united organization and the guidance of theory. In addition they must pursue an intransigently internationalist foreign policy opposed to one which involves 'pursuit of criminal designs, playing upon national prejudices, and squandering in piratical wars the people's blood and treasure' (PW 3:81). The Address ends with an allusion to the conclusion of the *Manifesto*: 'Proletarians of all countries, Unite!'.

4

The 'General Rules' of the Association (PW 3:82-84, 269f) based upon Marx's 'Provisional Rules', and finally adopted in September 1871, with an addition one year later, have a very dense political content. But the following are main points of principle.

1 *Working-class self-emancipation*. The preamble begins with a fundamental thesis: 'The emancipation of the working classes must be conquered by the working classes themselves'. This is a cornerstone of Marx's political thinking from the beginning, the rationale of which is deeply rooted in the idea (already discussed in Chapter 17) that social change can be thoroughgoing only if it is a result of a practice which simultaneously changes not only people's conditions but the people themselves. In a speech on the seventh anniversary of the organization (1871) Marx says that 'what was new in the International was that it ws established by the working men themselves and for themselves' (PW 3:271) — that is, its very existence and special mode of functioning was a crucial achievement quite apart from what it actually accomplished in detail. This principle applies in particular to all 'substitutionist', 'putschist' tendencies.

2 *Communism as goal*. This is the thrust of what is said, though it is not spelled out: 'the struggle for the emancipation of the working classes means ... a struggle for ... the abolition

of all class-rule'. Marx thus formulates a programme of opposition to all perspectives of social harmony through reconciliation of classes.

3 *The primacy of economic oppression.* '... the economical subjection of the man of labour to the monopoliser, that is, the sources of life, lies at the bottom of servitude in all its forms, of all social misery, mental degradation, and political dependence'; therefore 'the economical emancipation of the working classes is ... the great end to which every political movement ought to be subordinate as a means'. The polemical point of this was primarily directed at the anarchists with their thesis of the primacy of political oppression and hence of political emancipation and political struggle's being the primary end.

4 *Internationalism.* This goal of emancipation requires not only 'solidarity between the manifold divisions of labour in each country', but 'a fraternal bond of union between the working classes of different countries', for 'the emancipation of labour is ... a social problem, embracing all countries in which modern society exists, and depending for its solution on the concurrence, practical and theoretical, of the most advanced countries'.

5 *The necessity for autonomous political organization of the working class.* 'In its struggle against the collective power of the possessing classes the proletariat can act as a class only by constituting itself a distinct political party, opposed to all the old parties formed by the possessing classes'. The contemporary thrust of this was against, for example, both the followers of Proudhon, who were opposed to all forms of politics, and to certain mainly French and Italian trends which opposed an independent workers' movement.

5

I said at the beginning that the IWMA was from the start marked by many different and often conflicting views. It was inevitable that its history would be partly one of struggle between these trends for influence over the policies and practice of the organization. Marx's work within it in particular was marked by a series of conflicts with various tendencies, the main opponents being, in the earlier period, the followers of Proudhon, and in the later the anarchists led by Bakunin. There is no question here of following these disputes. Instead I shall simply pick out some of the leading points of principle.

1 *The positive role of reform.* With regard to such things as the limitation of the working day, provision of education, and so on, Marx stresses the necessity for struggling to win reforms from the existing state. For 'converting *social reason* into *social force*' there exists:

under given circumstances...no other method of doing so, than through *general laws*, enforced by the power of the state. In enforcing such laws, the working class do not fortify governmental power. On the contrary, they transform that power, now used against them, into their own agency. (PW 3:89)

2 *The significance of trade unions.* Marx writes that the contract for the sale of labour-power can never be struck on equitable terms because of the inequality of power on the two dies. The workers' only weapon, their numbers, is usually weakened by disunity, stemming from competition among themselves. Trade unions originated in an attempt to decrease this competition and hence increase the bargaining power of workers. But this gave rise to another function of unions:

Unconsciously to themselves, the trade unions were forming *centres of organisation* of the working class, as the medieval municipalities and communes did for the middle-class. If the trade unions are required for the guerilla fights between capital and labour, they are still more important as *organised agencies for superseding the very system of wage labour and capital rule.* (PW 3:91)

Marx goes on to say that trade unions have not yet fully understood their power in this regard, and have therefore 'kept too much aloof from general social and political movements', though this has been changing. The future task lies with their being deliberately 'organising centres of the working class in the broad interest of its *complete emancipation*' (PW 3:92). Unionists must regard themselves and act 'as the champions and representatives of whole working class', looking after the interests of the least able members of the class. 'They must convince the world at large that their efforts, far from being narrow and selfish, aim at the emancipation of the down-trodden millions.' (*loc. cit.*)

3 *The Irish question.* On the question of Ireland Marx's position is a model of non-moralistic defence of an internationalist position. The English working-class, he argues, has a direct interest in the emancipation of Ireland, not in the first place on ethical grounds, but because Irish emancipation is a necessary condition for their own. 'The only point at which one can strike a major blow against official England is *Ireland*'. This is because 'England is the bulwark of European land-lordism and capitalism ... [and] ... Ireland is the bulwark of English landlordism'; because the immigration of Irish workers to England, driven from their home country by lack of work, divides the working class in England; and because Ireland provides the only excuse that England has for keeping a large standing army, which is a potential danger to revolutionary forces in England. 'What ancient Rome demonstrated on a gigantic scale can be seen in the England of today. A people which subjugates another people forges its own chains.' (PW 3:117f)[2]

6

By 1871 the high years of the IWMA were well and truly over. Its achievements had been considerable:

Over most of Europe the trade-union movement emerged in the period of the International [writes Eric Hobsbawm] largely under the leadership of the socialists, and the labour movement was to be politically identified with them, and more especially with Marxism. ...the most significant achivement of the International ... [was to have] ... made labour both independent and socialist.[3]

There were many reasons for its decline. Among them were increasingly bitter internal conflicts between the anarchists (largely grouped round Bakunin) on the one hand, and the supporters of Marx on the other; the moderating influence on the English working-class of the Franchise Bill of 1867; its continued failure to show any movement towards the foundation of an independent working-class party; the beginning of a period of economic decline, with a consequent tendency on the part of the trade unions to adopt a defensive rather than offensive stance; and, last but not least, the events of spring 1871 in France.

Notes

1   *A History of Socialist Thought*, Vol. II (London, Macmillan, 1954), p.92.
2   On the same theme see the long letter by Marx to S. Meyer and A. Vogt written 9 April 1870, about the same time as the above.
3   Hobsbawm, E. *The Age of Capital 1848-1875* (London, Weidenfeld and Nicolson, 1975), pp. 113f.

Chapter 21
Reflections on the revolution in France and the Gotha programme

1

Europe had been comparatively quiet since the defeat of the revolutions of 1848-1849. Bismarck's Prussian expansionism changed all that. In July 1870 he provoked a war with France. By the first week of September both the Emperor, Louis Napoleon, and his armies had been captured and the German army was marching on Paris. A republic had been declared there and a new French army created. But the military situation grew more and more grave. The conservative government concluded an armistice with the Germans. Thiers was elected Provisional President by the National Assembly in Bordeaux, and attempted to disarm the Paris workers organized as a National Guard. In March 1871 there was a rising in Paris; Thiers' government and regular army retreated to Versailles; a new democratic municipal government, 'the Paris Commune', was elected. This had a majority of Blanquists and Jacobins and a minority of members or supporters of the IWMA. Some other French cities followed suit but these Communes were quickly suppressed. In Paris itself the Versailles troops of Thiers advanced and a week of ruthless repression began on 22 May. Estimates of the number of Communards killed outright (in the fighting itself or in the extensive massacre of prisoners) vary between 20,000 and 50,000, with tens of thousands made prisoner or fleeing. The city was put under martial law and Thiers resumed power. The bourgeoisie had won again in the first major armed confrontation with the working class and its allies since 1848.

Marx himself became the object of hysterical public charges of being one of the instigators and leaders from afar of the Commune, though he had in fact considered the uprising to be doomed from the start. Of course he followed the events with the keenest interest and wrote three 'Addresses' for the General Council of the IWMA. The first two (in July and in September 1870) presented and commented upon what was happening; the third (in April-May 1871) amongst other things examined the Paris Commune from the point of view of what could be learned from it for the programme of a communist reorganization of society. In addition, there survive various drafts of this last address, as well as miscellaneous notes containing valuable material supplementary to the originally published version. This last address, entitled 'The Civil War in France', was very successful, quickly going through three editions and being translated. The work which is now known by that name is a collection of all three addresses.

The bloody repression of the Paris Commune meant that one of the chief original reasons for the existence of the IWMA — co-operation between the English and French working classes — had all but disappeared, the leading ranks of the French working-class having been decimated. For this and other reasons (some of them listed at the end of Chapter 20) the IWMA came effectively to an end at the Hague Congress of September 1872, though it was not formally dissolved until 1876.

2

With the debacle in France and the decline of the IWMA, the centre of political gravity shifted to Germany. About this time there were two main socialist parties there (in fact the only socialist parties in the European labour movement): the General Association of German Workers (*Allgemeine Deutsche Arbeiterverein*), led by Ferdinand Lassalle, and the German Socialist Workers' Party (*Sozialistische Partei der Arbeiter Deutschlands*) led by Wilhelm Liebknecht and August Bebel. The first party had links with Marx and the second was quite close to him. In 1875 a unification of the two parties was proposed, and a draft programme drawn up for presentation to a unity congress at Gotha.

In April or early May 1875 Marx wrote a sulphurous analysis of the document and sent it to Wilhelm Bracke, who had a leading role in the moves towards reunification. It was first published, by Engels (in a slightly toned-down form) as *Critique of the Gotha Programme* (1891). This, together with the last of the addresses on the Paris Commune written by Marx for the IWMA, are the central sources for the study of Marx's late thinking about socialism and communism. (To these may be added as supplementary material some marginalia that he wrote in 1874 to a book by Bakunin on *State and Anarchy*.) In the following I shall take these together and trace out some of their principal themes, focussing mainly however on the *Critique of the Gotha Programme*.

3

One of the most important innovations in the *Critique* is the introduction of a distinction between two phases of communist society, where up till now Marx had written simply of 'communism' as such. Speaking more accurately, Marx's terminology is uncertain. He sometimes calls the second the 'higher phase' of communist society, which contrasts with what is called 'the first phase'; sometimes the former he simply terms 'communism'. The terminology of two phases of communist society seems at least simple and clear and I shall adopt it in the following.

The crucial characteristic of the first phase is that it is a *transitional* society, one which is post-capitalist but not yet properly communist:

We are dealing here with a communist society, not as it has *developed* on its own foundations, but on the contrary, just as it *emerges* from capitalist society, thus in every aspect, economically, morally, intellectually, still stamped with the birth-marks of the old society from whose womb it has come.... Between capitalist and communist society lies a period of revolutionary transformation from one to the other. (PW 3:346, 355)

To say that it is a transitional society is to say that it is one which does not have a stable character of its own, that it is not an autonomous mode of production, though it is essentially characterized by a certain developmental tendency. Wholly in line with his radical anti-Utopianism, he does not see communism in its higher form being reached by some sudden

207

revolutionary stroke: it is said to be a period of 'trans-formation', that is, one in which each step is created by the making-over of previous circumstances. Marx does not say that he envisages that the transition will inevitably be made, nor, if it is in fact made, that the process will be a smooth, gradual one; on the contrary, he says that he envisages it as a period of 'revolutionary' transformation.

4

What does it mean to say that it is not an autonomous mode of production? This question can be answered in its economic aspects by considering its characteristic modes of production, circulation and distribution.

From the point of view of *production* and *circulation* the lower phase has a straightforwardly post-capitalist character. It is a 'co-operative society based on common ownership of the means of production'. Since the ownership is common, 'the producers do not exchange their products'. Hence the labour employed on the products does not appear here, as it does in capitalist society

as the value of these products, possessed by them as a material characteristic, for now . . . individual pieces of labour are no longer merely indirectly, but directly, a component part of the total labour. (PW 3:345)

With regard to the *distribution* of the social product Marx says that 'the individual producer gets back from society . . . exactly what he has given' minus his share of necessary deductions from the total social product to cover such things as replacement of the means of production used up, additional means for expansion of production, reserve or insurance funds to provide against such contingencies as accidents and natural calamities, general costs of administration not belonging to production, means for the satisfaction of common needs like education and health, funds for those unable to work, and so on. Individual workers by their labour receive an entitlement to means of consumption from the common stock equal as regards the labour represented in them to the amount of labour they have contributed (minus the deductions referred to above) (PW 3:346f).

But, Marx goes on to say, this principle of distribution is still in its fundamentals a bourgeois, a capitalist one, because it rests, like the exchange of commodities, and in particular like the sale of labour-power for a wage, on the exchange of equal amounts of labour in different forms. Certainly there is no expropriation of surplus for other than common purposes, and no exchange of means of production. Nevertheless it is still basically a matter of equal rights to the social product. This is inequitable, insofar as people with such equal rights have different capacities for working, and, more importantly still, different needs. Marx in fact says that *all* distribution according to 'rights' is in *principle* inequitable:

A right can by its nature only consist in the application of an equal standard, but unequal individuals (and they would not be different individuals if they were not equal) can only be measured by the same standard if they are looked at from the same aspect, if they are grasped from one *particular* side, ... if ... everything else is ignored. (PW 3:347)

But, again in his usual anti-Utopian spirit, he goes on to say that:

such defects ... are inevitable in the first phase of communist society, given the specific birth-pangs from capitalist society. Right can never rise above the economic structure of a society and its cultural development conditioned thereby. (PW 3:347)

This last sentence sums up very briefly one made at greater length in *Capital*:

The justice of transactions which take place between agents of production rests on the fact that these transactions arise as a natural consequence of the relations of production. ... legal forms ... cannot, being mere forms, determine ... their ... content.... They merely express it. This content is just whenever it corresponds, is appropriate, to the mode of production. It is unjust whenever it contradicts that mode. (C 3:460f)

5

It follows from this analysis that the overcoming of the above principle of distribution depends on the emergence, first, of a different economic structure and second, of a corresponding

209

'cultural development', or, as it might also be described, new forms of ideology. So it is not surprising that Marx goes on immediately to sketch the type of economic and cultural-ideological formation appropriate for the overcoming of the surviving bourgeois principle of distribution in the first phase of communism:

> In a higher phase of communist society, when the enslaving subordination of individuals to the division of labour, and thereby the antithesis between mental and physical labour have disappeared; when labour is no longer just a means of keeping alive but life's prime want; when with the all-round development of individuals their productive powers have also increased and all the springs of co-operative wealth flow more abundantly — only then can society wholly cross the narrow horizon of bourgois right and inscribe on its banner: From each according to his abilities, to each according to his needs! (PW 3:347)

This is an extremely significant passage. To start with, the theme of the division of labour, or more accurately, its abolition, which we saw earlier as a central one in Marx's thinking about communism in *The German Ideology*, returns to the forefront of attention. But the context is rather different now. Marx is not fully explicit here, but I think that his train of thought can be spelled out somewhat as follows. The principle according to which the individual draws from the stock of social wealth an amount strictly proportional to what he contributed to it has a practical anchorage in the situation in which contributing to that wealth through labour is something to be avoided. So, for that principle to be done away with it is necessary that labour not be something to be shunned: in such circumstances the amount of labour-time that people con-tribute to or take out of the social fund would not be of prime importance. It is only in the third part of the passage that the increase in the level of development of the productive forces is mentioned as a factor in a new principle of distribution. And note how this theme is actually introduced: Marx makes development of the forces of production a *consequence* of the 'all-round development of individuals'. This is another way of describing the abolition of the division of labour. Thus the latter is important not only from a 'humanistic' point of view, but because such individuals are envisioned as being more productive, and hence as themselves providing the material pre-conditions for their own all-sided development.

6

If the crucial feature of the post-capitalist, pre-(fully) communist society is that it is transitional, that it is one which has emerged from capitalism and is aiming at communism, but is not yet there, this transitional character comes out in the first place, as we have seen, in its not having an entirely autonomous mode of distribution of the social product. And if this form of society is transitional in its economic character, then it is to be expected, according to the general lines of Marx's thinking, that it will also have a transitional political form. And this is indeed what Marx affirms. Corresponding, he writes, to this social formation's being 'the period of the revolutionary transformation' from capitalism to communism, there is also a 'period of transition in the political sphere and in this period the state can only take the form of a *revolutionary dictatorship of the proletariat*' (PW 3:355). (On this term cf. Chapter 5.)

What is the character of this as a transitional form of state? To start with it is a *state* insofar as it is, in Marx's normal meaning of the term, an instrument for the coercion of one part of society by another, with the aim of maintaining prevailing relations of production or introducing new ones. To this extent a transitional state in the lower phase of communism is no more and no less a 'dictatorship' than a bourgeois state.

Why is a state necessary at all during this period? Marx's implicit answer is that it is necessary precisely because it is a transitional period, so that a development towards communism can be assured, rather than one backward to capitalism. Why is there a danger of such a movement? Marx does not take up the question in the *Critique*, but the elements of an answer to it are not difficult to supply. The post-revolutionary society will typically face, for a time anyway, wars of intervention from capitalist states; former owners of the now expropriated means of production and their supporters constitute a constant focus for possible counter-revolution; and, perhaps most importantly, there are tendencies backward

211

towards the old order springing from the inequalities which the principle of distribution by equal right makes possible.

7

So much for the character of the transitional state as a *state*. But what is its character as a *transitional* state? The idea of a state that, on the one hand, exercises traditional functions but, on the other, prepares its own demise, is not an easy one to construct, and the difficulty of it may be more obvious to us, living after 1917, than it was to Marx. He himself saw the Paris Commune as offering valuable lessons.

The first point to be made is a very general one. It is Marx's thesis that the bourgeois state cannot simply be taken over and modifed into the state which is the revolutionary dictatorship of the working-class and its allies. The working-class, he writes in *The Civil War in France*, 'cannot simply lay hold of the ready-made state machinery, and wield it for its own purposes' (PW 3:206). This idea is so central to Marx's later thinking that he (and Engels) wrote in the Preface to the 1872 edition of the *Manifesto* that it had to be added to the doctrine of that work as a consequence of the experience of the Commune (SW 1:99).[1] The underlying idea is that the very modes of functioning of the bourgeois state are such as to render it unsuitable for the role of a transitional one, so that it has to be dismantled and a new state-form constructed from the beginning.

What did Marx have in mind? Some idea may be gained from considering what he thought were some of the lessons of the Commune for a new political organization (PW 3:209f). First, the standing army was replaced by 'the armed people'. Second, political functionaries were not representatives, but delegates 'chosen by universal suffrage in the various wards of the town, responsible and revocable at short terms'. Third, the wages of public servants were limited to those of a worker. Fourth, there was an abolition of the separation of powers, so that legislative, judicial and executive powers were united in the same organs:

The Commune was to be a working, not a parliamentary body,

212

executive and legislative at the same time. .... The judicial functionaries were to be divested of that sham independence which had but
served to mask their abject subservience to all succeeding governments... Like the rest of public servants, magistrates and judges
were to be elective, responsible, and revocable.

Finally, there is the principle of decentralization and
federalism:

...the Commune was to be the political form of even the smallest
country hamlet.... The rural communes of every district were to
administer their common affairs by an assembly of delegates in the
central town, and these district assemblies were again to send
deputies to the National Delegation in Paris.... The few but
important functions which would still remain for a central government were ... to be discharged by Communal ... agents ... While the
merely repressive organs of the old governmental power were to be
amputated, its legitimate functions were to be wrested from an
authority usurping pre-eminence over society itself, and restored to
the responsible agents of society.

The continuity with the vision of 'On the Jewish question'
nearly three decades before scarcely needs to be underlined.

Notes

1 The germ of the idea is present in *The Eighteenth Brumaire of
Louis Bonaparte* (1852) when he writes that 'All revolutions
perfected this machine [sc. the 'state machinery' of France]
instead of breaking it.' (CW 11:186)

PART V: 1875-1883

Chapter 22
A farewell to arms

1

The German Socialist Workers' Party (known later as the German Social Democratic Party) the draft of whose founding document Marx had so trenchantly criticized in the *Critique of the Gotha Programme*, grew rapidly, polling round 500,000 votes in the elections of 1877; Bismarck's Anti-Socialist Law (1878) which prohibited socialist political activity was a blow, but also a testimony to the significance of the party as the first organized, independent, socialist mass labour-movement. But future developments were foreshadowed in a lengthy circular letter that Marx (and Engels) wrote to the leadership in 1879 on the theme of reformism in the party (PW 3:360ff).

Largely as a consequence of the temporary eclipse of public socialist political activity in Germany, Marx turned his attention to France, where energies were beginning to revive after the disaster of the Commune. In 1880 he contributed a theoretical introduction to the programme of the newly founded French Workers' Party. In the same year he wrote a detailed questionnaire to be completed by workers regarding their conditions of employment, as a way of getting to know about and making known the nature and extent of their exploitation.

He also turned special attention to Russia, traditionally the bulwark of counter-revolution, but now the site of revolutionary movements, and a place where his ideas found a ready welcome. He learned Russian and read a prodigious amount of socio-economic material on the subject. He also corresponded with many people there, including Vera Zasulich, a letter to whom in 1881 (together with three individually important drafts), concerning the perspectives for social development in Russia, is of great significance. The Preface to the second edition of the Russian translation of the *Manifesto of the Communist Party* (1882) contains thoughts in the same direction, and is the last of Marx's works published during his lifetime.

Not unconnected with this study of Russian conditions, including the nature of the Russian village community, were wide-ranging researches into ancient societies, particularly primitive ones; Marx's manuscripts on this material have been only quite recently published as his *Ethnological Notebooks.* (Part of this, especially the work on Lewis Henry Morgan's *Ancient Society*, served Engels as some of his raw material for his later book *The Origin of the Family, Private Property and the State.*)

2

On the central work of his life — *Capital* — he made little headway; I have said something about the work of those years towards the end of Chapter 6. He studied mountains of material (the above-mentioned work on the situation in Russia fed into it) and pottered away at the manuscripts which were later to become, under Engels's inspired editorial hands, the second and third volumes of *Capital*. (The only piece that he actually published on the theme of political economy was a chapter for Engels' *Anti-Dühring* in 1877.) In this regard it is essential to mention a long series of marginalia, written during 1879-1880, to one Adolph Wagner's textbook of political economy. These are precious for the light they cast on some basic questions about the subject, even if they do not break new ground.

For the rest, a great deal of energy went into his correspondence, and he continued his lifelong habit of prodigious miscellaneous reading. ('I'm a machine condemned to devour books and then to throw them in a changed form on the dunghill of history', Marx wrote to his daughter Laura some years before.[1]) The approximately 3,000 extant pages of extracts and notes which date from this period include studies in chemistry (especially agrochemistry, relevant to his work in political economy), physiology, geology and even mathematics (algebra and calculus).

218

3

But a life-long of overwork and neglect of his health was at last taking a decisive toll, a situation exacerbated by domestic grief. His wife Jenny was buried in December 1881 and his daughter of the same name little more than a year later. The springs of Marx's life finally snapped, and he himself died just two months later on 14 March 1883.

He left a world which now had independent working-class parties with socialist programmes, and also powerful new forms of the capitalist state; a world recovering from the massive economic crisis of the second half of the 1870s, and entering a new period of capitalist development, marked by monopolization and imperialism, which would bring in its wake international competition between rival national econ-omies and wars on a scale hitherto inconceivable; a world which was incubating ideologies appropriate to the new developments (both anti-liberal and anti-socialist typified by Nietszche). And the history of 'Marxism' had already begun.

Notes

1   Marx to Laura and Paul Lafargue, 11 April 1868 (W 32:545).

Guide to further reading

Guide to the Guide

The following guide to further reading offers a briefly annotated classification of the items in the list of works on Marx that follows. It is broken up according to themes which only partly correspond to the breakup of the main text of the book.

The mode of reference is fairly obvious. When there is only one item by the author in the list the reference is by name of author only, in upper case; when there is more than one the items are distinguished by the date of publication after the name of the author. Exceptions are works by Marx (and Engels), referred to either as explained in the note towards the beginning of this book or in self-explanatory fashion.

1 Bibliographical Aids
EUBANKS. See also AIMS [American Institute of Marxist Studies] *Newsletter*, a bimonthly listing of current articles and books, and containing relevant items.

2 Editions of Marx in English
What will be the standard English edition of the works of Marx (and Engels) for the foreseeable future is the *Collected Works* which began publication in 1975 in Moscow (Progress Publishers), and which appears in England and the United States under other imprints (Lawrence and Wishart and International Publishers respectively). At the date of writing fifteen volumes of a projected fifty have appeared. (It is based upon, but by no means follows in every respect, the standard German edition of the Marx-Engels *Werke* in thirty-nine numbered and four supplementary volumes published by Dietz in the German

Democratic Republic from 1956 onwards and frequently reprinted. Another edition of the Marx-Engels works as definitive as can be achieved at the present time is now in process of publication in the GDR.)

Moscow also publishes a Marx-Engels *Selected Works* in three volumes and another less comprehensive one in a single volume, as well as numberless editions of particular works and collections on particular themes. The translations (especially of *Capital*) are often not as good as in other editions (for example the Pelican Marx Library in eight volumes) but they are accessible and widely referred to.

3   Predominantly Biographical and Historical Works on Marx and Background

Of the older biographies prime place must be given to a brief sketch by Engels published in 1878 (SW 3:78-87). The first large-scale biography was that by MEHRING (1981). Though first published in 1918 and therefore in many respects out-of-date (though recently republished with supplementary material), it is still eminently worth reading if only because of the author's personal and political feel for his subject. Similar remarks apply to the much briefer work by RIAZANOV which first appeared in English in 1927. Of the more recent works BLUMENBERG is very brief and highly readable. The best general biography, as up-to-date as any available, is that by McLELLAN (1973), who has also edited a book of source-material — McLELLAN (1981). RUBEL and MANALE is a mine of well-arranged facts about Marx and Marxiana. The life by NICOLAIEVKSY and MAENCHEN-HELFEN is especially good on the political side. SEIGEL's is an attempt at psychobiography. PRAWER's is an exploration of one facet of Marx's work — fascinating because of, rather than despite, the jungle of detail. Almost as indispensable for knowledge of the life of Marx as for that of his favourite daughter is the first volume of KAPP's superb biography of Eleanor Marx. Gustav Mayer's great life of Engels is full of information also relevant to the life and times of Marx but unfortunately has only appeared in an abridged translation (MAYER) of the original, *Friedrich Engels. Eine Biographie* 2nd ed., two volumes, 1934, reprinted by Ullstein, 1975.

The best general sources for the entire historical background are HOBSBAWM's two volumes together covering the period 1789-1875. MEHRING (1975) covers the German historical background 1525-1848, whilst HAMEROW covers the period 1815-1871. The crucial events of 1848-49 in particular are best studied to begin with in the contemporaneous or nearly contemporaneous writings by Marx and Engels themselves, and especially Engels' series *Revolution and Counter-Revolution in Germany* (CW 11). It is hoped that the outstanding work by CLAUDIN on the period will soon find an English translator. The period of the First International is covered in COLLINS and ABRAMSKY.

Information on intellectual background can be found in CORNU, LOBKOWICZ, LÖWITH, McLELLAN (1969) and (1972), MARCUSE, TAYLOR, THERBORN (1976) and WARTOFSKY.

4 Predominantly Systematic Works on Marx's Thought as a Whole or in Large Part

There is a great number of these and selection is correspondingly difficult. Of the older works the various articles and excerpts collected in LENIN are of great importance. KORSCH and MARCUSE present distinctive pictures. POPPER's criticisms have had an influence out of all proportion to their merits. The work of ALTHUSSER and of BALIBAR (see especially his work of 1974 which contains an excellent synoptic piece on 'Marx and Marxism') signified something of an epoch in thinking about Marx: whether people agreed with it or not discussion tended to be framed to a great extent in the terms they laid out. CUTLER *et al.,* especially Vol. 1, is a criticism of Marx by former 'Althusserians'. COLLETTI (and his introduction to Marx's *Early Writings*) presents views stemming from the Italian school inspired by Della Volpe; BLACKBURN is a criticism. COHEN's is a much praised recent work defending a fairly traditional 'technological' view of Marx; the work by McMURTRY is along similar lines. The works by MESZAROS and OLLMAN focus their expositions of Marx on the notion of 'alienation'. GODELIER (1977), HELLER, KRADER and the various articles in MEPHAM and RUBEN, Volume 4

Marx: An introduction

focus on particular aspects of Marx's general conceptions of society and history.

5 Marxist 'Philosophy'
Much of the recent debate in this area has been touched off by the work of ALTHUSSER. On the areas of materialism, epistemology, methodology, RUBEN and TIMPANARO defend fairly traditional positions, SCHMIDT gives a view highly influenced by 'critical theory', HALL (1974) analyses the '1857 Introduction'; there are many different stances in MEPHAM and RUBEN Volumes 2 and 3. Works making special reference to the methodology of *Capital* include ALTHUSSER and BALIBAR, CLEAVER, GERAS, GODELIER (1972), SAYER and ZELENÝ. The literature in the area of dialectics is in general very poor. The best single work is still the relevant essays in MAO ZEDONG (MAO TSE-TUNG). These had considerable influence on the very difficult but seminal papers 'Contradiction and overdetermination' and 'On the materialist dialectic' in ALTHUSSER (1969) in connection with which see GODELIER (1967) and (1972). MEPHAM and RUBEN, Volume 1 is a patchy collection of essays by several hands. The most recent work on the subject is by NORMAN and SAYERS: the contributions by the first are the most rewarding.

6 Marx's Political Economy
Very brief introductions include FINE, JALÉE and MANDEL (1970). The latter's excellent introductions to the three volumes of *Capital* in the Pelican Marx Library are more advanced. More detailed treatises include the now quite old SWEEZY and MANDEL (1962) which are still very useful however. HARVEY is a superb restatement and rethinking of Marx's political economy in a contemporary context. The older but quite indispensable work by RUBIN has a title that makes its subject-matter sound much narrower than it in fact is; the volumes of essays by ELSON and by STEEDMAN and others are contemporary contributions to the continuing controversies round Marx's concept of 'value', the historical affiliations of which are explained in MEEK. Critics stretch from BOEHM-BAWERK, who determined, already in

224

1894, much of the subsequent course of criticism of Marx's political economy, to CUTLER *et al.* (especially Volume 2). On the development of Marx's economic thought there is MANDEL (1971), taking the story up to the *Grundrisse*, ROSDOLSKY, centred upon that work, and VYGODSKI (to 1863). For literature on the methodology of *Capital* see the preceding section.

7 Classes and the State

The central work on Marx's political theory is DRAPER (1977-1978) (still unfinished). See also BLACKBURN, LENIN and MILIBAND (1977), and on the earlier works, HUNT and (especially) CLAUDIN and GILBERT. AVINERI is a 'standard' work which should be used with great care if only because of his playing down of the politically revolutionary character of Marx's thought. Presentations of Marx's thinking on the state in particular may be found in CORRIGAN *et al.*, JESSOP and MILIBAND (1965). A collection of texts on Marx's (and Engels') thinking on law is to be found in CAIN and HUNT. Later Marxist thinking on the subject, relating itself to Marx, may be found in MILIBAND (1969) and in POULANTZAS (1973) and (1978), together with the controversies between them in POULANTZAS and MILIBAND (continued in *New Left Review*, Numbers 82 and 95) and the discussion in LACLAU. See also HOLLOWAY and PICCIOTTO, THERBORN (1978) and WRIGHT. On Marx's thinking regarding classes see GIDDENS, Chapter 2 and HALL (1977). Later work is represented in CARCHEDI, GIDDENS and POULANTZAS (1975).

8 Ideology

As mentioned in the text Marx's writing on the subject of ideology is very sketchy. There is an attempt at a synoptic treatment in LARRAIN. Mepham studies the theory of ideology in *Capital* in his contribution to MEPHAM and RUBEN, Volume 1, and there is an inquiry into Marx's doctrines of fetishism in *Capital*, in relation to his concept of ideology and related matters with special reference to anthropology in GODELIER (1977), especially Chapters 6 and 7. Also GERAS. The framework for much of the contemporary broadly Marxist discussion of the topic was set up in the paper 'Ideology and ideological apparatuses of the state' in ALTHUSSER (1971). References to the critical literature on this may be found in the excellent survey of the topic which is THERBORN (1980). Perhaps relevant here is LIFSCHITZ on Marx's thinking about art.

9 *'Base' and 'Superstructure'*
See GODELIER (1978), HALL (1977a) and WILLIAMS.

10 *Socialism/Communism*
Historical background may be found in COLE and LICHTHEIM. BALIBAR (1977) has careful exegeses of texts relevant to the title of his book. See also DRAPER (1970). MOORE argues, with detailed references to Marx's texts, that his arguments do not justify 'communism' rather than 'socialism'. The work by BAHRO, highly significant on its own account, has many important pages of commentary on Marx-texts regarding socialism/communism. POULANTZAS (1978) has relevant contemporary discussions.

Further reading

What is and is not in the following list

The literature on Marx (not to speak of that on Marxism) is huge and increasing by the minute. As this book is intended to be genuinely introductory the following list is also meant to be an introduction: I have assumed that the reader wanting to win a foothold on the subject will prefer some general orientations rather than highly specialized guidance. (More extensive references can be obtained from the catalogue of any good library or the bibliographies of many of the more comprehensive works on Marx and Marxism that are available.)

More specifically, I have not tried to list even all the more or less 'standard' works on Marx. Rather, within certain limits (to be mentioned in a moment) I have tried to make a reasonably brief list of some works on the subject that I think may well be useful to someone studying Marx for the first time. Some are included more because they are representative of influential trends than because I think highly of them, and for other such reasons; but by and large it is a personal selection of what I think worthwhile.

As regards the limits on the choice, I have, with just a very few exceptions, confined the list to texts which are available in English and in books: the first because works in languages other than English will certainly be inaccessible to the majority of readers, either because of language-barriers or because of difficulties in obtaining them, and the second because journals are comparatively difficult to come by even in many University libraries. (An appendix lists some relevant journals though.) I have also not listed works dealing with topics on which Marx wrote only in passing — for example, the question of women.

Althusser, L. *For Marx* (Harmondsworth, Penguin, 1969).

Althusser, L. *Lenin and Philosophy* (London, New Left Books, 1971).

Althusser, L. *Essays in Self-Criticism* (London, New Left Books, 1976).

Althusser, L. and Balibar, E. *Reading 'Capital'* (London, New Left Books, 1970).

Avineri, S. *The Social and Political Thought of Karl Marx* (Cambridge University Press, 1968).

Bahro, R. *The Alternative in Eastern Europe* (London, New Left Books, 1978).

Balibar, E. *Cinq Etudes du matérialisme historique* (Paris, Maspero, 1974).

Balibar, E. *The Dictatorship of the Proletariat* (London, New Left Books, 1977).

Blackburn, R. 'Marxism: theory of proletarian revolution', in R. Blackburn (ed.) *Revolution and Class Struggle: A Reader in Marxist Politics* (London, Fontana/Collins, 1977).

Blumenberg, W. *Karl Marx. An Illustrated Biography* (London, New Left Books, 1971).

Boehm-Bawerk, E. von *Karl Marx and the Close of His System* (New York, A. Kelly, 1949). This volume also contains Rudolf Hilferding's reply.

Cain, M. and Hunt, A. (eds) *Marx and Engels on Law* (New York, Academic Press, 1979).

Carchedi, G. *On the Economic Identification of Social Class* (London, Routledge and Kegan Paul, 1977).

Claudin, F. *Marx, Engels et la révolution de 1848* (Maspero, 1980).

Cleaver, H. M. *Reading 'Capital' Politically* (Brighton, Harvester Press, 1980).

Cohen, G. A. *Karl Marx's Theory of History. A Defence* (Oxford, Clarendon Press, 1978).

Cole, G. D. H. *A History of Socialist Thought* Volumes I and II (London, Macmillan, 1953-1954).

Collins, H. and Abramsky, C. *Karl Marx and the British Labour Movement. Years of the First International* (London, Macmillan, 1965).

Colletti, L. *From Rousseau to Lenin* (London, New Left Books, 1972).

Cornu, A. *Karl Marx et Friedrich Engels: Leur vie et leur oeuvre*, 4 volumes (Paris, P.U.F., 1955-1970).

Corrigan, P., Ramsay, H. and Sayer, D. 'The state as a relation of production', in P. Corrigan (ed.) *Capitalism, State Formation and Marxist Theory* (London, Quartet Books, 1980).

228

Cutler, A., Hindess, B., Hirst, P. and Hussain, A. *Marx's 'Capital' and Capitalism Today*, 2 volumes (London, Routledge and Kegan Paul, 1977, 1978).

Draper, H. 'The death of the state in Marx and Engels', in R. Miliband and J. Saville (eds) *The Socialist Register 1970* (London, Merlin, 1970).

Draper, H. *Karl Marx's Theory of Revolution*, 2 volumes in 3 (New York and London, Monthly Review Press, 1977-1978).

Elson, D. (ed.) *Value: The Representation of Labour in Capitalism* (London, CSE Books/Atlantic Highlands, N.J., Humanities Press, 1979).

Eubanks, C. L. *Karl Marx and Friedrich Engels: An Analytical Bibliography* (New York, Garland, 1977).

Fine, B. *Marx's 'Capital'* (Basingstoke, Macmillan, 1975).

Geras, N. 'Marx and the critique of political economy', in R. Blackburn (ed.) *Ideology in Social Science* (London, Fontana/Collins, 1972).

Giddens, A. *The Class Structure of the Advanced Societies* (London, Hutchinson, 1973).

Gilbert, A. *Marx's Politics. Communists and Citizens* (Oxford, Martin Robertson, 1981).

Godelier, M. 'System and contradiction in *Capital*', in R. Miliband and J. Saville (eds.) *The Socialist Register 1967* (London, Merlin Press, 1967) and in R. Blackburn (ed.) *Ideology in Social Science* (London, Fontana/Collins, 1972).

Godelier, M. *Rationality and Irrationality in Economics* (London, New Left Books, 1972).

Godelier, M. *Perspectives in Marxist Anthropology* (Cambridge University Press, 1977).

Godelier, M. 'Infrastructure, society and history' *New Left Review*, No. 112, November-December 1978.

Hall, S. 'Marx's notes on method: a reading of the 1857 Introduction' *Working Papers in Cultural Studies* (Centre for Contemporary Cultural Studies, Birmingham), No. 6, 1974.

Hall, S. 'The "political" and the "economic" in Marx's theory of classes', in A. Hunt (ed.) *Class and Class Structure* (London, Lawrence and Wishart, 1977).

Hall, S. 'Rethinking the "base-and-superstructure" metaphor', in J. Bloomfield (ed.) *Class, Hegemony and Party* (London, Lawrence and Wishart, 1977a).

Hamerow, T. S. *Restoration, Revolution, Reaction: Economics and Politics in Germany 1815-1871* (Princeton, Princeton University Press, 1958).

Harvey, D. *The Limits to Capital* (Oxford, Basil Blackwell, 1982).

Heller, A. *Marx's Theory of Needs* (London, Alison and Busby, 1974).

Hobsbawm, E. *The Age of Revolution 1789-1848* (London, Weidenfeld and Nicolson, 1962).

Hobsbawm, E. *The Age of Capital 1848-1975* (London, Weidenfeld and Nicolson, 1975).

Holloway, J. and Picciotto, S. (eds) *State and Capital: A Marxist Debate* (London, Edward Arnold, 1978).

Hunt, R.N. *The Political Ideas of Marx and Engels* Volume I: *Marxism and Totalitarian Democracy* (Basingstoke, Macmillan, 1975).

Jalée, P. *How Capitalism Works* (New York, Monthly Review Press, 1977).

Jessop, B. 'Marx and Engels on the state', in S. Hibbin (ed.) *Politics, Ideology and the State* (London, Lawrence and Wishart, 1978).

Kapp, Y. *Eleanor Marx* Volume 1 (London, Lawrence and Wishart, 1972).

Korsch, K. *Karl Marx* (New York, Russell and Russell, 1963).

Krader, L. *The Asiatic Mode of Production* (Assen, Van Gorcum, 1975).

Larrain, J. 'Marx's theory of ideology', in *The Concept of Ideology* (London, Hutchinson, 1979).

Lenin, V.I. *Marx-Engels-Marxism* (Moscow, Progress Publishers, 1968).

Lichtheim, G. *A Short History of Socialism* (London, Weidenfeld and Nicolson, 1970).

Lifschitz, M. *The Philosophy of Art of Karl Marx* (London, Pluto Press, 1973).

Lobkowicz, N. *Theory and Practice from Aristotle to Marx* (Notre Dame, University of Notre Dame Press, 1967).

Löwith, K. *From Hegel to Nietzche. The Revolution in Nineteenth-Century Thought* (Garden City, New York, Doubleday, 1967).

Mandel, E. *Marxist Economic Theory* (London, Merlin Press, 1962).

Mandel, E. *An Introduction to Marxist Economic Theory* (New York, Pathfinder Press, 1970).

Mandel, E. *The Formation of the Economic Thought of Karl Marx* (London, New Left Books, 1971).

Mao Zedong (Mao Tse-Tung) *Four Essays on Philosophy* (Peking, Foreign Languages Press, 1968).

Marcuse, H. *Reason and Revolution. Hegel and the Rise of Social Theory* 2nd ed. (London, Routledge and Kegan Paul, 1960).

230

Marx, K. *Early Writings* (Harmondsworth, Penguin/New Left Books, 1975).

Marx, K. *Political Writings* Volume I *The Revolution of 1848;* Volume 2 *Surveys from Exile;* Volume 3 *The First International and After* (Harmondsworth, Penguin/New Left Books, 1973-1974).

Marx, K. *Grundrisse. Foundations of the Critique of Political Economy (Rough Draft)* (Harmondsworth, Penguin/New Left Books, 1973).

Marx, K. *Capital. A Critique of Political Economy*, 3 volumes (Harmondsworth, Penguin/New Left Books, 1976-1981).

Marx, K. *Texts on Method* (ed. T. Carver) (Oxford, Basil Blackwell, 1974).

Marx, K. *Value: Studies by Karl Marx* (ed. A. Dragstedt) (London, New York Publications, 1976).

Marx, K. *Theories of Surplus-Value*, 3 volumes (Moscow, Progress Publishers, 1963-1971).

Marx, K. *A Contribution to the Critique of Political Economy* (Moscow, Progress Publishers, 1970).

Marx, K. *The Ethnological Notebooks* (ed. L. Krader) (Assen, Van Gorcum, 1972).

Marx, K. and Engels, F. *Collected Works* (Moscow, Progress Publishers, 1975ff).

Marx, K. and Engels, F. *Selected Works in Three Volumes* (Moscow, Progress Publishers, 1969).

Marx, K. and Engels, F. *Selected Correspondence* (Moscow, Progress Publishers, n.d.).

Mayer, G. *Friedrich Engels: A Biography* (New York, Knopf, 1936).

Meek, R.L. *Studies in the Labour Theory of Value* (London, Lawrence and Wishart, 1956).

Mehring, F. *Absolutism and Revolution in Germany 1525-1848* (London, New Park Publications, 1975).

Mehring, F. *Karl Marx. The Story of His Life* (Brighton, Harvester Press, 1981).

Mepham, J. and Ruben, D.-H. (eds) *Issues in Marxist Philosophy,* 4 volumes (Brighton, Harvester Press, 1979-1981).

Mészáros, I. *Marx's Theory of Alienation* 4th ed. (London, Merlin, 1975).

Miliband, R. 'Marx and the state', in R. Miliband and J. Saville (eds) *The Socialist Register 1965* (London, Merlin Press, 1965).

Miliband, R. *The State in Capitalist Society* (London, Weidenfeld and Nicolson, 1969).

Miliband, R. *Marxism and Politics* (Oxford, Basil Blackwell, 1977).

Moore, S. *Marx on the Choice Between Socialism and Communism* (Cambridge, Mass., Harvard University Press, 1980).

McLellan, D. *The Young Hegelians and Karl Marx* (London, Macmillan, 1969).

McLellan, D. *Marx Before Marxism* (Harmondsworth, Penguin, 1972).

McLellan, D. *Karl Marx: His Life and Thought* (Basingstoke, Macmillan, 1973).

McLellan, D. (ed.) *Karl Marx: Interviews and Recollections* (Totowa, N.J., Barnes and Noble, 1981).

McMurtry, J. *The Structure of Marx's World-View* (Princeton, Princeton University Press, 1978).

Nicolaievsky, B. and Maenchen-Helfen, O. *Karl Marx: Man and Fighter* (Harmondsworth, Penguin, 1970).

Norman, R. and Sayers, S. *Hegel, Marx and Dialectic: A Debate* (Brighton, Harvester Press, 1980).

Ollman, B. *Alienation: Marx's Conception of Man in Capitalist Society* (Cambridge University Press, 1971).

Popper, K.R. *The Open Society and Its Enemies* Volume 2 5th ed. (London, Routledge and Kegan Paul, 1966).

Poulantzas, N. *Political Power and Social Classes* (London, New Left Books, 1973).

Poulantzas, N. *Classes in Contemporary Capitalism* (London, New Left Books, 1975).

Poulantzas, N. *State, Power, Socialism* (London, New Left Books, 1978).

Poulantzas, N. and Miliband, R. 'The problem of the capitalist state', in R. Blackburn (ed.) *Ideology in Social Science* (London, Fontana/Collins, 1972).

Prawer, S.S. *Karl Marx and World Literature* (Oxford, Clarendon Press, 1976).

Rosdolsky, R. *The Making of Marx's 'Capital'* (London, Pluto, 1977).

Rubel, M. and Manale, M. *Marx Without Myth. A Chronological Study of His Life and Work* (Oxford, Basil Blackwell, 1975).

Ruben, D.-H. *Marxism and Materialism. A Study in Marxist Theory of Knowledge* 2nd ed. (Brighton, Harvester Press, 1979).

Rubin, I. *Essays on Marx's Theory of Value* (Detroit, Black and Red, 1972).

Riazanov, D. *Karl Marx and Frederick Engels. An Introduction to Their Lives and Work* (New York and London, Monthly Review Press, 1973).

Sayer, D. *Marx's Method. Ideology, Science and Critique in 'Capital'* (Brighton, Harvester Press, 1979).

Schmidt, A. *The Concept of Nature in Marx* (London, New Left Books, 1971).

Seigel, J. E. *Marx's Fate: The Shape of a Life* (Princeton, Princeton University Press, 1978).

Steedman, I. and others *The Value Controversy* (London, New Left Books, 1981).

Sweezy, P. *The Theory of Capitalist Development* (New York and London, Monthly Review Press, 1970).

Taylor, C. *Hegel* (Cambridge University Press, 1975).

Therborn, G. *Science, Class and Society* (London, New Left Books, 1976).

Therborn, G. *What Does the Ruling Class Do When It Rules?* (London, New Left Books, 1978).

Therborn, G. *The Ideology of Power and the Power of Ideology* (London, New Left Books, 1980).

Timpanaro, S. *On Materialism* (London, New Left Books, 1975).

Vygodski, F.S. *The Story of a Great Discovery: How Karl Marx Wrote 'Capital'* (Tunbridge Wells, Kent, Abacus Press, 1974).

Wartofsky, M. *Feuerbach* (Cambridge University Press, 1978).

Williams, R. 'Base and superstructure in Marxist cultural theory', in *Problems of Materialism and Culture* (London, New Left Books, 1980).

Wright, E.O. *Class, Crisis and the State* (London, New Left Books, 1978).

Zelený, J. *The Logic of Marx* (Oxford, Basil Blackwell, 1980).

Appendix

The following are some relevant journals of a fairly general nature:

Berkeley Journal of Sociology (annual)
Canadian Journal of Political and Social Theory
Capital and Class (before 1977: *Bulletin of the Conference of Socialist Economists*)
Critique (Glasgow)
Critique of Anthropology
Dialectical Anthropology
Economy and Society
History Workshop
Ideology and Consciousness
The Insurgent Sociologist
Kapitalistate
Monthly Review
New German Critique

New Left Review
Past and Present
Philosophy and Political Affairs
Philosophy and Social Criticism
Politics and Society
Race and Class
Radical America
Radical Philosophy
Radical Science Journal
Review of Radical Political Economics
Science and Society
Social Policy
Social Praxis
Social Theory and Practice
Socialist Register (annual)
Socialist Review (formerly: *Socialist Revolution*)
Telos
Theory and Society
Thesis 11 (Melbourne)

Index

structure of 89
and surplus-labour 187
and surplus-value 85, 87,
89-91
technical composition 95
value composition 95
variable (*v*) 87, 179
capitalism 56
and the bourgeoisie 56-7
defined in the *Manifesto*
55-6, 171
'historic destiny' 187-8, 189
historical development 174
nineteenth-century devel-
opment 69
and production forces 56
centralization 57
change, tendency to 169
civil society
and power 147
and the state 115, 146
class chapter 11
abolition of 115
development of 69, 106,
110-11
and economic theory 132
and executive function 150
formation of 114
and ideological form 143
relationships 36-7, 52, 114,
143
and revolution 65
ruling, and ideology 139
and the state 147, 150
-struggle 36, 66
and ideology 143
and relations of produc-
tion 113-14
class-structure 150
class-theory 114-15
commodity (*C*)
defined 78, 84-5
and exchange-value 81, 182
fetishism 125, 128
and labour-power 90
as product of labour 82

as use-value 81, 126, 135,
182-3
communism
analyzed 39
and dogma 22-3
early 22, 30
French 14, 31, 49
and historical development
190-1
and historical materialism
Chapter 4
Marxist 51
and private property 39
and social organization 200
transition to 64, 207
Communist Corresponding
Committee (1846) 53, 54
Communist League (1847)
54, 70
2nd Congress 55
dissolution 61
in Paris (1848) 60
contradiction, dialectical
180-4, 190
critical method 17
and dialectics 180
Hegelian 20-1, 23, 124
and political economy 124

Darwin, C., influence of
161-2
determinism, materialist
166-7
dialectics chapter 18
in Engels 184
Hegelian 178-9, 181
material 179, 180
method 178
and social change 177
and surplus-value 179
'dual power' 64

economic base
and fetishism 142
and ideological form 142

and commodities 84, 98
and exchange-value 98
as reification of species-
essence 27
as use-value 98
monopoly 100
of capital 192

nationalization 60
necessity, realm of 193-4
and capitalism 194
New Rhenish Gazette 60, 62

objectification 41

Paris Commune (1871) 205-6,
212-13
philosophy
abolition of 33
idealized 33, 138
in Marx's doctoral thesis
9-10
and politics 33
realization of 33, 34
and revolution 34
and the working class 34
political economy 35, 71,
chapter 13
bourgeois concept of 132,
133-4
and class-struggle 134
'classical' 131-3
and mercantilism 35
and the Physiocrats 35
and private property 37
politics
and economics 20
German 33
Hegelian 16
and religion 26-7
and social organization 25
positivism 41
practice, primacy of chapter
12
character of 120

and commodity-exchange
122
economic 121, 124
and the individual 119-20
material 122
and relations of production
120
revolutionary 168
production
agents of 76
analyzed 74, 133
and base 104
and capital 87
capitalist mode of (*CMP*)
75, 76, 77-8
and dialectics 179
transitory 134
and class-struggle 115
and distribution 208-9
factors of 76-7
forces of 52, 56, 77, 210,
chapter 11
and base 109
means of (*MP*) 76, 90
ownership of 78
'price of' 96
as social determinant 49
social relations of 75, 76, 78,
chapter 11
and base 109
and technology 111-12
see also property relations
technical, relations of 76-7
profit (*p'*)
average rate 87, 95-6
'law of motion' 94
surplus 99, 100
and surplus-value 88, 93,
95
tendency to fall 100
proletariat, *see* working class
property, common 39
property, private
abolition of 20, 39, 40, 57
and division of labour 51
and estrangement 39

Principal References to Marx's Writings